THE ARGENTINE ECONOMY

THE

ARGENTINE

ECONOMY

ALDO FERRER

Translated by MARJORY M. URQUIDI

UNIVERSITY OF CALIFORNIA PRESS • BERKELEY AND LOS ANGELES 1967

University of California Press
Berkeley and Los Angeles, California
Cambridge University Press
London, England
Copyright © 1967 by The Regents of the University of California
Translated from *La Economía Argentina*
First published in Mexico City and Buenos Aires by
Fondo de Cultura Económica, 1963
Published with the assistance of a grant
from the Rockefeller Foundation
Library of Congress Catalog Card Number: 66-25669
Printed in the United States of America

*To Susana, Carmen, Amparo,
and Lucinda*

Preface

Since I finished writing this book, revised statistics on the Argentine national product for the postwar period and important contributions by several economists have appeared. These, together with my own recent research, highlight some problems that were not emphasized in this book—among them, the low level of efficiency in manufacturing and the new prospects for agricultural production and exports. A very active discussion on the strategy of industrial growth and the importance of foreign trade in manufactures to promote expansion and greater efficiency has been taking place. Furthermore, recent data show a better record of economic development than the one considered in this book, which is based on earlier data. I have added a few footnotes to take this into account.

The recent contributions and data mentioned above do not change the essential facts I deal with in the final chapters of this book. My basic conclusions on the current problems and prospects of the Argentine economy remain unchanged. That is why I prefer to introduce only minor changes into this edition. I have included statistical tables with economic and social data of special interest, and I have eliminated, as unnecessary in this edition, an appendix explaining the principal economic terms used in the text. Furthermore, I have condensed or discarded a few footnotes and paragraphs in the Spanish edition which I considered superfluous to this one.

A. F

Buenos Aires, September, 1966

vii

Preface

Argentina presents one of the most paradoxical cases in contemporary economic experience. Although a country with all the conditions necessary for rapid and sustained development, its rise in output since 1948 has barely kept up with its population increase, and the living standards of large sectors of its society have not advanced or have even deteriorated.

Furthermore, recently there has been a pronounced contraction in economic activity with a consequent unemployment of labor and productive capacity and a drop in income levels. There is little doubt that these trends are directly related to the country's prolonged political crisis and instability as well as to the loss of a feeling of common destiny among its different social groups.

I am convinced that there can be no adequate understanding of the reasons for this stagnation (including current short-term problems) without an analysis of the historical roots of the present situation and the changes in the world economy that traditionally have played a leading role in Argentine development. Ultimately, current problems are explained by the country's inability to readjust its economic structure to the conditions of modern economic development and to a new international situation.

In this book I shall try to analyze the economic formation of Argentina. Nearly two decades of work on the country's problems, in both an academic and an official capacity, have persuaded me that only a historical approach permits a systematic and broad understanding of the problems of national development and, therefore, the framing of a policy to strengthen the economic structure, to accelerate the rate of development, and to raise the living standard of the population. I hope that this work will stimulate empirical research and an analysis of Argentine development, making clear its trends and defining its objectives in this second half of the twentieth century.

In Argentina there is an increasing interest in economic topics, particularly those related to present conditions. Of course, no intense process of growth and of national purpose is possible unless the Argentine people are educated in the causes of growth so that they may acquire a "development mentality." My book is an attempt to satisfy the rising concern with these topics and to make them comprehensible to the general public. For this reason, I have added an explanation of terms commonly used in macroeconomic analysis which are indispensable to the text. The economist will find that some passages go into too much detail and that others are not technical enough.

The available bibliography on Argentine economics is still inadequate for the student of the economic and social sciences who wishes to view the problems of Argentine development in their historical perspective. Irrespective of the wide range of readers for whom it is intended, this book may fill part of the void by encouraging new generations of students and specialists in the social and economic disciplines to build a framework of reference permitting the tools of economic analysis to be usefully applied to the realities of my country.

A. F.

Washington, D.C., December, 1962

Contents

Introduction

The method followed in this book is to analyze the formation of the Argentine economy by differentiating between the historical stages within which the economic system has developed according to a certain pattern. This method can easily be applied to Argentina where the various structures and processes are distinctly separate.

The work of Celso Furtado on the Brazilian economy[1] underlines the value of this type of approach to the formation of an economy. Dispensing with the traditional economic historian's mass of data, the economic system can be defined in its different historical circumstances. This definition of stages or models enables the economist to apply modern analytical tools to the basic information and estimates available and to describe development in terms intelligible to the contemporary reader. Furthermore, this type of approach permits a more penetrating analysis of the causes of the present situation and of how these causes have evolved over the years. In this way, problems that cannot be examined systematically and thoroughly by short-term analysis are made much clearer and placed in their proper perspective. This method also compels the economist to define the role of social forces in development. Although these forces, which actually determine the process of history, are outside the sphere of problems that the economist usually deals with, they must be understood in order to correctly interpret the formation of an economy.

By the above method, four separate stages in the economic development of Argentina can be distinguished. The first covered the period from the sixteenth to the end of the eighteenth century. I designate it the "stage of regional subsistence economies" because it was characterized by the existence in different parts of the country of several regional socioeconomic units of very low productivity, mainly supplying domestic consumption. In this stage, these re-

---

[1] Celso Furtado, *The Economic Growth of Brazil* (Berkeley and Los Angeles: University of California Press, 1963), chap. 1, and *A economia brasileira* (Río de Janeiro, 1954).

gional economies were not affected by the period's dynamic element, which was the expansion of markets.

The second stage extended from the end of the eighteenth century to about 1860, and I call it the "stage of transition." This period marked the beginning of an activity, the production of hides and other livestock products, that brought Argentina an increasing share of world trade. Moreover, after the liberalization of the Spanish commercial system at the end of the eighteenth century and independence in 1810, the port of Buenos Aires could take full advantage of its geographic position and act as an entrepôt for foreign trade.

The third stage, which I call the "economy of primary exports," started around 1860, when Argentina began to participate actively in the expanding international trade, and ended with the world depression of 1930. This was the period when the increase in agricultural and livestock exports, the arrival of large groups of immigrants, and the inflow of foreign capital transformed the economic and social structure of the country in just a few decades.

The stage that I refer to as the "nonintegrated industrial economy" began in 1930 and has not yet ended. It is characterized by the existence of a diversified economic and social structure in many ways comparable to that of the advanced economies. The Argentine economy, however, is not integrated because it has not developed basic industries, and therefore, its growth and level of employment depend on imports financed by agricultural exports.

Within these four stages can be clearly defined the role of the economic system and of the factors that determine its evolution and transformation. It is also possible to analyze in each stage the level of development reached and the function of the country's regions. The reader will see that my analysis of the experience of the last decades, that is, the stage of the nonintegrated industrial economy, leads me to the conclusion that the system has entered a crisis that impedes further evolution and growth. In the face of this development crisis, I try to identify the different courses marked out by the social forces operating in Argentina. I also argue that the future growth of the national economy and a rise in material and cultural living standards can be achieved only through integration of the economic structure, that is, the formation of an integrated industrial economy. And I end by discussing the conditions needed to make this possible.

I have a final warning for the reader who now embarks on my attempt to interpret the formation of the Argentine economy. Because external factors have always played a decisive role in the country's development, I begin each part with the setting of the stage that will be analyzed. This description necessarily involves a series of data and details about the world economy of each period that are probably already familiar to the reader.

PART I

THE
REGIONAL SUBSISTENCE
ECONOMIES

(The Sixteenth to Eighteenth Century)

1. TRADE AS A FACTOR IN THE DISSOLUTION OF THE FEUDAL SYSTEM

The Dynamic Role of Trade

From antiquity until the Muslim expansion of the seventh century, the Mediterranean was the natural means of communication between all the civilizations of the Ancient World. After the fall of Rome, the barbarian kingdoms founded in the fifth century preserved "the most evident and essential feature of ancient civilization: its Mediterranean character."

The Muslim conquest gave control of the Mediterranean to the Arabs who, established in Africa and Spain and with strongholds in the Balearic Islands, Corsica, Sardinia, and Sicily, cut Western Europe's traditional line of communication with the outside world. Only Constantinople managed to maintain its position in the Aegean, the Adriatic, and on the southern coasts of Italy.

The isolation imposed by the Arab expansion on the peoples of Western Europe laid the bases of the social order of the early Middle Ages[1] and of the closed economies that produced for local consumption. These economies were characterized by a lack of external markets and the almost complete absence of trade with other regions. Economic activity depended on agriculture, and almost all the working population was engaged in rural production. Landownership, concentrated in the hands of small groups, was the mainspring of the political and social order. The feudal lord used his share of the production of the economy of his fief to support the court and its retainers, who not only performed personal and military services, but also did craft and construction work for the ruling class. The active population not engaged in agriculture was mainly composed of the feudal court and its retainers. Goods, other than food, consumed by the agricultural workers were produced domestically.

From a dynamic point of view, the distinctive feature of the

---

[1] Henri Pirenne, *Economic and Social History of Medieval Europe*, English transl., 1936.

feudal economy was the absence of any technical progress and the consequent stagnation of productivity. With no outside trade and no improvement in the methods and organization of rural activities, production varied according to the effect of climate and other circumstances on the harvest.

Capital accumulation was almost nonexistent. The low level of productivity barely allowed rural workers to subsist and to pay tribute, mainly in the form of crops, to their feudal lord. The latter, the only component of the feudal economy who could have accumulated capital, used his agricultural surplus to supply his court. In this way, no portion of available labor was used to expand the capital existing in the economy through improvements in agricultural methods and the production of tools and equipment for farmers and artisans. Surpluses belonging to the Church did not alter the system.

In the absence of technical progress and of capital accumulation in the feudal-closed economy, there was no possibility of a rise in the farmer's productivity and income. Such low levels of productivity meant that the economic structure could not change, because most of the population had to work in the fields to produce basic food crops. The lower the level of productivity in an economy, the higher the proportion of the active population employed in producing food and other articles essential to subsistence. With agricultural productivity at a standstill, there could be only a limited transfer of the active population to crafts and services. This transfer would have been the logical answer of supply to the diversification of demand created by a rise in the living standard.

Given these conditions, there was only one way to increase the productivity of the system: by carrying on trade with other regions. Because the difference in natural resources and in the knowledge of acquired techniques determined different cost structures among the various economies, a given commodity could be produced and traded advantageously and a greater volume of goods made available to the community. The promoters of this precarious division of labor among the different regions were the traders themselves. Since trade was the only way to increase productivity within the feudal economy, it became the dynamic sector par excellence, and it made possible the accumulation of capital by those who were not feudal lords. The role of these surpluses was altogether different from that of the surpluses appropriated by the feudal class. The latter were consumed, whereas the former went back into economic activity and intensified trade. The accumulation of wealth in the hands of emerging commercial groups, the rise in productivity generated by their activities, and the consequent changes in the social and economic structure opened the way for the dissolution of the feudal system and the birth of commercial capitalism, which had as one of its results the colonization of America.

Trade Routes

The renaissance in trade during the Middle Ages was associated with maritime traffic. The two centers of commercial expansion were the Baltic and the North Sea to the north and the eastern Mediterranean to the south. Travel along these waterways gradually re-established the trade between East and West that had been interrupted by the Muslim conquest. In the ninth century, the expansion of the Scandinavians brought the peoples of the Carolingian Empire, England, Scotland, and Ireland into contact with the Slavs and, down the Dnieper and Volga rivers, with the trade of the Orient in the Bosporous and the Caspian Sea. By way of the North Sea and the Baltic, the Orient exchanged its spices, medicines, porcelains, and fine fabrics for the furs, slaves, lumber, metals, and cloth produced by the Slavs and the peoples of northeastern Europe.

To the south in the eastern Mediterranean, Constantinople maintained the Christians' commercial positions against the Arab onslaught. After Constantinople, Venice on the Adriatic coast was the most important city in the region. The great markets of Byzantium encouraged the growth of active trade.

From the ninth century on, the cities of the Italian peninsula— Naples, Gaeta, Amalfi, and Salerno to the west; Bari and especially Venice to the east—no longer limited their trade to Constantinople and the Christian ports of Asia Minor, but dealt increasingly with the Arabs of Africa and Syria. Venice thus became the leading commercial city of the Middle Ages, a position it held until the fifteenth century, when new routes to the Orient and the discovery of America shifted the center of gravity of trade. These cities, but principally Venice, created economic units that were engaged in commerce and the crafts rather than in subsistence agriculture.

They generated the forces that spread out and destroyed the feudal system.

In the Mediterranean, the resurgence of trade among the Christian peoples, which had been initiated by Venice and the cities of the Byzantine Empire, received a strong impulse from the defeats suffered by Islam after the tenth century. The victories of Pisa and Genoa were followed by the First Crusade, which restored control of the Mediterranean Sea to the Christian world. The reconquest of Corsica, Sardinia, and Sicily in the eleventh century assured Christian supremacy.

Trade between the Christian peoples of the West and the peoples of the Orient was intensified with the liberation of the Mediterranean from the Arabs. Venice and the Italian cities were joined by other centers of growing commercial importance like Marseilles and Barcelona.

The products exchanged were chiefly luxury articles from the Orient and raw materials and food produced in the West. Western Europe imported from the Orient spices, medicines, sugar, precious stones, and, to a lesser degree, dyes, cotton and silk for its textile industry, fine fabrics, and gold and silver ornaments. The West exported wool, hides, metals, food products, and wool and linen cloth.

Trade in the north of Europe, which had originated with the Scandinavians, was newly spurred by the Germanic thrust to the east. The founding of Teutonic cities on the Baltic Sea and their monopoly of Slavic trade was consolidated, from a commercial standpoint, when the new cities banded together. The ports on the North Sea became members of this confederation of Baltic cities known as the Hanseatic League, which maintained its commercial hegemony in the north of Europe until the end of the Middle Ages.

The Scandinavians were supplanted by the Germans as the result of the opening of a new line of contact with the Orient. The traditional trade routes they had established along the Dnieper and Volga rivers were closed in the twelfth century. Communication between northern Europe and the Mediterranean was reestablished by maritime route around the Spanish Peninsula, with Bruges emerging as the entrepôt for traffic from north and south.

The trade of the Hanseatic League differed substantially from Mediterranean trade. The Hanseatic cities exported products from their undeveloped hinterland, mainly food, raw materials, and ship stores. From England and France they imported wheat, wine, salt, metals, cloth, and beer. Bruges became an important trading center where products of northeastern Europe were exchanged for those of the Slavs as well as for articles brought from the Orient by Venetian and other Mediterranean merchants.

Limitations on Structural Changes

The impact of the commercial expansion of the eleventh to the fifteenth centuries on the social and economic structure of Western Europe was conditioned by the very real difficulties of trade in that period. The primitive methods of land transport, the hazards of maritime navigation owing to imperfect nautical instruments, and the dangers of piracy made transportation extremely expensive; and the high profit margins of the traders—largely justified by the risks of their activity—multiplied the cost to the consumer. The levies and abuses imposed on trade by the fragmented political power of feudalism also impeded commercial development.

These conditions meant that only merchandise of small bulk and great value would be worth the expense of medieval commerce. A few raw materials were also imported that were essential to the work of the artisans in the cities of Western Europe, especially of those who produced for external markets.

The composition of demand corresponded logically to this structure of supply. Given the low living standards of the agricultural sector, which represented more than 90 percent of the total population, the only people who could purchase luxury imports were members of the feudal landowning class, in part ecclesiastical, and —as the process of urbanization intensified and commercial groups gained importance—the new merchants. Raw materials for industry, principally the textile industry, were mainly bought by artisans who were able to sell their products abroad or to local wealthy groups for high prices.

From the time that European trade began to revive until the technological revolution of the eighteenth century, the expansion of markets through Europe's widening commercial contacts was the dynamic element in development. Even at the end of the eighteenth century, Adam Smith attributed economic progress primarily to specialization created by the expansion of markets.

Technical progress, with its revolutionary effect on the functions of production and the economic structure, still had not become the main stimulus to development. The lack of technological advances restricted the impact of widening markets on the transformation of the internal productive structure and, ultimately, on the rate of growth in output. It operated on two planes: agriculture and the creation of food surpluses, and the urban activities producing exportable goods.

The emergence of cities with populations engaged in crafts and services related to commercial traffic posed problems of supply that were never solved in the Middle Ages. Supply was limited in two ways. On the one hand, low agricultural yields prevented the creation of surpluses to feed the cities, and the great difficulty of transporting bulky and heavy products over long distances restricted the area of urban supply to adjacent fields. On the other hand, the same conditions prevented the importation of food. Regular supplies of food from abroad, which began in the second half of the nineteenth century, were to influence profoundly the economic structure of England and the countries of Western Europe.

Technical progress and improvements in the organization of the crafts and other urban activities were also slight. Therefore, any increase in the volume of exports involved a proportional increase in labor. This is typical of the development in Western Europe of certain domestic crafts and activities producing for external markets, particularly the textile industry. The latter concentrated the first large groups of workers dedicated to a specific activity, as in the cities of Flanders and Spain, especially in Toledo where the production of cloth began to flourish in the thirteenth century. Because of lack of technical progress, the expansion of export activities in the Middle Ages was characterized by the employment of more labor at the same levels of productivity.

As noted before, commercial activities were the dynamic sector par excellence in the feudal economy because, although their effect was limited by extrinsic conditions, they were the only sector that raised over-all productivity. Another factor that influenced the transformation of the internal productive system was demographic pressure. With technological levels and feudal institutions unchanged, the available land could not absorb all the population growth. Consequently, the peoples of Western Europe were driven to emigrate, chiefly toward the east, and to extend occupied territory.

On the other hand, part of the excess population moved to urban centers and entered commercial activities. According to Henri Pirenne, the first commercial nuclei of the early Middle Ages were the result of demographic pressure.[2]

[2] *Ibid.* It is important to point out that, although demographic pressure played a different role after the eighteenth century, its role in the structural changes of the economy of medieval Western Europe is pertinent to the experience of some present-day countries defined as "underdeveloped."

Actually, beginning with the nineteenth century, the changes in the economic structure of Western Europe, insofar as they implied a rise in the relative importance of manufacturing and services and a fall in the relative importance of agriculture, with urbanization as a consequence, received their principal impulse from technical progress and world economic integration, which opened up external sources of food and raw materials and made possible a decrease in the proportion of active population engaged in primary activities. A typical example of this process was the English agricultural crisis of 1870.

However, the experience of some underdeveloped countries, particularly those of high population density, is more like—although in completely different historical conditions—the experience of the countries of the Middle Ages. It is not basically technical progress or the expansion of external markets that stimulates a shift in the distribution of active population from agriculture to other sectors. Demographic pressure on low-yield agricultural activities is the main force that drives people to the cities.

2. FORMATION OF THE ECONOMY
OF COLONIAL AMERICA

New Problems of European Commercial Expansion

As commercial capitalism grew, it inevitably sought to broaden its markets. Trade was the prime dynamic sector and the chief source of increases in productivity, profits, and capital accumulation. In the fifteenth century, Turkish expansion and the fall of Constantinople cut off traditional routes to trade with the Middle East and the Orient, thereby contracting the field of operations of the commercial cities, especially the Italian and the emerging nation-states.

In the second half of the fifteenth century, Western Europe devoted most of its energy to searching for a sea route to replace the overland bridge of Asia Minor and northeast Africa. Portugal, through the expeditions of Henry the Navigator and his successors, opened a maritime route to the Orient around Africa; and Spain, England, France, and Holland followed its lead.

The shift in the center of gravity of trade from the eastern Mediterranean to the Atlantic Ocean transferred the commercial scene from the Italian cities to the European countries of the Atlantic coast and the North Sea. The discovery of America was a key episode in the European trade expansion that had been halted abruptly by Turkish control of Asia Minor and the eastern Mediterranean.

But economic exploitation of the recently discovered lands presented entirely new problems, which subsequently required the European commercial powers to adjust their policies. In order to understand the nature of these problems, it should be remembered that until the discovery of America the economic relations of the Europeans with the peoples they dealt with in the Middle East and the Orient and in Eastern Europe were based on trade and/or plunder. Piracy and pillage dominated the first stages of the expansion of the mercantile cities and the maritime powers. Later, they established more or less normal trade relations, exchanging products from the West for the spices, sugar, and luxury goods produced in the Orient. Given these conditions, their policy was to set up trading posts that served both as a center of exchange and frequently as a fortified base for defense and for attacking commercial rivals.

With this kind of a policy, European commercial capital did not participate in the productive activities of the peoples with whom they maintained economic relations. They ruthlessly despoiled them of part of their wealth or, when this was not possible, they traded with them. But as a rule, western merchants did not organize "peripheral" industrial or agricultural activities and, as authentic entrepreneurs, combine productive factors in a specific branch of production.

The situation in America broke the traditional patterns of European commercial expansion. On this continent, the Europeans found indigenous civilizations (some as advanced as the Inca and the Aztec) that could be subdued by force, or they found regions of vast unexplored natural resources.

Given the existing conditions, the first type of economic relations was one of plunder. But this period was necessarily limited by the amount of treasure that had been accumulated by the conquered people, and America soon represented a new and different undertaking for the colonial powers. In order to exploit the natural resources, the conquerors and colonizers would have to organize production directly, that is, combine the productive factors of capital and labor. The situation posed concrete problems that over a period of time each one of the colonial powers energetically solved in its own way, but only by modifying their usual rules of political practice.

It may be said in summary that these problems were as follows: (1) labor and the organization of the production unit; (2) large-scale territorial occupation; (3) political and institutional organization of the new territories; and (4) collection of wealth for the metropolitan countries.

The need to organize production was primarily a question of available labor. In the various colonial empires, the problem was solved differently in the light of prevailing circumstances. The Spanish Empire could count on the most abundant supply of native labor, and the main objective of colonial policy and of the colonizers was to mobilize the labor for production. The relations of the indigenous workers with productive enterprise were governed by the traditional practices of the *mita* [forced labor] and the *yanaconazgo*,[1] among others.

Almost none of the other colonial nations found a ready supply of labor. Portugal, England, France, and Holland, therefore, had to bring in outside labor: white indentured servants to the English colonies in the north and, of course, slaves, especially to the coasts of the Caribbean, the West Indies, and Brazil.

Each colonial power tried different systems for organizing and financing their production units. England set up colonial companies as a not very successful way of transporting labor and capital to its American possessions. Portugal and Holland put their capital, commercial methods, and technical experience in the production of sugar into joint ventures to form the sugar economy of the northeast of Brazil.

The economic exploitation of natural resources required large-scale occupation of the conquered territories. The colonial policy was to send advance missions of conquest and colonization and subsequently to settle the unoccupied territories. Actually, population centers grew up wherever productive activities were located.

The political and institutional organization of the new territories operated on two planes. On the one hand were the institutions and agencies created to uphold the sovereignty of the metropolitan country in the dependent territory. In general, the European countries tended to transplant their own institutions to their American colonies. On the other hand were the measures used to establish a political balance between the predominant social forces in the colonies. In Spanish America, the administration (representing the Crown), the clergy, and local oligarchies were forces in colonial life that frequently clashed and that forced the central power to constant political regulation in order to maintain its supremacy. These conflicts, which occurred to varying degrees in all colonial America, culminated in the revolutions of independence at the beginning of the nineteenth century and the victory of the interests of the creole groups.

In their relations with their American possessions, the colonial powers aimed at creating channels that would efficiently fill their

---

[1] *Yanaconazgo* was personal service of the Indians in exchange for clothing, a wage, and even land; later the Indians, including their descendants, were attached to the land and were not permitted to leave.

coffers with part of the wealth obtained in the New World. This was accomplished indirectly through taxes and levies, or it was accomplished directly through the exploitation of certain natural resources by officials of the Crown (as in the mining of gold and silver in Spanish America) or through the participation of public capital in private productive enterprises.

Throughout the colonial period, the mainspring of economic organization in America was the monopoly imposed by the metropolitan country. At the height of mercantilism, the enjoyment of an economic or commercial position implied the exclusion of any competition from another country. The political history of Europe and America from the sixteenth to the eighteenth century largely reflects the constant struggle between the European powers to increase their relative share of the colonial economy.

Nevertheless, the trend in those centuries was toward a very marked decline of the foremost colonial powers, Spain and Portugal, and toward the ascendancy of Holland, France, and England. By the beginning of the eighteenth century, England had taken the lead. At the end of that century, however, the revolution of the English colonies in the north caused the first rupture in the system of the New World.

Colonial Production and Its Location

An analysis of the development of the colonial economy should take into account its setting. The main characteristics of that economy were the following: (1) the metropolitan countries were primarily agricultural, and their imports were limited to a number of exotic food products and luxury goods for the politically and economically privileged groups, in addition to a few raw materials; (2) the uncertainty of transport, in view of the primitive state of navigation and the dangers of maritime traffic, made transportation so costly that only products of high value per unit of weight could be profitably traded.

Thus, the colonial powers sought in America the traditional merchandise of the period: gold, precious stones, and metals; sugar and other tropical crops; spices and furs; fish and naval stores. But the discovery of gold was their main concern, and they only began to develop other activities in those lands when they had discarded, at least temporarily, the possibility of finding precious minerals.

The relative success of Spain in this undertaking was one of the reasons for its supremacy in the sixteenth century and also of its subsequent decline.

The flow of labor and capital from Europe to America was explained partly by the policy of the metropolitan countries to consolidate their territorial possessions and partly by their expectation that productive factors would yield higher profits in the New World. The use of those productive factors in the development of specific branches of production and their geographic location were influenced by the above-mentioned characteristics of the economy of the period. Apart from gold and silver mining, economic activity was concentrated in such tropical crops as sugar, which gave rise to the plantation system with slave labor typical of the colonial economy. In North America different resources like the fisheries, forests, and furs of Hudson Bay and New England, and the cotton, rice, tobacco, and sugar of the southern plantations were exploited.

The geographic location of the colonial populations and producing enterprises was determined by two main factors: natural resources and distance. Obviously, economic activity sprang up wherever there were natural resources for producing marketable goods—primarily gold and silver, then tropical crops and fish and lumber. But, except for precious metals, almost the only natural resources exploited were near the ocean or lake areas with access to the ocean. Distance prevented the development of resources found in the interior and far removed from waterways, because the cost of transportation, given the almost complete absence of roads and means of carriage, meant that the price of such products would be prohibitively high. This partly explains the low level of development reached in present Argentine territory during the colonial epoch.

Undoubtedly, other factors must have operated in the location of economic activities. In the case of precious metals, for example, it is possible that Europeans decided to exploit low-grade mines if labor was at hand, because this reduced the organization costs of the enterprise. Nevertheless, as Sergio Bagú points out, the history of Spanish America furnishes numerous examples of forced migrations of native workers to mines.[2] This shows that labor was, in the

---

[2] Sergio Bagú, *Economía de la sociedad colonial* (Buenos Aires: El Ateneo, 1949).

final analysis, a mobile factor that was moved about according to production needs.

The type of products in demand and the factor of distance limited the extent of occupied territory. To mine precious metals, the *conquistadores* pressed on to the most inaccessible and remote corners of the continent. Gold and silver were worth the expense of transport to seaports. Tropical crops were grown on islands or in coastal areas like the West Indies, the northeast of Brazil, and the Caribbean coast. At that time, settlement did not spread beyond a narrow strip along the coastline. The exploitation of fisheries, forests, and certain plantations of the temperate zone was likewise confined to areas near waterways. The economic and social physiognomy of several American countries, notably Brazil, still reflects the influence of this process.

Development of Colonial Economies

The dynamic economic activities of the colonial economy were those closely linked to foreign trade. Mining, tropical agriculture, fishing, hunting, and lumber were the expanding activities that attracted capital and labor. Some activities connected with export production also developed rapidly and were a significant source of profits and investment outlet. The outstanding examples were overseas transport and slave traffic, which, directly tied to colonial trade, became very important in the economy of the period.

Not all activities were, like mining and tropical agriculture, developed on a large scale with slave or servile labor. In the northern hemisphere, small- and medium-sized enterprises with independent workers grew out of the lumber and shipbuilding industries. The shipyards of New England were relatively complex activities that exploited several resources.

The production of a broad range of export goods was reinforced by the size of the market and the pattern of demand. The existence of small and large property owners and independent workers generated an internal demand that was met partly by local output. This early diversification of the internal productive structure, supported by expanding export activities that increased incomes and by the growth of domestic demand, opened the way to a rise in the technical and cultural levels of the population. Social groups were formed that identified with the community rather than with the mother country. This "national bourgeoisie," linked to the expansion of an internal market not dominated by the metropolitan power, was the dynamic nucleus of development, particularly in some of the English colonies of North America.

The experience of the colonies that exported only one or a few products like precious metals or tropical crops was very different. Their production was generally carried out in large-scale production units on the basis of servile labor. Associated with export activities were the wealthy property owners and merchants, together with high officials of the Crown and the clergy. These sectors created demand in the colonial economy and were the only ones that could accumulate capital. They were at the same time the internal colonial market and the source of capital accumulation. On the other hand, the mass of laborers supplied their own subsistence needs and remained almost outside the colonial economy.

Given these conditions, neither the export sector nor the pattern of demand favored diversification of the internal productive structure. As the small groups of property owners, merchants, and political figures acquired more wealth, they bought from abroad more manufactured consumer and durable goods (chiefly luxury articles that could not be produced domestically), thereby decreasing the proportion of total income spent internally.

Consequently, although increased exports and high incomes for the beneficiaries of this system could expand the export sector—through the employment of a greater amount of labor, capital, and natural resources—they did not help to diversify the internal productive structure. Export activities continued to be based on one or a few products, and most of the domestic income leaked into the purchase of imported goods. Once the basic export activity disappeared, as occurred when the northeast of Brazil could not compete with the sugar production of the West Indies, the structure disintegrated, and the labor force returned to subsistence activities.

Irrespective of the restrictions placed on colonial activities that competed with those of the metropolitan country, there is little doubt that both the structure of the export sector and the concentration of wealth were fundamental obstacles to the diversification of the internal productive structure, which would have led to a rise in technical and cultural levels and the emergence of social groups interested in developing a domestic market, as well as export items not controlled by the metropolitan power. This narrow prospect of economic and social development largely explains the experience of colonial America and especially of the Spanish and Portuguese possessions.

Actually, the process of urbanization in these colonies was due to an increase in the labor force employed by those who held political and economic power and to the demographic pressure of the excess population not absorbed by existing activities. Bagú notes that this waste of labor and productive capacity was typical of the colonial economy.[3] Whatever the nature of the export activities and the social structures they supported, the regions devoted to export activities developed most; whereas those that produced for internal consumption or subsistence had little relative importance in the economy of the period. Peru, Mexico, the English colonies of North America, the West Indies, and the northeast of Brazil belonged to the first group and the present Argentine territory to the second.

Of the activities producing for the domestic market, only those that were in some way linked to a dynamic exporting center developed to any extent. In Argentina, for example, mules were raised in the Litoral, and cloth was produced in Tucumán to supply the mines of Potosí. These were among the few activities developed in Argentina from the sixteenth century to the first half of the eighteenth century that enjoyed any prosperity.

---

[3] *Ibid.*

3. THE REGIONAL SUBSISTENCE ECONOMIES
OF PRESENT-DAY ARGENTINA

Location of Argentine Regions in the Colonial Economy of the New World

Geography and availability of resources for export production determined the location of economic activity in colonial America. Present-day Argentina, the territory to the south of the Tropic of Cancer, to the east of the Andes, and to the west of the Uruguay River, could not become an important center of the colonial economy because it offered fewer of these advantages than other parts of the New World.

The physically dominant region of this territory is the temperate zone Pampa, which is ideally suited to growing cereals and grazing livestock. Covering an area of about 56 million hectares [nearly 140 million acres], it is one of the world's most extensive natural prairies with a moderate climate.

During most of the colonial period, agriculture and livestock in the temperate zone, both in the north and south of the continent, had little to do with the dynamic sector: foreign trade. Until nearly the end of the eighteenth century, output of grain and livestock products—hides, meat, milk and dairy products, tallow, and so on—was principally consumed by the producers themselves and by the small local market. Although hides were a significant exception, this general observation is still valid.

The meager development of agricultural and livestock production in the temperate zone was essentially due to the low productivity of the sector and the difficulty of transporting over long distances such bulky products of low value by weight. In addition, this type of production was not adaptable to colonial export production, that is, to the employment of servile labor and of relatively large sums of capital to exploit vast areas.

The variety and complexity of the agricultural activities of the temperate zone demanded enterprising producers and a range of skills that could not be obtained under a system of Negro-slave and

Indian labor. Thus, small-scale agricultural production became the basic economic unit.

All these factors hindered the formation of large agricultural surpluses that could be collected and exported privately and limited consumption of the rural output of the temperate zone to producers and the local market.[1]

Toward the middle of the eighteenth century, the colonial livestock ranch appeared, which permitted some use of servile labor, but only on a small scale in comparison with the great production units in mining and in tropical agriculture.

Nor did present Argentine territory have deposits of gold and other precious metals in the cordillera of the Andes or the mountainous regions of the Center and Northwest. On the other hand, the subtropical lands and forests of the Northeast, despite their having an outlet to the sea by way of the Paraná River could not compete with Brazil, the West Indies, and the Caribbean coast, which were better suited to tropical crops and more accessible to seaports. Moreover, the Spanish Crown had no interest in this type of activity. To the south, almost one third of the present national territory consisted of the Patagonia Plateau, which was not occupied during the colonial period and is to this day sparsely populated.

The drive behind the conquest of these territories was, as in all

---

[1] In the English colonies of North America, cereal production did not become part of foreign trade. "The varied tasks of the small-scale northern agriculture were not adaptable to the gang labor of ignorant Africans." Edward C. Kirkland, *A History of American Economic Life* (New York, 1951), p. 60. Furthermore, the availability of so much land permitted both free workers and indentured servants sooner or later to become independent and to farm their own properties. For the same reason, it was difficult for large landowners, particularly in Pennsylvania and New York, to have their fields cultivated by tenant farmers and share in the crop. The steady expansion of the frontier and the incorporation of new lands prevented the exploitation of those already occupied.

Only in the nineteenth century, with the settlement of the Great Plains in the basin of the Mississippi and Ohio rivers and the completion of a waterway through the Hudson River, the Erie Canal, and the Great Lakes, did the agriculture of the temperate zone become part of the national market of the United States, which began to sell its surpluses on the world market. This process was promoted by an improvement in transportation facilities and a drop in freight charges for bulky products of little value by weight. At the same time, the industrialization of the European countries, particularly England, made possible increasing integration and specialization in the world economy.

the Spanish colonial empire, the search for precious metals and the occupation of Crown lands. Conquistadores and colonizers came from Peru, Chile, and Paraguay. From Peru came the settlers who founded Córdoba in 1573, Tucumán in 1565, Salta in 1582, and Jujuy and La Rioja in 1591; from Chile came the settlers who founded Santiago del Estero in 1553, San Juan and Mendoza in 1562, and San Luis in 1596; from Paraguay came the colonizers of the Mesopotamia and the Río de la Plata Basin, who founded Corrientes and Paraná in 1558, Santa Fe in 1573, and reoccupied the site of Buenos Aires in 1580.

During the Conquest, the indigenous population was concentrated in the present zone of Cuyo, the provinces of the Northwest on the outskirts of the Inca Empire, and in the Center of the country. The principal nuclei of pre-Hispanic population seem to have been located in Quilmes and La Paya in the Calchaquí Valley and in Tilcara in the Quebrada de Humahuaca. The entire indigenous population in present Argentine territory came to about 300,000 at that time. These Indians were useful to the conquistadores because they were pacific and organized. By the sixteenth century, 20,000 Indians had been allotted to encomiendas in Mendoza, 12,000 to Córdoba, and a like number to Santiago del Estero.[2] The tribes of the Pampa and the Mesopotamia, on the other hand, were very primitive and were never incorporated into the colonial economy. In Paraguay, the Jesuit missions were able to organize the Guaraní Indians for large-scale labor.

The expansion of the first settlements and of economic activity from the sixteenth to the eighteenth century was limited for the reasons already described. In those three centuries, no part of Argentine territory developed any activity closely linked to foreign trade. Therefore, these regions received very little labor and capital, and their closed economies fell far behind those of other areas of the colonial world that participated in foreign trade.

Within these regional economies, only activities associated with a dynamic exporting center enjoyed some degree of prosperity as occurred in Tucumán, where cloth was manufactured, and in Córdoba and the Litoral, where draft animals were raised to supply the mines of Upper Peru.

---

[2] An encomienda was a grant from the Crown to a conquistador of the right of the tributes of a native community in exchange for such benefits as the support of a priest and Christian indoctrination. [Translator's note.]

During the colonial epoch, in the absence of other forces of attraction, population and economic activity grew up around the first settlements. In this way, the regional economies emerged and remained unchanged in relative importance until the end of the eighteenth century.

The Region of the Northwest

This region includes the present-day provinces of Salta, Jujuy, Santiago del Estero, Catamarca, and Tucumán.[3] The total area covers about 470,000 square kilometers, of which three fourths are the mountainous and arid regions of the Andes and the rest the arid and semiarid regions of the Chaco. The former are from 1,500 to 6,000 meters above sea level, with from 200 to 500 millimeters of rainfall a year, except for the humid Tucumán-Salta section where precipitation amounts to 1,500 millimeters annually. It is an area of mining, forests, and intermontane valleys suitable for livestock and agriculture. The rest of the Northwest region shares the characteristics of the Chaco, which has seasonally flooded lowlands and natural forests, with an irregular rainfall of between 900 and 1,200 millimeters a year.

The climate is in general continental, dry, temperate, or temperate-torrid, with extremes of daily and seasonal temperature that range from a high of 47 degrees centigrade to a low of 10 degrees below zero. Winters are dry, and it usually rains in summer and autumn. Rivers are sluggish and unnavigable, which accounts for the shortage of surface water in the region.[4]

The first European settlements in the Northwest were established in the sixteenth century by immigrants from Peru, and it is estimated that early in the eighteenth century the total population of the region was about 130,000 inhabitants. The sixteenth century also marked the introduction into the area of the crops and range cattle that were later to develop into a major industry. From Chile came wheat and cotton; from Brazil, sugar cane; and from Peru,

---

[3] The region was smaller than the Gobernación del Tucumán created in 1563, which included in its political limits the provinces of Córdoba, La Rioja, and Chaco, in addition to the above-mentioned.

[4] For a description of the physical characteristics of the different regions, see: Bruno A. Defelippe, *Geografía económica argentina* (Buenos Aires, 1958), and Economic Commission for Latin America, *El desarrollo económico de la Argentina*, Vol. II (United Nations, México, Sales No. 59.II G.3, 1959).

livestock. Crops and livestock and, consequently, population, were distributed according to the suitability of the land. Sugar, rice, cotton, and tobacco were concentrated in the eastern lowlands. Orchards, vineyards, and wheat were planted in the valleys of the cordillera. Cattle, sheep, goats, and horses were raised in the lowlands and in the valleys of the cordillera.

Production of metals never became very important and was destined chiefly for domestic consumption. Along with livestock and agricultural activities, crafts, particularly the manufacture of cotton and wool cloth, carts, furniture, and the processing of livestock products like tallow and hides, were developed.

Output was organized along the following lines. On the one hand were the large plantations owned by Europeans, which produced cotton and pack animals for the mines of Upper Peru and grew food crops for local consumption. Labor was supplied by natives held in encomiendas that usually employed no more than 300 persons each. Toward the middle of the seventeenth century, from 30,000 to 40,000 Indians may have been allotted to the region's encomiendas. These great landed estates furnished the cotton that later was woven into cloth by the Indians. The rest of agrarian output was in the hands of farmers who produced mostly for their own subsistence and a limited trade.

Some of the activities of the region benefited from interregional trade. Nearby Potosí in Upper Peru, with an estimated 160,000 inhabitants in the middle of the seventeenth century, specialized in mining exportable products and generated a demand for cloth, foodstuffs, and livestock, particularly draft animals. Trade between other Argentine regions was scanty and comprised foodstuffs, livestock, and handicrafts.

During the entire colonial period, the Northwest was the most important region in present Argentine territory because of its proximity to a dynamic export center, Potosí. The region contained about 40 percent of the total population and, given its greater specialization, probably produced an even higher proportion of total output.

These facts do not mask, however, the essentially primitive and subsistence nature of the economic structure of the region. The expansion of export activities was restricted by low productivity in agriculture and crafts and by transportation difficulties and limited external demand.

The composition of output underwent some changes during the colonial period. Perhaps the most significant were the disappearance of cotton farming and cotton cloth manufacture as a result of the dying out of Indian labor and the introduction of sheep and wool production. But these changes did not modify the basic economic structure of the region or its limited development prospects.

The Region of Cuyo

Composed of the present provinces of Mendoza, San Juan, and La Rioja, the Cuyo region covers about 330,000 square kilometers. The western half is occupied by the Andes cordillera and the rest by sandy, stony plains with an irregular rainfall of between 200 and 500 millimeters a year. In the mountains the climate is dry with cold winters and cool summers, and in the piedmont the summers are hot and the winters cool. The annual temperature averages from 14 to 20 degrees centigrade. The eastern plains have saline groundwater and are covered with tall bunch grass (*pasto duro*). Surface waters are furnished by the mountain streams of the Desaguadero-Salado system, which has an average annual flow of 250 cubic meters per second. Agricultural and livestock production is possible in the intermontane valleys, and crops can be grown under irrigation in the eastern plains.

The first settlements of Europeans came from Chile in the sixteenth century, and it is estimated that by the middle of the eighteenth century the region's population reached about 70,000 inhabitants, of whom nearly 80 percent were Indian and *mestizo* [of mixed European and Indian blood] and the rest European and creole. The first immigrants to the region introduced the crops and range cattle that were to be developed later.

Livestock and agriculture were the principal activities. Crops were grown under irrigation in the valleys of the eastern piedmont, and cattle, goats, sheep, and horses were grazed on the tall bunch grass and irrigated pastures of the plains. In the urban centers textile, metal, and leather crafts grew.

Production was organized along the same lines as in the Northwest. On the one hand, there were great properties, encomiendas; it is estimated that in the sixteenth century 20,000 Indians were assigned to them in Mendoza. On the other hand, there were farmers producing for subsistence and the narrow local market.

Because the region was far removed from any dynamic exporting center, its foreign trade was even smaller than that of the Northwest. Cuyo exported chiefly wine, alcohols, and dry fruits to the Litoral and other Argentine regions. But the regional economy was essentially of a primary and subsistence nature.

The Region of the Center

The present provinces of Córdoba and San Luis are included in the center region. The total area is approximately 250,000 square kilometers. In the west and north are the mountains of the Sierra Grande, Sierra Chica, and San Luis, with an average altitude of 1,000 meters above sea level and with the Champaquí peak rising to almost 2,900 meters. Mountains occupy about half the region, and the rest is semiarid prairie.

Rainfall varies from 200 to 500 millimeters a year, and the climate is generally continental, dry, temperate, or temperate-torrid. There are very few streams, and they have an average flow of about 100 meters per second. Groundwater is usually saline.

Agricultural production was for the subsistence of the farmers and the consumption of a small local market. Córdoba, however, was a flourishing center of livestock production, especially of draft animals for Upper Peru. The raising of mules for Potosí mines was the most important activity of the region and the only one closely linked to the external market. The colonial ranch was typically organized on the basis of great extensions of territory and small-scale employment of servile labor. The only high-income groups in the region were associated with this sector. In addition, an artisan activity developed within the traditional patterns—the processing of leather, tallow, and cloth—to meet local consumption.

The Region of the Litoral

Historically, this region encompasses the present provinces of Buenos Aires, Entre Ríos, Corrientes, and Santa Fe. With an area of roughly 56 million hectares, it includes almost all the Pampa. The 35 million hectares of its humid zone receive 700 to 1,000 millimeters of rainfall evenly distributed throughout the year. The semiarid Pampa occupies 21 million hectares with a precipitation of 600 to 800 millimeters per year. The region has abundant fresh water just below the ground and surface streams of little volume that dry up in times of drought.

The humid Pampa covers the center and east of Buenos Aires, the center and east of Santa Fe, and Entre Ríos. The semiarid Pampa stretches from the west of Buenos Aires to the northeast of the Pampa Province and the southeast of Córdoba. The climate of the region is temperate with mild seasonal variations; the soil is ideally suited to agriculture and stock raising. It is an almost uninterrupted expanse of natural grassland.

Although Corrientes Province historically forms part of the Litoral, it is geographically part of the Chaco, with heavy rainfall of more than 1,000 millimeters per year. This area, which has zones of swamps and frequently flooded lowlands as well as natural forests, can support agriculture and livestock.

At the time of the Conquest, the indigenous population in the Litoral was nomadic and primitive, and its labor never could be organized by the colonizers. The latter came in the sixteenth century from Paraguay, bringing with them the crops and especially the cattle that formed the basis of subsequent livestock and agricultural activity in that region.

During the colonial period, the Litoral was the most backward and least populated region of present Argentine territory. It is estimated that in the middle of the eighteenth century there were 50,000 inhabitants, of whom around half were white and creole and the rest Indian and mestizo. By the end of the eighteenth century, barely 10 percent of the Pampa was settled by Europeans, the rest being left to the Indians. The absence of exploitable mineral resources and of a native labor supply accounted for this relative underdevelopment.

Farmers produced for themselves and for the small local market, and agricultural activity languished, making it periodically necessary to import flour and food. The wild cattle of the Pampa, descendants of stock brought by the first colonizers, were the basis of livestock production.

The meat, hides, lard, and hoofs obtained from the wild cattle were used for subsistence and for supplying the needs of the small urban centers. Some foreign trade was carried on in hides, but never to a significant degree. Because it depended so much on the exploitation of wild cattle, contemporary observers referred to the Litoral as a "civilization of hides" (*civilización del cuero*).

The expansion of livestock production was not only hindered by a lack of external markets but by the difficulties of securing labor. The boundless land and wide open spaces of the Pampa created the gaucho, who worked to eat and occasionally traded hides for articles to satisfy his "vices."

When systematic trade in hides became possible toward the middle of the seventeenth century, the authorities restricted the hunting of wild cattle to licensed groups. Later, the ranch emerged as cattle began to be raised and rounded up. Nevertheless, livestock production expanded very slowly until the end of the eighteenth century, when conditions arose that changed it into the dynamic sector par excellence of the development of the Litoral.

There was little urban formation during the entire period. Not more than 10 or 15 percent of the total population lived in Buenos Aires and other towns of the Litoral. It is estimated that as late as the eighteenth century, Buenos Aires had scarcely 1,000 inhabitants, and contemporary chroniclers agreed on the poverty of the city and the region. Some Litoral towns developed crafts for local consumption. Moreover, a commercial nucleus existed in Buenos Aires that tried to promote the port as a center for the exchange of products from the interior for articles imported from abroad. But the poverty of the region, its lack of exportable production, and its meager trade with other regions of Argentine territory, plus the monopoly imposed by the Spanish Crown, prevented the city from turning into a commercial port. Nor did the smuggling activities of the period change the basic conditions of that stagnation.

The Northeast and Patagonia

The Northeast covers the present provinces of Misiones, Chaco, Formosa, and northern Corrientes. When the Spaniards arrived at the beginning of the sixteenth century, about 50,000 primitive Indians inhabited these territories. Until the first half of the eighteenth century these tribes frequently attacked the neighboring regions of the Northwest, making forays as far as Tucumán, Córdoba, and Salta. Except for those who came under the influence of the Jesuit missions of Paraguay, they were not integrated into the colonial economy.

In Paraguay, until they were expelled in 1753, the Jesuits organized about 150,000 Indians to work in missions and supply their own needs. Trade with other regions was limited to exports of yerba maté which, although it still has a wide market throughout Argentina and the south of Brazil, never became a significant item in the trade of the American colonial world.

Patagonia, with an area equal to one third of the national territory, was not occupied permanently during the colonial period.

4. STRUCTURE AND DYNAMICS OF THE SYSTEM

During the period under review, that is, from the sixteenth to the end of the eighteenth century, there was no national economy, properly speaking, within the present geographical limits of Argentina, because there was no market in which reciprocal flows of capital, labor, and products could take place on a significant scale between the different regions. It is characterized, therefore, by the existence of self-sufficient regional economies separated by considerable distances, a lack of maritime or river communications, and the hazards of land transport. Consequently, analysis of the structure and expansion of the system can be made only at the regional level.

It is possible to deduce some of the structural features and to outline the dynamics of the system of regional subsistence economies by relating the information available for the period in question to the basic pattern of contemporary economies that have not yet advanced beyond the primitive stage of development reached by those territories at the end of the eighteenth century.

Demographic Stagnation

Population levels were largely determined by the number of natives working in the regional economies. Where large indigenous populations existed at the time of the Conquest, demographic change can be explained by their fate. For example, in the Northwest, high mortality among encomienda Indians, due to working conditions on cotton plantations and in textile factories, accounts for the decline in the total population of the region. The disappearance of native labor from the regional economies through death or flight to other areas, and the lack of immigration from Europe and other parts of the continent indicate that the total population of present Argentine territory remained stationary or even diminished from the sixteenth to the eighteenth century. Furthermore, during this whole period there was hardly any incorporation of Negro slaves. By the middle of the eighteenth century, the total number of inhabitants probably came to around 300,000, which was about equal to the pre-Hispanic population.

Weakness of the Export Sector and of the Structure of Domestic Production

Since the regions' economies were typically subsistence and their populations were stagnant or declining, it is unlikely that total output went up from the sixteenth to the second half of the eighteenth century. In all regions, essentially the same factors were responsible for stagnation and, above all, the absence of any growing export activity that might have increased total output. The ratio of exports to gross product must have been very low; and it could not have been significant even in the Northwest, where a certain amount of trade with Potosí had developed. At no time during the entire period was there a steady expansion of foreign trade sufficient to raise even temporarily the relative importance of the "external sector" in the regional economies. Another, although secondary, factor was the monopolistic system of the Spanish colonial empire, to which reference will be made later.

The weakness of the export sector explains why the various regional economies did not develop and also why each region diversified its productive structure and managed to become self-sufficient in the main commodities and services that it needed. With no capacity to import supported by a significant volume of exports and/or inflow of foreign capital, each region had to satisfy its own demand. The structure of supply fitted logically the diversification of demand and made available the foodstuffs, manufactures, and services the latter required. However, it must be remembered that only a small part of the population participated in the market economy and that incomes were so low that only a very reduced proportion could be spent on any consumption above the subsistence level. On the other hand, the demand exercised by the few landowners, *encomenderos,* and other "high-income" groups was insufficient to bring about a substantial diversification of output.

Because of the stagnation of population and productivity, effective demand in each region remained essentially unchanged, which prevented the high proportion of income spent domestically from generating a further flow of income, as occurs in a dynamic economy where capital formation and technical progress constantly expand.

Low productivity in the regional economies kept the domestic market narrow and thereby limited the possibilities of labor specialization and trade within each region. Most of output went to satisfy the subsistence requirements of the producers and the groups that controlled them, as in the case of the encomiendas. In fact, most of the productive effort of the population was outside the market economy. Therefore, diversification of the structure of output had little effect on the capacity of each regional economy to develop.

Manpower was probably allocated among the different activities as follows: from 80 to 90 percent was employed in agricultural and livestock production, while the rest was engaged in services and manufactures. Services were mainly government—defense and administration—and trade. It is possible that in regions containing an indigenous population, personal services to the encomenderos accounted for a significant proportion of labor; but this did not change the relative importance of the service sector in the over-all employment structure.

The low level of technology and the small amount of capital per person employed in the export sector meant that output per person in the most productive sector of the economy was not much higher than that of labor engaged in subsistence activities, services, or manufactures for the local market.

The importance of agricultural activity was also reflected in the large proportion of the population in rural areas. During the whole period, urban dwellers employed in nonagricultural activities never represented more than 10 percent of the total population of any region.

Income Distribution and Capital Accumulation

The distribution of income among the different social sectors of each region was largely determined by specific relationships between the different groups involved in production. But taking all the regions together, only the encomenderos and landowners and, to a lesser degree, the burgeoning merchant groups had an income above subsistence level. The indigenous population used as servile labor, the small farmers, and most of the artisans received incomes barely sufficient for subsistence and frequently below, particularly in the case of Indians assigned to encomiendas.

The importance of the subsistence sector outside the market economy also reduced the scope of the money economy. The indigenous laborer was paid in kind, or he derived an income from the work he did on the days he was free from service to the encomendero. Transactions among small rural producers and artisans were largely carried out on a barter basis. Money entered only into transactions relating to the foreign trade of the region, and for that purpose Spanish coins were used.

Given the low levels of productivity, the bulk of output was for consumption. A very small proportion must have been diverted from current consumption and appropriated by the high-income groups mentioned above. This saving was used mainly to employ manpower in the construction of houses and in a number of nonproductive public works. Restricted external and internal markets meant that there was little incentive to invest in order to expand installed capacity in agricultural activities and manufacturing or to undertake new enterprises. Investment in infrastructure capital—at that time mainly for improvements in transportation, particularly roads and canals—both by the private and the "public sector" was limited by similar factors. During the whole period, an insignificant share of the resources of the community was allocated to capital formation, so that the amount of capital available per person employed was very small and probably did not increase. Only in export activities was there any capital accumulation to expand productive capacity.

Public sector receipts, derived chiefly from taxes on external transactions and on certain items of consumption, were spent almost entirely on defense and administration, with a negligible amount left over as savings for the sector. Given the absence of technical progress in closed and stagnant economies and the prevailing levels of subsistence or less than subsistence, the distribution of income among the different social sectors and the manner in which savings were utilized is hardly relevant to development.

With no strong impulses from foreign trade, it was impossible to improve systematically the techniques and organization of the economic process and thereby help raise productivity and per capita income. The regional economies, closed by definition, did not receive any immigration or foreign-capital inflow worth mentioning.

Balance Between the Regional Economies

European immigration settled in areas having an indigenous population that could be used as labor. Argentina lacked the elements that attracted European population, capital, and economic activity to other parts of colonial America.

The various regions developed from the sixteenth to the eighteenth century without any significant change in their relative importance. As already indicated, the most important was the Northwest, with 40 percent of the total population. Next were Cuyo and the Center, until the Litoral began to advance in the second half of the eighteenth century due to forces that will be discussed later. The Northeast and Patagonia were not settled by Europeans and remained practically outside the colonial economy.

The balance between the different regional economies was maintained because no export activity arose in any one of them that could have brought about a massive displacement of the center of gravity of the economy. Brazil, for example, shifted from sugar to minerals to coffee; and its experience clearly shows the fundamental importance of exports in the location of economic activity and of the dynamic center of development. Argentina was not to undergo this process until the second half of the nineteenth century.

Lacking any outside stimulus for growth and any possibility of autonomous development on the basis of domestic demand and productivity, each regional economy was a closed and self-sufficient unit. Within present Argentine territory, the regional economies were independent of one another. There was no one predominant region, with the others as satellites, as was to occur later.

The importance of these features of the regional economies and of the aggregate picture, however, should not be exaggerated. Regional self-sufficiency and diversified production and the balance between the regional economies were not related to a development process in which productivity, income, and a national market expanded concurrently. To the contrary, the regional economies had these characteristics because they were unable to fit into the colonial market and participate in foreign trade, the mainspring of development at that time. Without foreign trade, the income of each region and, consequently, domestic demand could not increase, which eventually had an adverse effect on the diversification and growth of output and prevented the ultimate formation of a national market and a national economy. Self-sufficiency from the sixteenth to the eighteenth century was a feature of stagnation, not of development.

PART II

THE TRANSITION

(*The End of the Eighteenth Century to 1860*)

5. BUENOS AIRES AS AN ENTREPÔT

At the end of the eighteenth century, the regions that now make up Argentina began to change in character and in relative importance. First, the Río de la Plata was opened up to colonial trade, which meant that Buenos Aires emerged as a natural entrepôt for the trade of Spain's southernmost American possessions. Second, cattle production in the Litoral became increasingly directed toward exports. Thus, for the first time in history, these regions began to feel the influence of the basic dynamic element of development at that time: foreign trade. In this part, Part II, its effect on the conditions of development in each region and on the balance between them will be taken up.

Advantages in Location

The geographical location of the Río de la Plata made it the best route of access to the heart of the Spanish colonial empire south of Peru. The distance from Buenos Aires to Potosí was 1,750 kilometers over plains which took two months to cross. On the other hand, Potosí could be reached from Lima only after four months of travel over 2,500 kilometers of mountain trails. Therefore, the price of imported merchandise in Potosí varied according to whether it arrived via Lima or Buenos Aires. In Potosí a length of cloth coming from Lima cost six or seven times more than one from Buenos Aires. Mules, the basic draft animal in mining, were four times as expensive in Potosí if brought from Lima rather than from the Litoral or Córdoba.

The difference in the location of Lima and Buenos Aires with regard to the market of Potosí obviously affected all the regional economies—Cuyo, the Center, the Northwest, and the Litoral, as well as Paraguay. However, Buenos Aires could not benefit from its competitive advantage over Lima until the second half of the eighteenth century when the Bourbon kings instituted a number of liberal reforms.

During almost 250 years of colonial life, the Río de la Plata and particularly Buenos Aires did not fulfill their natural role as an entrepôt for the Spanish Empire south of Peru for the following reasons:

First, the scanty development of the Río de la Plata hinterland, that is, the Pampa region, and the closed character of the regional economies of the interior meant that no exportable surpluses were available for colonial trade.

Second, most trade in the produce of Mexico, the West Indies, and New Granada, as well as that of Peru, was concentrated in the Caribbean area. In fact, the Caribbean, especially in the sixteenth and seventeenth centuries, was the center of gravity of the whole colonial empire.

Third, as a consequence, the Río de la Plata was excluded from the trade channels of the colonial empire, which the economic regulations of the Spanish Crown limited to Central America.[1] The isolation of the Río de la Plata from the interior was reinforced by the establishment of the Aduana Seca [inland customs house] of Córdoba in 1622 and by regulations prohibiting imports of precious metals into the Río de la Plata area in order to prevent export of the mining output of Upper Peru by this route.

Spain made some exceptions to its foreign trade ban on the Río de la Plata, so that Buenos Aires and the miserable towns of that region might survive.[2] Since these towns had no exportable pro-

---

[1] From 1561 to 1739, Spain used a system of *galeones* and *flotas* to carry on its trade with America. [Two fleets were dispatched each year, one for Tierra Firme and one for New Spain. The fleet to South America was known collectively as the galeones from the type of vessel composing the armada of six or eight men-of-war that convoyed it. In contradistinction, the Mexican fleet became specifically the flota, being defended only by two warships, a *capitana* and an *almirante*.] Exclusive authorization for trans-Atlantic commerce was given in Spain in Cádiz and San Lúcar de Barrameda, the port of Seville, and in America to Cartagena, Portobello on the Isthmus of Panama, and the island of San Juan de Ulúa off the coast of Vera Cruz. All other Spanish and American ports were excluded from this trade, as well as any ship that was not part of the galeones and flotas. The most important trade fair of Spanish America was held in Portobello, where European wares were sold and distributed overland to Peru and the rest of the Spanish Empire south of Ecuador. On their return trips, the galeones and flotas transported to Spain the produce of the colony and the bullion of the Crown. This system was suspended in 1739, and trade was again entrusted to individual vessels chartered by the merchants of Seville and Cádiz.

[2] A few concessions were granted to the Río de la Plata which partially liberalized trade. In August, 1602, Phillip II authorized the inhabitants of the

duction to ensure their development, they could only subsist if allowed to take at least partial advantage of their location. Although such authorizations were limited, trade expansion through the Río de la Plata was actually held back by the lack of exportable surpluses and by the population's meager capacity to import.

Smuggling, although it alleviated the harshness of the royal regulations, never achieved a large volume because of the lack of development of those territories. Trade through the Río de la Plata, including smuggling, was always insignificant in relation to the total foreign trade of colonial America.

Changes in Spanish Policy

The change in the policy of the Spanish Crown toward the Río de la Plata was related mainly to a shift in over-all strategy.[3] Meas-

---

Río de la Plata to export annually in their own vessels to Brazil, Guinea, and "other neighboring vassal islands" 2,000 *fanegas* of wheat, 500 *arrobas* of tallow, and 500 *quintales* of jerked beef. [A fanega is 1.6 bushels; an arroba is 25.35 pounds or 11.50 kilograms; a quintal is a hundredweight.] These ships could bring back any commodities provided the goods were not reshipped to other Spanish colonies in America. Direct trade, as well as immigration and slave traffic, was forbidden. The concession was renewed for five year periods in October, 1608, and July, 1614. In 1616, a request by the inhabitants of the Río de la Plata for a permanent concession was refused. However, in compensation, for three years beginning in September, 1618, they were allowed two vessels a year of not over one hundred tons each. Of commodities imported in this way, a part might be transported overland to Peru, but a duty of 50 percent had to be paid at the inland customs house of Córdoba in addition to the *almojarifazgo* [duty] and *avería* [tax on exports and imports to maintain the convoys] already levied in Seville and Buenos Aires. These regulations remained in force until the liberal measures instituted by the Bourbons in the eighteenth century. See Elena F. S. de Studer, *La trata de negros en el Río de la Plata durante el siglo XVIII* (Buenos Aires: University of Buenos Aires, 1958).

[3] Trade liberalization permitted the principal Spanish ports to trade with the Indies and the principal ports of America, including Buenos Aires and Montevideo. But shipowners, captains, officers, and two thirds of the crew still had to be Spanish. Imports could be transshipped from Buenos Aires, which brought the inland market under the influence of that port. These measures were contained in the Free Trade Regulation of 1778. In 1791, Spaniards and foreigners were given the right to traffic in Negro slaves in Buenos Aires and other parts of America. In 1795, the Viceroyalty of the Río de la Plata was authorized on a temporary basis to trade with foreign colonies. The trade liberalization measures were supplemented with a simplification of the tax system.

ures favoring the estuary ports over Lima—the creation of the Viceroyalty of the Río de la Plata in 1776 and the Free Trade Regulation of 1778—were apparently not due to pressure exerted by the early commercial and livestock interests of the Río de la Plata. The decentralization of administrative, political, and military power was a response to strategic defense needs in those territories in the face of increasing penetration by the Portuguese and the British. The extension to Buenos Aires and Montevideo of the same conditions of trade granted to other ports of Spanish America was the material basis for the necessary development of this area, which was to continue relying on its role as an entrepôt.

It was, therefore, the growing threat of the Portuguese and the British that brought about the change of policy. In Brazil, during the second half of the seventeenth century, the *bandeirantes* [slave raiders, members of a military company of São Paulo] began to move south from São Paulo into Río Grande, Uruguay, and various parts of the Argentine Mesopotamia. At the end of the eighteenth century, the discovery of metals and precious stones over a large area stretching through the states of Minas Gerais, Matto Grosso, and Goias shifted the center of gravity of the Brazilian colonial economy southward.[4] Furthermore, owing to the dependence of Portugal and its colony on Britain, which crystallized in the Treaty of Methuen in 1703, the British became closely associated with Portuguese expansion to the south.

Luso-British penetration had two important centers in the Río de la Plata: the Sacramento colony established by the Portuguese in 1680 and the slave traffic conducted in Buenos Aires by the British under a concession granted them by the Spanish Crown in the Treaty of Utrecht in 1713. During most of the eighteenth century, the mainstays of contraband in the region were the colony and the slave traffic. In fact, the struggle against smuggling and foreign penetration only became effective whenever the authorities of the Río de la Plata took advantage of conflicts between the metropolitan powers to occupy the colony and interrupt the slave traffic.

---

[4] Celso Furtado estimates that in the eighteenth century total Portuguese immigration, attracted by mining development, was at least 300,000 and possibly as high as 500,000. See *The Economic Growth of Brazil* (Berkeley and Los Angeles: University of California Press, 1963) p. 81n.

The Rising Commercial Importance of the Port

In any event, the liberal reforms of the Bourbons opened the way for profound changes in the evolution of the regional economies of Argentina. Buenos Aires became the natural intermediary for domestic exportable production and a supply center for foreign imports. The role of Buenos Aires was strengthened by the War of Independence at the beginning of the nineteenth century, and free trade became the objective and the political philosophy of the merchant groups.

The expansion of Buenos Aires as an entrepôt was severely limited by its underdeveloped hinterland, the Pampa, which had no activity properly integrated into the colonial market and no exportable output. There was little to export and, therefore, little capacity to import. Some export-oriented activity within the port's zone of influence was needed to consolidate the foundations of development and to give predominance to that part of the country. Livestock production in the Litoral furnished this activity.

This new commercial importance of Buenos Aires was to largely determine Argentina's transition into a primary export economy. On the one hand, it gave rise to a commercial sector engaged in trading domestic production for imports. This sector gradually accumulated capital and gained influence in the development process. On the other hand, it forced the nearly self-sufficient regional economies of the interior into a situation in which they increasingly had to face foreign competition. The resulting conflict between the port and the regional economies conditioned the whole of Argentina's economic and political development from the end of the eighteenth to the second half of the nineteenth century. However, as will be seen later, this conflict was not to be solved simply by opening up the port or by expanding livestock production in the Litoral.

6. THE EXPANSION OF CATTLE RAISING

Conditions Favorable to Livestock Development

Livestock production was the first activity in the economic history of this region to be developed for export on a significant scale and at a rapid pace. As indicated before, its expansion in the Litoral from the end of the eighteenth to the middle of the nineteenth century was, together with trading activity at the port of Buenos Aires, the dynamic growth factor in the transition period.

Exports of hides, which were the leading trade item in the transition stage, rose from an average of 20,000 units per year in the seventeenth century, to 150,000 by the middle of the eighteenth century, and more than one million at the close of the eighteenth. Two and one half million hides were exported in 1850, a time when new livestock exports such as jerked beef and wool were beginning to appear. Jerked beef, which entered export data the end of the eighteenth century, represented about 10 percent of total exports by the middle of the nineteenth century. Wool exports also increased rapidly but did not have much impact until the second half of the nineteenth century. The effect of wool exports will be considered later in discussing the primary export economy.

The development of livestock raising was aided by the abundance of fertile land in the Pampa region; the expansion of world demand and the liberalization of trade; the relative simplicity of livestock raising; and the low labor requirements of this kind of production. Each of these aspects will be considered separately.

The abundance of fertile land in the Pampa region

The ecological conditions of the Pampa could not have been better suited to development of a livestock industry. Stock flourished on its grasslands and watering places almost without expense to the rancher. Only the presence of the Indian, who constituted a frontier to the production area, and the long distances with the ensuing transportation difficulties limited use of the Pampa lands.

In any case, for the first time in colonial history, the "useless territories" of the Pampa were profitably used on a fairly large scale.

The expansion of world demand and the liberalization of trade

The gradual improvement in maritime transport and the growth of demand for livestock products in Europe and North America opened up new markets for these products and expanded existing ones. World trade in products like hides and wool was encouraged by the early stages of industrialization in Europe. Production of jerked beef for the consumption of slave labor in the tropical agriculture economies was also stimulated by external demand. On the other hand, freer trade under the Free Trade Regulation of 1778 meant that the livestock products of the Pampa region had increasing access to overseas markets.

The relative simplicity of livestock raising

Large-scale livestock production was possible at the low levels of technology, organization, and capital prevailing in the Litoral at the end of the eighteenth century. Livestock could be raised, slaughtered, and processed on the basis of elementary techniques and organization. The amount of capital needed per person employed in livestock production probably was not much higher than the average for the whole economy. These features distinguished livestock production from other export activities developed in the rest of the colonial empire, particularly tropical agriculture, where capital requirements and technical and organizational complexity were much greater.

The low labor requirements

At the end of the eighteenth century, according to Félix de Azara, one overseer and ten laborers could take care of an *estancia* [grant of grazing land] holding 10,000 head of cattle and covering no less than 15,000 to 20,000 hectares. The practical significance of this is evident if it is recalled that at the time population density in the settled rural areas of the Pampa region must have been approximately one inhabitant per 500 hectares. When the National

Census of 1869 was taken, there was still only one inhabitant per 100 hectares in the rural areas of the province of Buenos Aires. Obviously, if livestock raising had required a large amount of manpower, its development would have been impossible without a massive immigration of foreign labor. National labor could not have moved into the Litoral in large numbers owing to its lack of mobility and to the low population density in Argentina generally.[1] Although the scarcity of labor for livestock production was not an insurmountable obstacle, it remained a problem throughout the transition stage and well into the second half of the nineteenth century. Legislation was repeatedly adopted during that period to prevent laborers from leaving the ranches on which they were employed and to recruit the potential manpower roving the countryside, the gaucho.

Ample land and low labor requirements reduced the cost of livestock raising in Argentina to below that in the importing countries; at the same time, growing external demand and gradual expansion of the domestic market centered in the city of Buenos Aires pushed up prices. Investments in livestock raising, therefore, were extremely profitable. In the years immediately following the trade liberalization of the 1770's, the price of hides multiplied from three to four times. As its profit margins widened, livestock raising, together with the commercial activity of the port, became one of the principal sources of capital accumulation in the Litoral.

To make good use of the new opportunities offered by livestock

---

[1] Labor actually became a problem in the second half of the nineteenth century, but in connection with agriculture rather than the livestock industry. As is well known, it was solved by vast immigration from Europe. However, until the middle of the century, agriculture was mainly for domestic consumption and had very little prospect of expansion. Furthermore, agricultural productivity was very low and barely provided a subsistence income for farmers. Its development required that large numbers of farmers be settled on land already used for livestock grazing, which explains why so many landholders opposed immigration. But after 1860, world markets for the agricultural production of the Pampa opened up, and better techniques substantially raised productivity. Large proprietors responded to these new circumstances by renting their land, thereby participating in the growing agricultural output. The system of tenant farming also allowed a more rational use of land through the rotation of cereals and forage crops, which supplemented agricultural and livestock output. This change in the conditions of the development of agriculture and livestock accounts for the new attitude of landholders in the Litoral after 1860, when they converted to a policy of immigration and of settlement in the Pampa region.

development, however, the frontier had to be extended into new territory, and productivity in the livestock industry itself had to be increased.

Extension of the Frontier and Appropriation of Land

During the eighteenth century, the settlers left most of the Pampa to the Indian because they had sufficient land for their primitive pastoral activities. Very little of the cattle was utilized at that time—only hides and tallow for limited exports and the domestic market, and meat for local consumption. The "technique" of production consisted in hunting wild cattle and skinning it on the site.

Beginning with the seventeenth century, local authorities prohibited the free hunting of cattle and awarded permits to private individuals who thereby, in effect, became the owners of the wild cattle that roamed the Pampa prairies. Because of these conditions, the possession of land to raise and fatten cattle was of secondary importance.

After 1750, however, the rise in exports of hides led inevitably to a need to organize livestock raising. The few remaining wild cattle had to be hunted and slaughtered farther and farther away from population centers. According to Emilio A. Coni, by 1720 almost all cattle had owners. The roundup became the basis of livestock raising and the estancia the unit of production.

With huge tracts taken over in order to establish privately owned estancias and herds, it was soon apparent that more land would have to be made available. Thus, the initial thrust to obtain *acciones de vaquería* [cattle equity] was transformed into expansion of the frontier of the Pampa and the private appropriation of new lands. This twofold process was of utmost importance in the stage of transition and was to exert a profound influence on the later development of rural production and of the country as a whole.

Occupation of land in the Pampa area went on uninterruptedly throughout the nineteenth century, culminating with the Roca campaign of 1879 when the Indian was decisively defeated.[2] At

---

[2] The occupation of the rest of the territory still controlled by the Indian was accomplished during the last two decades of the nineteenth century, when Patagonia and the interior of the Chaco were settled. The latter comprised the area north of parallel 30°, east of Santiago del Estero and Salta, and the present provinces of Chaco and Formosa.

the close of the eighteenth century, which marked the end of the regional subsistence economies, the southern frontier of the Pampa stretched along the Salado River, Carmen de Areco, Salto, and Rojas in the province of Buenos Aires. Of the total area of this province, amounting to 300,000 square kilometers, only about 10 percent was integrated into the colonial economy.

By 1830, the frontier had moved southward to a line running through Junín, Bragado, 25 de Mayo, Tapalque, Azul, and Tandil in the province of Buenos Aires, reaching the Atlantic Coast at the level of Mar del Plata. According to Ramos Mejía, the estancias in the province of Buenos Aires then covered an area of more than 100,000 square kilometers.

The Indian campaigns of 1876 pushed the frontier southward and westward until it ended at Truenque, Lauquen, Guamini, Carhue, Puan, Bahía Blanca, and Carmen de Patagones. This territory included nearly all the humid Pampa of 35 million hectares. The 1879 expedition of Roca crushed the Indians and completed the process of land occupation.

As stated before, land occupation was accompanied by private land appropriation. The policy of distributing public lands, particularly in the province of Buenos Aires, meant that most of the Pampa region rapidly fell into the hands of a small number of people. By 1840, about 8,600,000 hectares had been disposed of, principally through the sale of land that had been rented by the state to private corporations and individuals under the emphyteusis system followed in the 1820's by the governments of Martín Rodríguez and Rivadavia. That amount of land was divided among 293 proprietors, giving each one an average of 30,000 hectares. National territory beyond the frontier, which had been freely used under legal provisions adopted in 1857, was subsequently converted into the property of little more than 300 persons. If these 3 million hectares, mainly awarded for military services rendered in the campaign against the Indians, are added to the sales of the public domain, aggregate private appropriations in the province of Buenos Aires amounted to some 12 million hectares.

Distribution of public lands did not usually involve such large areas nor was it done as rapidly in other provinces of the Pampa region—namely, Córdoba, Santa Fe, and Entre Ríos. However, a small number of proprietors accumulated a considerable amount of land as a result of the allotment of Crown lands during the colonial period and of national territory after independence.

By the middle of the nineteenth century, all the most fertile and well-located land of the Pampa region had been privately appropriated. Most of the humid zone was in the hands of large proprietors. The legal occupation of these lands was largely completed in the 1860's, when the stage of primary exports brought the Argentine economy into the world economy. As shown below, this process shaped the land tenure system which has prevailed in Argentina ever since.

Capital Formation and Technical Improvements

In order to consolidate its development, the livestock sector had to be made more profitable by means of better organization and improved techniques. This required an adequate flow of savings into livestock enterprises.

The estancia, a vast property under a single administration and employing wage labor, was the first large-scale and expanding capitalist enterprise to be organized in Argentina's economy. As regards techniques, the system of roundups arose at the same time that the first blooded stock began to be imported to improve domestic herds. After 1850, the introduction of wire fences was an important technical advance that helped raise the yields of the estancia because it permitted a consolidation of legal property rights, a better use of land, and a reduction in the employment of labor by eliminating the burdensome "night watches" on the open range.[3]

The growing importance of jerked beef initiated the integration of the livestock economy; its processing supplemented cattle raising and generated a demand for salt. It was the only aspect of livestock development that went beyond the simple pattern of producing meat for local consumption and hides and tallow for export and the internal market.

The flourishing livestock sector attracted the savings needed for the modest levels of development of the time. Expansion of productive capital was chiefly financed by reinvestment of profits, but the

---

[3] Horacio Giberti, *Historia económica de la ganadería argentina* (Buenos Aires, 1954).

commercial groups of Buenos Aires also put part of their savings into livestock, thereby linking *porteño* business interests with the cattle-raising economy.

Infrastructure investment, particularly in highways, was insignificant throughout the period. Private investment in this field was limited to the needs of the estancia, whereas the public sector expended its savings on extending the frontier and exterminating the Indian.

There were changes in the structure of livestock production as the prices of different exports fluctuated and as such new lines as jerked beef emerged. A notable change was the rise in the output of wool after 1850. During the wool boom, sheep displaced cattle on much of the Pampa.

However, the next stage brought the most striking changes in the structure of livestock production and the utilization of land. With the integration of world markets, price fluctuations and technical progress exerted much more influence. As a result, Argentina's agricultural output, which in 1850 chiefly supplied the local market and utilized only the greenbelts around the population centers, increased enormously. By the end of the century, it made up no less than one half of the nation's exports, which by then had reached record levels.

7. DEVELOPMENT OF THE LITORAL

A national economy was not created during the transition stage because of the continued isolation of the regional economies which prevented interchange among them of capital, labor, and goods. However, after leaving the subsistence stage, the various regional systems no longer followed similar patterns of growth. Expansion of trade and livestock production brought dynamic elements into the Litoral's development process which were clearly to distinguish it from that of other regions.

These differences must be further analyzed in order to understand how new conditions upset the balance that had existed among the different regional economies. It is also important to note that the centralization of foreign trade in Buenos Aires and the restrictions imposed on navigation on the Paraná and Uruguay rivers pitted the interests of the province of Buenos Aires against those of Santa Fe, Entre Ríos, and Corrientes. Buenos Aires not only appropriated all customs revenues but also received a large income from the commercial activity generated by the foreign trade that had to go through its port. Although these circumstances limited the impact of livestock expansion, the dynamic forces of development also exerted an influence on these provinces and differentiated their growth from that of the regions of the interior. Therefore, this chapter will deal with the development of the Litoral as a whole, with special reference to the province of Buenos Aires.[1]

The Increase in Population

The population of the Litoral provinces increased steadily throughout the transitional period, particularly in the city of Buenos

---

[1] The scanty information available for this period—mainly on foreign trade, population, public finance, and money—has been used to make quantitative estimates of growth in accordance with logical relationships to be expected between different economic variables in an economy at the level of development reached by Argentina during the period under study. In any event, the reader is warned of the nature of the data with which the author has established a working hypothesis and a framework for the analysis he attempts in this chapter and the following one.

Aires and the surrounding countryside. The first national census, taken in 1869, showed that the combined population of the Litoral provinces—Buenos Aires, Santa Fe, Entre Ríos, and Corrientes— had risen from an estimated 100,000 inhabitants in 1800 to 850,000, that is, at a compound rate of growth of slightly above 3 percent. Part of the demographic expansion may have been due to foreign immigration as well as to migration from the interior. Although the data for that period do not permit firm conclusions, for the purposes of this analysis they can be used to indicate trends. Within the Litoral region, the province of Buenos Aires, comprising the city and its environs, had the most striking increase. Its population, which in 1800 was about one half of aggregate Litoral population, grew at a rate of close to 3.5 percent annually until by 1869 it accounted for almost 60 percent. This may be somewhat over-estimated, in view of the lack of reliable information, but it denotes the trend of the period.

It must be remembered that demographic increase was accompanied by extension of the frontier, so that population density in occupied territory rose much less than might otherwise be assumed.

The Growth of Exports and Changes in the Structure of Output

The opening of the Río de la Plata ports in the second half of the eighteenth century, the general liberalization of trade after independence, and the expansion of livestock raising in the Litoral naturally were reflected in the growth of exports. Toward 1850, exports amounted to about 10 million *pesos fuertes*, equivalent to some 35 million present-day dollars.[2] At the end of the eighteenth century, exports had represented approximately 5 million pesos fuertes, or 17 million dollars. Thus, over a fifty-year period marked

---

[2] The gold content of the peso fuerte was similar to that of the American dollar of the same period. An ounce of gold weighing 25 grams, 0.875 fine, was worth 17 pesos fuertes. On the other hand, an ounce of fine gold weighing 25.8 grams was worth 20.66 dollars. In 1934, the price of gold was raised to 35 dollars per ounce, making the 1850 peso fuerte equivalent to 1.70 post-1934 dollars. However, for present calculations, reference is made to the purchasing power of the dollar between 1850 and 1962. Using wholesale price series in the United States and taking into account the limitations of such comparisons over long periods of time, it is estimated that an 1850 dollar was equivalent in purchasing power to 3.3 dollars of 1962.

by sharp fluctuations, Argentina roughly doubled the value of its imports.

Estimating exports at 15 percent of gross product in 1830,[3] the latter was 250 million present-day dollars.[4] Given Argentina's population of 1,200,000 inhabitants, the per capita product was approximately 200 dollars, or 1,000 pesos at 1950 prices.[5]

During the transition period, the origin of exports shifted from the interior regions to the Litoral, and most of the gain in foreign trade took place in the latter. At the same time, the Litoral's population gradually entered the market economy, forsaking the subsistence activities that continued to prevail in the interior. It is, therefore, likely that per capita income in the Litoral was higher than in the rest of Argentina.

The growth of exports stimulated production and income through a process that will be analyzed in detail when the primary-exports economy is discussed. Of immediate interest is the extent to which the increase in exports and income in the Litoral influenced the structure of output.

In the Litoral, at the beginning of the transition period, there was hardly any economic activity directed toward supplying domestic consumption. Actually, consumption in excess of subsistence levels was largely met from imports which, until the end of the

[3] Exports were 25 percent of gross domestic product in 1900. It may be assumed that the ratio of exports to product in 1850 was less than in 1900, in view of the national economy's lower degree of integration into world markets and the continued employment in subsistence activities of a large part of the active population in the interior. As explained in the next footnote, there is evidence that a 15 percent ratio was the approximate figure for 1850.
[4] There are no data on gross product for the middle of the nineteenth century. The first fairly reliable figure is for 1900, estimated by ECLA as equivalent to 2.1 billion dollars for gross product and 440 dollars for per capita product. This would indicate that gross product had increased at a compound rate of 4.5 percent annually from 1850 to 1900, which seems reasonable considering the rapid growth of the last few years of the century. With an annual population increase of approximately 3 percent between 1850 and 1900, the growth in per capita product was about 1.5 percent per annum during that period.
[5] The purchasing-power parity rate in 1950 was 1 dollar to 6.3 pesos. A comparison of the 1950 peso with the 1962 dollar, taking into account the latter's loss of purchasing power, raises the parity to approximately 1 dollar to 5 pesos. In the text, figures are given in 1950 pesos because of the acute inflation that has occurred in Argentina and the need to make comparisons in real terms. However, data in dollars are taken at their present-day purchasing power, so that the reader can relate the information to the present situation.

eighteenth century, came principally from the interior and consisted of cloth, wine, dried fruits, yerba maté, and tobacco. The
rising income of the Litoral during the transition period obviously
generated a greater and more varied demand, as always happens
when better living conditions make necessities relatively less important and increase the importance of manufactured goods and
services, as well as machinery, equipment, and other capital goods
for domestic investment.

The merchants and livestock owners, who were the dynamic
forces in the development of the Litoral, were chiefly interested
in the expansion of exports. Free trade thus became the philosophy
and practical policy of these groups. In fact, the economic purpose
of the War of Independence was to finally eliminate the obstacles
to trade still existing under colonial regulations in spite of the
liberalization of 1778. Free exports also meant freedom to import.
Because production in the Litoral had not kept up with growth
in local demand and because output in the interior was also insufficient as well as expensive to transport, imported products took
over the Litoral market.

The proportion of the Litoral's gross income spent on imports
must have been similar to its ratio of exports, that is, from 15 to 20
percent.[6] The more complex manufactures (textiles, beverages,
metal articles) were largely purchased abroad, thereby discouraging
domestic production. Development of these industries locally was
prevented by free importation and by the application of low import
duties designed to provide revenue rather than to protect domestic
manufacturing. Therefore, the structure of output in the Litoral
had limited prospects of diversification.

The sectors that grew during the transition stage were livestock
production strongly oriented toward exports, manufactures and
crafts (such as the construction and repair of vehicles and me-
chanical parts) responding to local demand, and certain services.
Lucrative customs revenues and monetary expansion enabled the
provincial governments of the Litoral, especially Buenos Aires, to
augment their expenditures and services. Employment rose not

---

[6] During the transition period, there was hardly any inflow of foreign capital,
with the exception of the 1824 loan. There were, therefore, no remittances
abroad for amortization, profits, and interest that would have drained the gold
and foreign exchange generated by Argentina's exports and thus have reduced
its capacity to import.

only in the public sector but also in the commercial activities related to foreign trade, population growth, and higher income.

As commercial and urban employment became more important, the Litoral cities swelled in size. The 100,000 inhabitants of Buenos Aires alone represented 50 percent of the total population of the province. In the Litoral as a whole, 25 percent of the population must have lived in cities with the remaining 75 percent in rural areas. Urbanization was also linked to traffic on the Paraná and Uruguay rivers, particularly in the cities of Rosario de Santa Fe, Gualeguaychú, and Concepción del Uruguay.

Income Distribution and Capital Accumulation

Because the livestock industry, which generated 30 to 35 percent of gross product in the Litoral, was conducted principally in large properties belonging to a few owners and because commercial activity was dominated by a few groups connected with foreign trade, income was concentrated in a small part of the population—cattle raisers and merchants. After independence, government deficits and the issue of paper money led to currency depreciation, especially in the province of Buenos Aires. The wages of agricultural and urban workers went up less than the general price level, which was closely tied to export prices[7] and to the prices of imports required for domestic consumption. As export prices and consequently the incomes of cattle raisers and merchants increased *pari passu* with currency devaluation, there was an internal transfer of income from one social group to another, which led to further concentration of income.

High- and low-income groups differed appreciably in their pattern of consumption. The former spent a large proportion of their income on manufactured goods, including luxury articles, which were almost entirely imported from abroad; whereas the foodstuffs and cheaper consumer goods purchased by low-income groups were for the most part domestically produced. It may be assumed, therefore, that income inequality stimulated imports of relatively elaborate manufactures and luxury articles. Add to this the absence of a restrictive tariff policy to encourage domestic output, and it is

---

[7] As the peso depreciated, the domestic price of exports increased, raising the price of internal consumption of livestock products. Domestic prices of imports also went up, of course, proportionately to the depreciation of the currency.

clear that the structure of internal production could not change significantly during the transition period.

The practical impossibility of developing manufacturing activities of any complexity meant that most of the savings of the high-income groups were used to finance expansion of the livestock and trading sectors and also, to a large extent, urban construction, especially in Buenos Aires. Little private investment went into manufacturing to supply the domestic market.

On the other hand, as a result of the expansion of income and savings in the Litoral, especially in the province of Buenos Aires, and of the existence of profitable investment opportunities in cattle raising, trade, and urban construction, there was considerable mobility of funds available for investment in those fields. At the same time that stock ranchers and traders linked directly or indirectly to urban centers accumulated savings for use in alternative investment opportunities, a system of banking and financial intermediaries evolved. In this way, a financial and capital market, subsequently consolidated during the stage of primary exports, was initiated in the Litoral, especially in the city of Buenos Aires.

At this point, the problem of alternative investment opportunities should be related to the comparative productivity of the various sectors of economic activity.

The population of the Litoral became progressively integrated into the market economy during the transition period, so that by the middle of the nineteenth century, there were few important centers of population that did not produce commodities for sale or that did not include in their consumption a substantial proportion of goods imported from abroad or produced domestically. The relationship between entrepreneur and worker was a purely capitalist one, even in the livestock industry where the labor force was paid partly in kind.

Primary activity, chiefly livestock production, was oriented toward exports, and output per person was relatively high.[8] If account

---

[8] Assuming that the active population in 1850 was 50 percent of the total population, product per person employed must have been about 400 dollars per year, that is, 2,000 pesos at 1950 prices. On the other hand, because no less than 30 percent of the value of exports went into trading expenses, only about 25 million dollars accrued to the livestock sector, of which about 20 million dollars went to the cattle raisers of the Litoral. In view of the level of domestic demand for livestock products at the time, the internal market probably consumed an amount equivalent to that exported by the ranchers of

is also taken of the mobility of labor within the Litoral and of the expansion of urban employment in trade and government services, the level of wages was similar in the different sectors of activity.

Due to the near equality of their productivity levels and profit margins, the various sectors of activity did not differ much in capital accumulation and technical improvements. Within the existing structure of output, returns on capital were similar in all sectors, and, therefore, capital accumulation and, in turn, labor productivity were fairly uniform throughout the economic system of the Litoral.

This was to distinguish Argentina's economy from that of countries in which an efficient export sector of high capital formation and output per person employed coexisted with widespread subsistence sectors of low output and income per worker.

The Public Sector

During the transition period, the role of provincial governments, particularly of the province of Buenos Aires, was to consolidate the position of the livestock and trading sectors and thereby strengthen the dynamic elements in the development of the Litoral. Public expenditure was high during the whole period because of the War of Independence, domestic conflicts, and the Indian campaigns. No less than 60 percent of the expenditure of the Litoral governments was for military purposes. The remainder was allocated to maintain and expand the administrative machinery of the state.

Customs receipts and port levies provided about 90 percent of the current revenue of the Litoral governments. This reliance on current trade taxes made fiscal revenue very unstable. A contraction in exports affected the volume of imports, and a reduction in total trade was immediately reflected in fiscal revenue. The ratio of customs taxes to total revenue was so high that the indirect effect of a fall in exports on internal economic activity and, therefore, on other tax revenues was almost nil.

There was hardly any recourse to other sources of funds, such

the Litoral. Therefore, the product generated by the livestock sector of the region in 1850 must have been close to 40 million dollars, or 200 million pesos at 1950 prices. Furthermore, stock raising in the Litoral must have employed around 100,000 persons, so that product per worker was roughly 400 dollars per year, or 2,000 pesos at 1950 prices. This is the same figure as the one arrived at for total gross product per person employed for the whole economy.

as the placing of public bonds abroad or the sale of government lands. With the exception of the loan floated through Baring of London in 1824, Argentina was not to have access to international markets until after 1870. The sale of lands was not actually a fiscal measure, but was used to facilitate private appropriation of the new land along the Pampa frontier that had been occupied by influential groups.

In addition to customs receipts and port levies, there were two other important means of finance available, particularly in the province of Buenos Aires: the floating of domestic bond issues and the printing of currency. Domestic issues were frequently forced contributions imposed upon the wealthy merchants and landowners. Some bond issues were bought voluntarily by the public, especially in the province of Buenos Aires, but at a great discount of usually no less than 40 percent. That is, on a nominal issue of 100 pesos, the government received only 60 but had to pay interest and amortization on the face value of 100. Naturally, currency depreciation, stimulated by monetary policy, reduced the real value of the domestic public debt.

Until long after the May revolution, Spanish gold and silver coins continued to circulate in Argentina. After 1810, several provinces, chiefly in the Litoral, and among them Buenos Aires, set up their own monetary system by establishing banks with the right to issue paper money. The Bank of the Province of Buenos Aires in 1822 was the first one to exercise this right.

Governments found it convenient simply to issue paper money to finance public expenditures because they received money that did not have to be repaid and they were spared the effort of selling bond issues. But these are secondary reasons. The real supporters of the policy of monetary expansion as against the issue of domestic debt were the cattle ranchers and the merchants, for obvious reasons. These were the wealthy groups who were forced to buy bond issues, and the printing of currency relieved them of this burden. Furthermore, the inflation resulting from currency issues also favored them, because the prices of their products increased proportionately to currency depreciation, whereas wages and other costs increased less than proportionately and lagged behind the devaluation of the peso.

Miron Burguin has written an excellent account of this situation. He discusses the debates in the 1837 legislature of the province of Buenos Aires, when the congressmen representing the ranchers and merchants of the province advocated a policy of monetary expansion in order to meet the government deficit.[9]

During the Rosas government, from 1836 to 1851, a total of 125 million paper pesos was issued. Such currency expansion affected both the domestic purchasing power of the peso and the rate of exchange. There was a drastic depreciation of the province's paper currency. Taking 1826 as a base year, it was 594 percent by 1836 and had reached a high of 2,100 percent by 1840. The domestic price level adjusted fully to the external devaluation of the currency.

To the extent that fiscal policy was designed to finance government deficits with currency issues rather than with domestic bond issues, the burden was shifted from the landholding and merchant groups to the low-income groups of the population. The latter thus had to make "forced savings" as rising prices reduced their real income.

The effects of monetary expansion on the economy in terms of transfer of income were soon exhausted, and its compensatory effect at a time of declining foreign trade was slight. When exports fell, domestic consumption could not absorb the surplus of livestock products. Capital and labor could not move from cattle raising to other types of production required to meet domestic demand for goods that could no longer be imported due to diminished export earnings. The Litoral economy was so undiversified and so lacking in an industrial base that it was impossible in the short run to bring about an appreciable shift of productive factors from the export sector into the sectors working for domestic consumption. In other words, import replacement was impossible. The rise in the domestic prices of traditionally imported commodities could not, therefore, attract capital funds into new enterprises to manufacture those commodities.[10] Thus, inflation raised prices and money income, but real income and output could not go above the levels deter-

---

[9] M. Burguin, *Aspectos económicos del federalismo argentino* (Buenos Aires: Hachette, 1960).

[10] Because the prices of imported goods rise more than wages and more than at least part of the raw materials necessary for production, it is assumed that inflation increases the profit margins of enterprises undertaking domestic production of such goods. Inflation can, therefore, stimulate import replacement by attracting capital to such industries.

mined by the volume of exports. Inflation could have stimulated diversification only if there had been a parallel policy of restrictions on imports that could be replaced; but this was not the policy nor the long-range objective of the dominant groups of the Litoral.

The public-sector savings, that is, the difference between current revenues and current expenditures, were negligible during the transition period. In fact, the long-standing deficits of the provincial treasuries indicated their inability to raise sufficient funds to finance their current expenditures. The lack of savings in the public sector meant that there were practically no public works during the period, particularly infrastructure investments such as highway development. Nevertheless, expenditures in the province of Buenos Aires, insofar as they served to finance the Indian campaigns and to extend the frontier, were in a sense real investments by the public sector that raised the productive capacity of the province through the incorporation of new land. Subsequent private appropriation of this land transferred these government "investments" to the private sector at almost no cost to the latter.

By extending the frontier and establishing political and administrative machinery, the public sector, especially the government of the province of Buenos Aires, finally ensured the expansion of cattle raising and trade during that period and gave control of the Pampa prairie, the Litoral's basic resource, to privileged groups.

Limitations to the Development of the Litoral

Although substantial, the process of change and growth in the Litoral economy was subject to limitations throughout the transition period. Population in the region was sparse, and living conditions, particularly in areas distant from urban centers, were primitive. At midcentury, the desert and the "civilization of hides" still predominated in the rural areas of the Litoral. As late as 1896, there was not more than one inhabitant per square kilometer in the countryside of the province of Buenos Aires, which was the heart of the Pampa region. This is clearly reflected in the writings of contemporary observers such as V. Martin de Moussy and Woodbine Parish. Domingo F. Sarmiento's "barbarism" continued to reign in large areas of the Litoral.

The limitations to development of the Litoral were as follows: In the first place, the formation and integration of world markets had not yet been accomplished. The industrial revolution had not transformed the economic structure of the European countries. Maritime transport was only beginning to make use of the technical advances of steel and steam that would later bring down overseas shipping costs for a number of agricultural and livestock products. Another technical innovation still to come was the refrigeration of meat, which would open up revolutionary prospects for livestock production. Meanwhile, Argentina's exports were kept within definite bounds.

Second, and as a consequence of the above, not enough capital and manpower had entered Argentina to settle the Pampa and make rational use of available land. In fact, land utilization throughout the transition period was haphazard and extensive. The level of technology in livestock production was low, and agricultural output was oriented toward the domestic market. There was little rural population, and the infrastructure capital necessary for the integration of the Litoral economy—namely, transport and communications—had barely progressed beyond the stage it had reached during the period of regional subsistence economies.

Such were the factors that limited the development and structural change of the Litoral economy. Nevertheless, for the first time in Argentina's economic history, the dynamic element of growth—expansion of external demand—exerted an influence on development. During the subsequent primary-exports stage, this dynamic element was intensified and, together with massive incorporation of technical innovations and capital, contributed to rapid, vigorous, economic development.

The transition stage also marked the consolidation of a system of land tenure which was to have a major effect on the growth of the agricultural and livestock sector, the mainspring of Argentina's later development. The government's sale to large proprietors of vast tracts of fertile land in the Pampa region, particularly in the province of Buenos Aires, was a basic factor in the evolution of the national economy during the next stage. Land concentration meant a concentration of rural income in a few hands; it provided the legal framework for the settlement of immigrants; it established the large production unit as the typical farm enterprise, particularly

in cattle raising; it determined the pattern of land utilization as
between stock grazing and agriculture; and, finally, it shaped the
social and political structure which from then on was to condition
the country's development.

8. STAGNATION IN THE INTERIOR

Population Growth

Once the decline in indigenous population had spent itself, the population of the interior regions began to increase during the transition stage. This was essentially the result of natural growth, since immigration was slight. The expanding activities of the Litoral may even have attracted population from the interior.

In the Northwest, population increased from some 150,000 inhabitants in 1800 to 450,000 in 1869, according to the census of the latter year. In Cuyo, it increased from 40,000 to 184,000 and in the Center, from 60,000 to 264,000 inhabitants over the same period. Thus, total population in the interior regions went up from 250,000 to 900,000 inhabitants, and the annual rate of growth for the interior as a whole was 1.9 percent.

Population in the interior, which was 70 percent of Argentina's total of 1800, had declined to only 50 percent by 1869, due largely to the fall in the Northwest's share from 43 to 26 percent. The Northwest, which had been the most populous and prosperous region during the colonial period, lost importance because, more than the rest of the interior, it remained isolated in its self-sufficient economy. On the other hand, the Litoral accounted for most of the population increase of Argentina, and its share in the total went up from 30 to 50 percent from 1800 to 1869.

Obstruction of the External Sector

During the transition period, there was a radical change in the type and regional origin of exports from the port of Buenos Aires. In the middle of the eighteenth century, 80 percent of exports was silver from Upper Peru and 20 percent was agricultural products, which were, in fact, mostly hides. According to estimates made by Coni, the export of silver at that time amounted to some 1,600,000 pesos fuertes, or 5.6 million present-day dollars. Therefore, export of hides must have been worth about 300,000 pesos fuertes, or 1 million dollars of today's purchasing power.

An analysis of the composition of exports, including silver from Upper Peru, shows that they came chiefly from the interior. It is almost certain that a substantial proportion of the silver exported by the entrepreneurs of the Northwest and Córdoba had been received by them in payment for the mules, textiles, and other products they sold in Potosí. If all the silver and at least one half of the hides came from the interior, it may be assumed that around 90 percent of total exports originated in the interior and only 10 percent in the Litoral. Consequently, out of total exports of 5.6 million dollars from the port of Buenos Aires in the middle of the eighteenth century, commodities from the interior represented 5 million and from the Litoral 600 thousand dollars.

A century later the pattern was radically different. Exports of silver had almost disappeared as a result of the decline in the output of Upper Peru, and agricultural products made up almost all exports. Hides continued to be the most important item, accounting for 60 to 70 percent of total exports, but such new products as wool, jerked beef, and tallow were appearing in foreign trade.

Statistics on so-called overland imports of livestock products to the province of Buenos Aires reveal that toward the middle of the nineteenth century around 30 percent of exports abroad from the port of Buenos Aires must have originated in the rest of the country. Assuming that at least one half of that 30 percent came from other Litoral provinces—Entre Ríos, Santa Fe, and Corrientes—only 15 percent of livestock exports came from the interior. Since overseas exports in 1850 were about 35 million present-day dollars, it is likely that only 5 million dollars of that total accrued to the interior provinces. Obviously, the income actually received by the entrepreneurs of the interior must have been further reduced by the high transportation costs of the time and the high margins charged by intermediaries in the port.[1]

---

[1] Another factor that may have reduced the amount of income actually received by these entrepreneurs was the rising price level in the province of Buenos Aires from 1810 to the end of the transition period. The Buenos Aires merchants were intermediaries for output coming from the interior and probably paid for the latter in paper pesos, while they collected gold, dollars, sterling, and other foreign currencies for their exports. They exchanged their foreign currencies for paper pesos at the going rate, and, therefore, as the peso depreciated, their earnings increased proportionally; at the same time,

The overland imports of the province of Buenos Aires also included products used to meet ordinary consumption needs: yerba maté, tobacco, beverages, *ponchos* [wool blankets] and other unspecified goods. According to data for 1837, these imports were about 2 million dollars of present purchasing power, and they undoubtedly did not substantially exceed that level until the end of the transition stage. On the other hand, there was probably little trade between the regions of the interior.

It may be estimated, therefore, that by midcentury the interior's total exports, including overseas exports through the port of Buenos Aires, amounted to some 7 to 8 million present-day dollars per year, or 35 to 40 million pesos of 1950 purchasing power. This meant that over a period of one hundred years, exports had increased only slightly. In the particular case of the Northwest, which had supplied a large part of eighteenth-century exports, the value of foreign trade must have diminished with the loss of the Upper Peru market.

One of the basic factors affecting exports from the interior was the free-trade policy followed by the province of Buenos Aires since independence. Although export expansion in the Litoral was accompanied by a growth in local demand, that demand was met by imports from abroad rather than by increased purchases from the interior. Thus, the port's policy of free imports blocked any possibility of spreading the dynamic impulse generated by the Litoral's export expansion.

Available data on imports through the port of Buenos Aires show that toward the middle of the nineteenth century about 50 percent of such imports were textiles, beverages, sugar, yerba maté, and tobacco, all of which competed directly with the production of the interior. Furthermore, many of these imports, especially the textiles, were superior in quality and lower in price than the articles produced by the inefficient craft industries of the rest of the country.

---

prices paid in paper pesos to producers in the interior rose less than the devaluation of the peso, so that the Buenos Aires merchants made immediate windfall profits. This frequently occurs in countries in which exportable output is supplied by a large number of domestic producers and the marketing of that output is handled by intermediaries. Furthermore, when consumers in the interior purchased foreign goods, they had to pay the Buenos Aires importers as many paper pesos as the latter needed in order to pay the foreign supplier in gold or foreign exchange.

Nevertheless, in some of the interior provinces, certain activities producing for interregional trade survived and were even consolidated during the transition period. Such was the case, for example, of sugar production in Tucumán; and the growth of livestock raising in the southeast of the province of Córdoba played a role similar to that in the rest of the Litoral. In any case, these exceptions do not alter the general stagnation that characterized the export sector of the economies of the interior.

As seen earlier, the situation in the Litoral was quite different. Overseas exports originating in the region rose from 1 million dollars of present-day purchasing power in the middle of the eighteenth century to about 30 million dollars in 1850.

Persistent Stagnation

Throughout the transition period, the stagnation of the interior's exports was a barrier to any development within the regional areas, nor was there a prospect of growth through the introduction of technical innovations and a consequent rise in productivity, income, and effective demand. Not only did the free-trade policy of Buenos Aires prevent the expansion of the Litoral from being reflected in purchases of commodities from the rest of the country, but the goods imported into Buenos Aires and distributed from there to the interior provinces competed with local production within each region and affected the traditional interregional trade flows. However, this should not be exaggerated. Because of their limited exports, the inland provinces had a very low capacity to import. Their low capacity to absorb foreign goods was also due to the protective tariffs and restrictions imposed by the provincial governments and to the extremely high prices charged for imported commodities in order to cover the costs of transporting them over such long distances. Therefore, the policy of Buenos Aires was an obstacle to the development of the other regions mainly in that it made the Litoral market—the only one susceptible to increasing volumes of trade—available to overseas production.

The concentration of livestock exports in the Litoral and the opening up of this market to foreign goods completely blocked development of the interior provinces. Population increase may have partly offset this external factor, but in the absence of the dynamic effect of expanding exports, the consequent rise in the labor force could only be absorbed according to the traditional pattern of subsistence occupations outside the market economy. In this manner, population growth was largely sterilized and did not generate an increase in incomes and domestic demand.

Given the factors conditioning its development, the economy of the interior did not change during the transition period. The output of each region went to the local market, and a large part of the working population continued in subsistence activities. In the Northwest, where exports actually declined during the transition stage, it is likely that the economy regressed from the levels it had reached in the eighteenth century and that the proportion of the labor force occupied in subsistence activities even increased. Thus, the level of income per capita must have remained the same or have fallen, except perhaps in those provinces where some industry was oriented toward the expanding Litoral market, as was the sugar industry in Tucumán.

With no external dynamic impulse and with the stagnation of domestic demand and incomes, the structure of production in the interior could not change. Agricultural and livestock output must have employed from 70 to 80 percent of the active population and services, crafts and manufacturing the remainder. The degree of urbanization corresponded roughly to the structure of output, and on the average more than 80 percent of the population continued to live in rural areas.

Income distribution and capital accumulation evolved according to patterns already analyzed in the discussion of the stage of regional subsistence economies. It should be pointed out that the gradual disappearance of the indigenous population, particularly in the Northwest, heralded the end of the servile labor that had been characteristic of the colonial period in Argentina.

Financial Weakness of the Governments of the Interior

The governments of the inland provinces played a minor role in the development process of this stage. Due to the lack of any expanding activity and the low prevailing levels of income, they could not do much to reallocate economic resources or to promote development. This situation was in sharp contrast to the active part taken by the public sector in the Litoral provinces, especially in the province of Buenos Aires.

Fiscal resources were severely limited, mainly because of the low level of exports and imports with the attendant low level of customs receipts. Whereas in the Litoral customs duties accounted for 70 to 90 percent of current fiscal revenues, in the interior the proportion was 40 to 50 percent. Furthermore, the low level of income and trade prevented other taxes, particularly stamp and business taxes, from yielding appreciable amounts. Finally, given the high percentage of the population engaged in subsistence activities outside the market economy, the government could not add much to its resources through the issue of paper money. In fact, these impoverished communities were of little use to the authorities. Although the government could issue currency, it could not greatly increase its expenditures on goods and on salaries of public employees. If inflation through monetary expansion is to bring about a transfer of income from the community to the government, there must be a minimum level of income. When a community lives entirely at the subsistence level, this transfer is not possible; and many of the poorer provinces of the interior approached this condition. Of course, the monetary system in these provinces continued to operate throughout the transition stage on the basis of gold and silver coins.

In spite of the small amount of tax revenues and the limited possibility of an inflationary use of currency, the level of expenditures of the inland governments was subject to the same pressures as that of the Litoral governments: the War of Independence, the federal conflicts, and, later, the Indian campaigns. Fiscal poverty was common to all the interior provinces. In extreme cases, forced loans were levied on the population, specifically on the merchants and landholders who were the only groups able to subscribe them. The poorer sectors could only cooperate by providing personal services to the army. But the general penury of the times restricted the use of forced loans. There were many cases of "loans" of only 1 or 2 thousand pesos fuertes, that is, 5 to 10 thousand pesos of 1950 purchasing power.

The sole alternative was to keep public-sector activity to a minimum. In 1839, Jujuy, one of the poorest provinces in the confederation, had a budget of 9,040 pesos; the ministry of government received 2,860, of which 1,500 pesos was the salary of the governor.

The appropriation for public education was 480 pesos per year! [2]

Not only were public payrolls in the provinces very low, but defense was reduced to the primitive *montonera*.[3] In the absence of a proper military organization, the maintenance of law and order fell to the local *caudillos,* the landowners. The outcome of federal conflicts was predetermined by the interior's lack of fiscal resources, which in turn reflected its general poverty.

The situation in the province of Buenos Aires and the Litoral as a whole was quite different. As the focal point of dynamic activity —livestock raising for export—these governments commanded abundant resources through customs duties and other levies and through the placing of internal loans or the issue of currency. The privileged position of the province of Buenos Aires also resulted from the foreign trade monopoly held by the port, although this was of secondary importance. Recalling that 90 percent of exports originated in the province and the rest in the Litoral and that this region absorbed a similar proportion of imports, it may be assumed that the share of customs receipts obtained by Buenos Aires from duties on products derived from or destined for the interior accounted for no more than 10 percent of total revenues.

To conclude this brief analysis of the fiscal evolution of the interior, mention should be made of the policies followed to protect local markets from the competition of foreign products that entered via Buenos Aires. Each province had its own customs tariffs restricting imports of competitive goods. But in practice, this protectionist policy was narrow in scope. Purchases of foreign goods were limited by the region's small volume of exports and, consequently, its very low capacity to import. In addition, foreign goods were subject to such high transportation charges from Buenos Aires to the interior that many of them were unable to compete with local production, in spite of the latter's inefficiency.

Increasing Interregional Imbalance

The interior provinces realized that the solution to their economic problems did not lie within their own borders. They, therefore,

---

[2] M. Burguin, *Aspectos económicos del federalismo argentino* (Buenos Aires: Hachette, 1960). Expressed in 1950 pesos, these figures would be approximately 45,000, 14,500, and 2,200, respectively.

[3] Armed groups, mostly of rural workers, who followed a political leader who might or might not be the landowner for whom they worked.

tried to force a protectionist policy on the province of Buenos Aires in order to give their inland production an outlet in the growing Litoral market. They also claimed a share in the customs receipts of Buenos Aires as another way to benefit from the expansion of trade in the Litoral.

Independence gave rise to the "problem" of the province of Buenos Aires and thereby upset the traditional equilibrium that had existed during the colonial period. The autonomy of this province permitted it to be the sole beneficiary of its position with regard to world markets as well as to the livestock raising that took place largely within its territorial limits. The province, naturally, was firmly committed to a defense of its autonomy under the banner of federalism.

The "federalism" of Buenos Aires after independence was the most intelligent way for the province to maintain its privileges and to avoid adopting a broader policy that would have allowed a gradual integration of the national economy and a more equitable distribution of fiscal revenues. The expanding sectors of the province—the livestock and commercial interests linked to foreign trade —supported federalism as long as they were not strong enough to impose a national solution entirely to their advantage. It was only later, during the stage of primary exports, that conditions favored integration of the national economy and market, but within a framework definitely subordinating the interior to Buenos Aires and the Litoral, or more precisely, to the agricultural and livestock economy of the Pampa.

The position of Buenos Aires during the transition stage was expressed not only in its free-trade policy and its arrogation of customs revenues but also in its denial of the right of other Litoral provinces to use the rivers for direct access to world markets. Representing the province of Corrientes, Pedro Ferré was one of those who fought for extension of the benefits of free trade to all the Litoral, in opposition to the vested interests of the porteño merchants.

However, during the transition period, the balance between the different regions that had prevailed since colonial times was not entirely disrupted. The major protectionist barrier was still distance, and in any case, the Litoral was not to enter its period of spectacular growth until after 1860.

The subordination of the interior was sealed during the primary-export stage, when immigration and rapid expansion of agricultural and livestock exports from the Pampa region turned the Litoral into the undisputed dynamic center of Argentine development. The railroads were finally to do away with distance, which was the last line of defense of the interior's isolation.

An economic analysis of the period, then, confirms the reasons deduced by historians for the decline in the provincial autonomy of Argentina.

PART III

THE EARLY
EXPORT ECONOMY
(1860–1930)

9. TECHNICAL PROGRESS AND THE INTEGRATION OF WORLD ECONOMY

After 1860[1] Argentina entered a new stage of economic development based on two concurrent circumstances: growth and integration of the world economy, and extension of the fertile and sparsely populated land of the Pampa.

The technological revolution in Europe at the end of the eighteenth century and the industrialization of the more advanced countries of the Old World resulted in the opening up of development possibilities in areas suitable for temperate-zone agriculture and livestock raising. The fertile Pampa plains became the focal point of European interests, particularly the British. These useless territories of the colonial period, which during the transition stage had launched a modest livestock industry, now became the nucleus of a rapid process of development.

The speed with which Argentina integrated into the world economy after the middle of the nineteenth century completely altered the social, political, and economic fabric of the country in a few decades. Part III will attempt an analysis of the period of Argentine development which I have defined as the stage of the primary-exports economy. Throughout this period agricultural and livestock production was the most important sector of national output, and exports of both products were the dynamic element in development.

The experience of Argentina at this time was an episode in the expansion of the European economy, particularly the British. Consequently, the principal changes that occurred in the world economy after 1850 should be discussed first.

The Dynamic Role of Technical Progress

As pointed out earlier, even in the conditions of the medieval world, trade helped to raise the level of productivity of the Euro-

---

[1] The beginning of this stage coincided with the inauguration of the Mitre administration in 1862 after the province of Buenos Aires had reunited with the Federation.

pean economies. In America, the development of certain export activities, such as mining and tropical agriculture, was the basis of growth during the colonial period. Both in Europe and America until the end of the eighteenth century, trade expansion and export activity provided the dynamic impulse that unshackled the subsistence economy and made it possible to accumulate capital, diversify the structure of output, and raise the levels of income.

But the economic horizon of trade expansion was necessarily circumscribed. Productivity and income remained at very low levels until almost the end of the eighteenth century, because of the slow improvement in agricultural and manufacturing techniques, the limited amount of capital per person employed, and the risks of transoceanic navigation. Such levels were naturally reflected in the economic structure, and no less than 70 percent of the total labor force of Western Europe continued to be engaged in agricultural activities.

Commercial expansion alone could not raise productivity and incomes beyond the limits set by the technological development of the times, even assuming a maximum division of labor and specialization through trade. Furthermore, up to the end of the eighteenth century, the national economies were far from integrated internally, nor were they closely linked to world commerce. Most of the active population was occupied in subsistence activities or in trade between narrow local markets.

In the final anlysis, it was the lack of technical progress that constituted an insurmountable barrier to a generalized and steady increase in productivity and income. Toward the end of the eighteenth century, a series of technical innovations known as the Industrial Revolution broke down that barrier and opened up boundless prospects for economic development.

Technological improvement, which advanced rapidly from then on, brought new production methods as well as better organization and led to a substantial rise in labor productivity. In turn, the greater volume of goods available made it possible to allocate relatively larger amounts of manpower and other economic resources to the production of machinery, equipment, and other investment goods giving material expression to the improved techniques.

As a result of the productivity and income generated by the

technological revolution, the domestic markets of developing countries expanded. In fact, technical progress is a specific form of market expansion, because it raises incomes and, thereby, effective demand. It also revolutionizes the conditions of development by permitting an indefinite expansion of the market within national borders and by creating incentives for private investment, which until the end of the eighteenth century had been a function of geographical expansion of the market. As Furtado says: "the entrepreneur no longer needed an expanding frontier, that is, new lines of trade. Now he could apply his capital in depth within the established economic frontier."

Under capitalism, effective demand is curtailed because a substantial part of total income accrues to capitalists and entrepreneurs who do not consume or invest all of their income. Because high-income groups were unable to consume all of their income, the economic variable determining the level of demand was investment; and investment possibilities derived not only from growth in domestic demand for consumer and investment goods but also from external demand. Expanding world markets at the end of the eighteenth century broadened opportunities for investment in activities specializing in the export market and enabled the capitalist system to develop far beyond the possibilities afforded by the domestic market. The pronounced inequality of incomes which characterized the initial development of capitalism did not retard growth through its restriction of domestic demand and investment opportunities; on the contrary, it stimulated growth by increasing savings and available resources for capital accumulation. From another point of view, the expansion of trade at the end of the eighteenth century and especially after the middle of the nineteenth century, which was a direct result of technical progress, in turn strengthened the system's capacity to assimilate technological innovations by creating new opportunities for investment.

Technical progress and the rise in incomes are the dynamic basis for a change in the structure of output. As incomes increase, the pattern of demand shifts from foodstuffs and other essential commodities to manufactured goods and services. In order to meet these changes in demand, more capital and labor are required in the growth sectors, and the relative amounts of these inputs vary to the extent each sector has advanced technically.

The most striking example of this process is the evolution of agriculture. On the one hand, agriculture loses importance because consumers spend proportionately less on food as their incomes rise. At the same time, improved farming methods reduce labor used per unit of output. In the developing countries, the steady decline in the proportion of the labor force employed in agriculture is a consequence of this parallel process of changes in the pattern of demand and the introduction of better techniques. On the other hand, technical progress engenders new lines of production and modifies existing ones. In short, at the end of the eighteenth century it replaced extension of the geographical frontier as the agent to increase productivity, and from then on it was the dynamic element of development.

Integration Through Technology

Technological progress contributes to the integration of economic activity. By increasing productivity, income, and specialization, it furthers the complementarity of different types of economic activity, the division of labor, and the interdependence of producers. For example, a farmer who works the land mostly with his own hands is less integrated into the economic system than one who uses a tractor and fertilizers. The former is entirely self-reliant; the latter is dependent on the industry that supplies him with machinery and other farm implements, on the market that buys his output, and on the economy as a whole that sells him the goods and services that he consumes.

Technical progress in transportation and communication has played a definite role in the integration of all national economies. Beginning with the construction of canals in the eighteenth century, through the expansion of railroads in the nineteenth century, and up to the dramatic development of motor and air transport and highways in this century, the technological revolution in transportation has been the mainspring of the integration of national economies and markets. In addition, improvement in communications has provided one of the services essential to the functioning of the economic system.

The integrating effect of technical progress was not and is still not limited to the increased interdependence of producers and different regions within a national territory. It also extended into the international sphere and, in fact, was instrumental in the formation of a world market after the middle of the nineteenth century.

The radical change in overseas shipping during the last decades of the nineteenth century sharply reduced transportation costs as well as travel time. Not only could larger volumes of traditional products be transported at lower freight rates, but other commodities—principally the agricultural and livestock products of the temperate zone and minerals—could also be shipped abroad.

In a broader sense, technical progress and the ensuing increase in incomes and effective demand within each country made it possible to create reciprocal markets. Furthermore, movements of capital and population meant integration, in terms of the productive process, of the interests of the countries participating in the world market.

Capital Flow, Migration, and Trade Expansion

The integration of the world economy was accomplished by three important means: capital movements, migration, and the expansion of world trade. Through these means, the process of integration reached its peak between the last decades of the nineteenth century and 1914. From the end of World War I until the breakdown of the multilateral trade and payments system in 1930, the forces of integration steadily lost the impetus they had shown in the previous period.

International capital movements

From 1874 to 1914, that is, over a period of some forty years, total long-term foreign investment rose from 6 billion to 44 billion dollars at current prices; at today's prices, the latter figure would be about 120 billion dollars. It was financed chiefly through reinvestment of profits and interests earned on foreign investment already existing in the debtor countries. Great Britain, France, and Germany accounted for 27 of the 38 billion dollar increase during that period. By 1914, 38 percent of foreign investment had been made in North America, Oceania, and Argentina; 34 percent in

Africa, Asia, and Latin America (excluding Argentina); and 27 percent in Europe.

On the whole, capital movements during the few decades preceding 1914 tended to favor the integration of various national economies into what may be called an expanding international economy. . . . It should be observed, however, that foreign capital was absorbed primarily by sparsely populated countries with large natural resources, the exploitation of which could easily increase the export of primary products.[2]

Such was the case of North America, Oceania, and Argentina, which were regions of "open spaces" at that time.

This concentration of investment is even more striking if it is remembered that in 1914 foreign investment in those open spaces was around $190 per capita, whereas it was only $30 per capita in Africa, Asia, and Latin America (excluding Argentina).

With industrialization, increasing specialization in manufacturing, and drastically reduced shipping costs, European markets were opened to foodstuffs and raw materials from overseas. The so-called peripheral countries that had not experienced the technological revolution and industrialization of that period now offered broad investment possibilities in activities that could supply the markets of the industrialized countries. The best opportunities were found in countries having vast natural resources and small populations. Such opportunities arose not only in activities oriented toward exports but also in the expansion of infrastructure capital, particularly transport, which helped the countries fulfill their role of producers and exporters of primary products. At the same time, there were good prospects for investment in commercial and financial mechanisms, as well as in activities and services supplying local demand in the peripheral countries. Thus, the increase in the international flow of capital during the second half of the nineteenth century was both cause and effect of the integration of the world economy.

After World War I, the relative positions of the creditor countries shifted, and Great Britain, France, and Germany had to liquidate part of their foreign investment. Most significantly, the United States emerged as the principal creditor country with long-term investments abroad. The international flow of long-term capital did not recover its prewar volume until the end of the 1920's.

---

[2] United Nations, *International Capital Movements During the Inter-War Period* (Lake Success, New York, October, 1949), p. 4.

Migration

Overseas migration from Europe during the nineteenth century and up to the outbreak of World War I was a basic component of integration of the international economy. The great migratory stream began around 1830 with an annual average of 100,000 persons, increasing steadily through 1914 when migration reached a maximum of 1,500,000.

From 1820 to 1920, 30 million Europeans migrated to the United States. However, substantial numbers also went to other countries in the Western Hemisphere—especially Argentina, Canada, and Brazil—and to Australia and South Africa. The main consequence of European migration overseas was that it enabled countries with large natural resources and little population to enter into the formation of the world economy.

World trade

The picture of the integration of the world economy is completed by the expansion of world trade during that period. From 1870 to 1913, the volume of world exports increased almost five-fold and by 1929 six-fold. Between 1870 and 1929, the average rate of growth per annum was, therefore, above 3 percent, which implies a rapid and constant expansion over a total of six decades.

The volume of international trade in 1870, which was already several times what it had been in recent years, by then was growing at a much faster rate than it had during the whole period of European trade expansion from the fifteenth to the eighteenth century. From 1700 to 1820, that is, in over a hundred years, the volume of exports had increased by approximately three times. But in the fifty years from 1820 to 1870, it expanded by nearly five times. After 1870, world trade soared as a result of the technological revolution at the end of the eighteenth century.

There were also important changes in the composition of world trade. Until the end of the eighteenth century, trade was concentrated in such traditional products as spices, textiles, precious metals, beverages, handicrafts, naval stores, and sugar. European output was undiversified and largely devoted to primary products; and both land and sea transport were expensive and inadequate for perishable products. Therefore, commodities of low value per unit of weight—including all agricultural and livestock products from temperate climates and all minerals except precious metals—were virtually barred from world trade.

During the last few decades of the nineteenth century, economic diversification in Europe, especially in Great Britain, the development of the railroad, the technological revolution in overseas shipping, and the refrigeration of perishable commodities led to a swift growth in exports of agricultural and livestock products and minerals. By 1913, agricultural and livestock exports from temperate climates, added to those customarily exported from tropical regions, made up 30 percent of total world trade. Exports of minerals and petroleum evolved similarly.

The Multilateral Trade and Payments System

The growing interdependence of countries within the world economy through trade, capital flows, and migration meant a higher volume of international payments to finance not only capital flow and the transfer of profits and interest earned by such capital but also ordinary trade transactions and the remittance of funds by immigrants to their homelands. Payments between countries did not have to balance bilaterally, and each country usually had a surplus with one group and a deficit with another. Therefore, international accounts were settled within the framework of a broad multilateral trade and payments system. Currency convertibility and a single standard, gold, facilitated transactions and payments. Later, in discussing Argentine development during this period, it will be seen that the domestic monetary system of each participating country fitted into the functioning of the multilateral trade and payments regime and the gold standard mechanism.

Although 75 percent of trade transactions was settled bilaterally, the remaining 25 percent was multilateral and vital to expansion of commerce and world financial relations.[3] From the close of the

---

[3] League of Nations, *The Network of World Trade* (Geneva, 1942), p. 88. This report also states (p. 88):

> We may imagine a system of bilateral exchange between countries, with no possibility of triangular or multilateral settlement of accounts. There would thus be no 'world market'; prices woud be determined in the various local markets represented by one country's supply and another's demand. Transactions in each market would be disconnected from those in others; there would be no international trade in the sense of an organic entity. It is

nineteenth century until its breakdown in the 1929 depression, the multilateral system of trade and payments operated on a progressively wider scale.

The Paths of Economic Integration

The discovery of America and the formation of the colonial economies of the New World were part of the European trade expansion that began in the eleventh century. From then until the middle of the nineteenth century, when world economic integration was thrust forward by the technological revolution, Europe remained the dynamic center of development and of the world economies. The Industrial Revolution grew out of Europe's merchant capitalism and, in turn, assured capitalism a predominant role during the period that began in the middle of the nineteenth century. The fact that in 1913 European exports were one half of world exports should give an idea of the quantitative importance of the continent during this stage.

At this time, Great Britain was a leading exporter of capital and emigrants. Its overseas investments in 1914 not only came to more than 40 percent of all foreign investment, but they had been made mostly in the developing countries, both in the open spaces already mentioned and in the less developed, more densely populated, countries of Asia, Africa, and Latin America. "During the period considered British foreign investments were redirected from Europe to non-European countries, and a part of the new investment in the latter was financed by the liquidation of British investments in Europe. In fact, it was largely through British capital that non-European countries were brought into the orbit of the international economy. . . ."[4]

Great Britain also furnished a high proportion of the people who migrated to the new countries. Furthermore, its exports before World War I were 15 percent of total world exports, and its imports were 18 percent. Great Britain had a large import surplus which was paid for out of income from overseas investment and from the

thus multilateral trade, in a general sense, that is responsible for the world-wide integration of the economy of different countries.

[This quotation and those in the notes below are taken from the original publications in English; page numbers supplied by translator.]

[4] United Nations, *op. cit.*, p. 3.

commercial and financial services that London provided as the center of the multilateral trade and payments system. This "invisible" income not only offset the trade deficit but also made possible further British investment abroad. The role of Great Britain in the world economy of that time should be borne in mind because of its influence on the primary-exports stage in Argentina.

The most important aspect of the integration of the world economy during the last few decades of the nineteenth century was the incorporation into that economy of a large group of countries then representing the bulk of world population. These countries, which were producers and exporters of raw materials and foodstuffs, will be referred to as primary-producing or peripheral countries. The latter's trade with the industrialized countries of Europe and, increasingly, with the United States accounted for more than one half of total world exports in 1914.

The United States played a dual role in the integration process because, although it began as a leading exporter of foodstuffs and raw materials, its rapid industrial development soon turned it into a heavy exporter of manufactured products. The industrialized countries of Europe, particularly Great Britain, France, and Germany, defined their roles much earlier as net exporters of manufactures and net importers of primary products.

As stated before, the trend toward integration originated mainly in the industrialized countries of Europe, especially in Great Britain. This meant that the primary-producing countries had to follow the paths to economic integration marked out for them by the policies of the industrialized countries.

Europe adopted three lines of action incorporating the peripheral countries into the world market. First, it sought foodstuffs and raw materials from such countries at a lower cost than it could produce them internally or obtain them from traditional suppliers. Second, it tried to expand markets for its manufactured products by penetrating the domestic markets of the primary-producing countries. Third, it channeled capital into those economies in order to secure higher yields and to equip them for the above functions.

The last aspect is worth considering more fully. By 1914, one half of all overseas investment by the industrialized countries was in Africa, Asia, Latin America, and Oceania, that is, in countries producing primary products; and approximately one half of this investment was in portfolio issues of the governments or in transportation and other public utilities. The debtor governments used most of the funds thus obtained abroad for infrastructure investments such as ports and communications. On the other hand, direct foreign investment was largely in transportation and public utilities, commerce, finance, miscellaneous services, and agricultural and mining activities for the export market. In brief, foreign investment helped the debtor countries to perform their function as exporters of foodstuffs and raw materials by providing them with resources for social overhead capital and by establishing financial and commercial machinery for the marketing of exportable output, the distribution of imports in local markets, and the direct development of production for export.

This process gave rise to an international division of labor under which the world economy was broadly composed of countries producing and exporting primary products and importing manufactures on the one hand, and countries importing primary products and exporting manufactures on the other. The latter group also exported capital to the former. As a return on such capital, the primary-producing countries transferred profits and interest to the capital-exporting countries, which reinvested such funds or used them to finance exports from the debtor countries. Integration and the international division of labor were responsible for profound structural changes in the economies participating in this system and influenced the course of their future development.

In the industrialized countries, integration of the world economy speeded up change and diversification of economic structures and resulted in a higher rate of growth. The importation of foodstuffs and raw materials at prices lower than those of domestic output led to a decline in the relative importance of the primary sector of those economies and to a shift of manpower into manufacturing activities and services in which productivity was greater. The most striking example of this process was the 1870 crisis in British agriculture, which collapsed under the impact of imports of agricultural and livestock products from the fertile regions of North and South America and Oceania. The industrial sector was stimulated further by the rising demand for manufactures in the primary-producing countries. Furthermore, earnings from overseas investment had a multiplying effect on the income of the industrialized countries and increased the amount of resources available for capital accumulation. The emigration of surplus agricultural labor that could not be absorbed by the new industries also spurred the process of industrialization and urbanization in the European economies.[5] Therefore, integration of the world market intensified structural change and accelerated the rate of growth more than would have been possible solely through the higher productivity and income derived from industrial development and the technological revolution.

In countries producing primary products, integration of the world economy also profoundly altered the economic structure and rate of development. But this change varied according to whether they were countries with a moderate climate, abundant natural resources, and scanty population (the open spaces) or densely populated countries. (The case of Argentina, which typifies integration of a country of open spaces into the world economy, will be discussed in some detail in the remaining chapters of this part.) Integration of the densely populated countries took place generally through the formation of a specific economic structure: on the one hand, a sector producing for export with a large amount of capital per person employed, modern technology, and high productivity; on the other, a mass of people engaged in traditional subsistence activities outside the dynamic scope of export expansion. Because the two sectors were not integrated into a single economic system, these economies developed slowly, and living standards remained low for most of the population.

To conclude this rapid sketch of the development of the world economy during this period, it should be remembered that just as technical progress released in the European economies forces of expansion that were to further integrate the world market, so also the resulting international division of labor established relations that were to condition the future ability of countries to generate and assimilate technical progress and ultimately to promote their own economic and social development. In fact, the so-called underdeveloped world of today, comprising two thirds of the world's population, consists of the same group of countries that were incorporated into the world economy in the second half of the nineteenth

---

[5] On the other hand, "Migration was an integral part of the process of industrialization; overseas colonization supplied the European industry with food, raw materials and markets for finished products, and rural-urban migration furnished the needed manpower." ("Migration," *Encyclopaedia Britannica* [1964 ed.], Vol. XV.)

century as producers and exporters of primary products and importers of manufactures.

Contemporary literature on economic development has thoroughly explored the reasons for the close relationship between primary production and underdevelopment. Economic integration, insofar as its paths led the peripheral countries toward specialization in primary production and away from a diversified economic structure and industrialization, was largely responsible for compartmentalizing these economies. The cumulative effect characteristic of economic development helped to reinforce the trends set in motion by the initial impulse.

The Place of Argentina in the World Economy

The case of the Argentine economy is a significant one in the integration of the world economy. Argentina's 56 million hectares of Pampa plains, ideally suited to livestock raising and temperate-zone agriculture, acted as a magnet for European migration and capital. The purpose and the result of this attraction was a sizable increase in Argentine exports and an important position for Argentina in the world economy in terms both of the volume of its foreign trade and the amount of foreign capital invested there.

After three centuries of regional subsistence economies, when it was considered a useless territory for the economic activity of the time, and after a transition period of only incipient livestock development, Argentina took its place in the second half of the nineteenth century as a dynamic and expanding economy closely linked to the world market.

The importance of the role played by Argentina in the integration of the international economy can be appreciated in the fact that between 1857 and 1914 that country received a net total of 3,300,000 immigrants, chiefly from Europe. Furthermore, foreign investment in Argentina beginning in the 1860's had by 1913 reached 10 billion dollars in present-day purchasing power, which was 8.5 percent of all foreign investment carried out by capital-exporting countries. This figure also represented 33 percent of aggregate investment in Latin America and 42 percent of the investments of the United Kingdom in the same region. In certain years during this period, the flow of foreign capital to Argentina was very high. In 1899, for example, it came to 40 or 50 percent of all overseas investment by the United Kingdom, then the major source of international capital.[6]

As a natural consequence of this process, Argentina emerged from insignificance to occupy a prominent position in world trade throughout the period. Exports of certain products like corn, wheat, flax, meat, and wool accounted for most or a substantial share of world exports.

[6] H. S. Ferns, *Britain and Argentina in the Nineteenth Century* (London, 1960).

10. EXPANSION OF AGRICULTURAL AND LIVESTOCK PRODUCTION

The Conditioning Factors

Argentina's participation in an expanding world market during the second half of the nineteenth century was based on the growth of its agricultural and livestock exports. This enabled the country to increase its payments to the rest of the world, both for imports of goods and services and for meeting commitments on external debts. The rise in exports and in capacity to make external payments engendered a complex system of economic and financial relations with the rest of the world. Therefore, during the primary-exports stage, the inflow of foreign capital and the servicing of such capital (interest, profits, and repayments) grew in importance along with exports.

As indicated before, the expansion of exports was possible for two main reasons. First, due to the increasing integration of the world economy, world demand for agricultural and livestock products from the temperate zones soared. Second, large tracts of fertile land were available in the Pampa that were either untouched or only partially exploited. But these circumstances alone could not raise the output of agricultural and livestock products or set into operation the system as a whole. In 1860, conditions in Argentina were actually unfavorable to such developments.

At that time, the Pampa region was sparsely populated, with not more than one inhabitant per 100 hectares in rural areas. This scarcity of manpower prevented a substantial increase in output and exports. Furthermore, overland transportation had changed little since the colonial period; traffic moved on carts and over dirt roads. High transportation costs meant that producers, especially in agriculture, who were far away from Buenos Aires had to accept such low prices that they were not encouraged to expand output.

Finally, when the province of Buenos Aires separated from the Federation and civil war broke out, the ensuing climate of political instability seriously hampered the settlement of the Pampa region, the construction of railroads, the inflow of capital, and the functioning of the system itself.

These problems had to be solved, and they were. This chapter will deal briefly with each and analyze growth in the output and exports of agricultural and livestock products in the primary-exports stage. In addition, it will consider the role played in this process by the land-tenure system carried over from the transition stage.

Immigration and Railroads

It would have been impossible to overcome the labor shortage in the Pampa region through natural population growth alone. The obvious solution was to bring in outside manpower, but not from the interior where population was small and relatively immobile. It therefore became necessary to attract large numbers of foreign immigrants.

It is estimated that 90 percent of the 3.3 million people who immigrated between 1857 and 1914 settled in the Pampa region and that about one quarter of that amount, or 800,000 people, went to rural areas. Largely as a result of immigration, total rural population in the region increased from approximately 600,000 inhabitants in 1869, to 1,300,000 in 1895, and 1,900,000 in 1914, when migration and development reached a peak. The rate of population growth during the whole period was 2.6 percent per year, and the number of inhabitants per 100 hectares rose from 1.1 to 2.3 and 3.4 on the dates indicated.

In spite of growth in population and available manpower in the Pampa region, agriculture continued to show a low ratio of labor per unit of farmland. Even so, the increase in this ratio, together with improved techniques and the introduction of mechanized farming, permitted a considerable expansion of output during the period.

The railroad was the answer to the transportation problem. It brought down freight rates and, by its mere existence, made possible the cultivation of land farther away from ports and consumption centers. In 1857, there were only 10 kilometers of railroads in Argentina; thirty years later, in 1887, there were 6,700. By 1900 the lines had spread to 16,600 and by 1914 to 33,500. At the end of the stage of railway expansion in 1930, 38,634 kilometers had been constructed.

Investment in railroads was financed mainly with foreign capital. Argentine private capital never contributed significantly to railway expansion; and the public sector, except in secondary and isolated cases of construction and administration, did no more than create favorable conditions for the flow of foreign capital into railway activity. Among the incentives offered were land grants, a guarantee of minimum rates of return, and unrestricted transfer abroad of the service on invested capital. In 1913, railroads absorbed 36 percent of all foreign capital invested in Argentina.

National Organization

Provincial autonomy, as it existed before the fall of Rosas and the subsequent clash between the province of Buenos Aires and the Federation, prevented the institutional, administrative, and political stability indispensable for development in this new stage. The country had to achieve peace and centralize in a national government the sources of its political power and economic policy. The reincorporation of the province of Buenos Aires into the Federation in 1861 and the election of Mitre as president of a united nation in 1862 provided the institutional framework for development of a primary-exports economy.

Obviously, domestic peace was essential in order to ensure minimum conditions of security for recent immigrants and to attract future labor, as well as to give foreign investors confidence in their investments and to permit the free movement of persons and goods through the national territory. However, it is necessary to study in more detail how closely stability and institutional organization—particularly the budget and the monetary system—were related to the economy in this new stage.

The budget

Until the fall of Rosas, every province had its own budget, and there was no national budget. The functions delegated to the province of Buenos Aires by the other provinces—for instance, in foreign affairs—were paid for out of provincial budget appropriations. After the fall of Rosas and the secession of Buenos Aires from the Federation, the province continued to maintain its own financial system. Although the Federation established the first national budgets, the component provinces of the Federation kept their own fiscal laws.

Of course, the basic issue was control of the source of revenue. The Buenos Aires customs contributed no less than 80 to 90 percent of consolidated public revenue, that is, the sum of the fiscal receipts of all provinces, including that of Buenos Aires, and the Federation government. But the province of Buenos Aires embraced only a part of the Pampa. Agricultural and livestock output was to increase, and railroads were to be constructed, not only in Buenos Aires, but in other provinces of that region. The new stage brought to the public sector vast possibilities of expanding current expenditures (in education, public health, administration, defense, and so on) and investment, which affected the whole country and not just the province of Buenos Aires. A federal budget was needed that would include all current and investment expenditures and that would centralize all fiscal resources, that is, nationalize the Buenos Aires customs. This was done in 1862 under the Mitre administration.

From another point of view, the budget reform meant that the problems of Argentine development would now be considered those of the country as a whole and would no longer come under the jurisdiction of each province.

With the nationalization of customs receipts and the establishment of the first effective federal budget, foundations were laid for a fiscal sector that would augment its resources as foreign trade and general conditions improved. The treasury was able to undertake commitments abroad through the sale of its issues in London and other international financial markets. Total government expenditures grew rapidly, and large amounts of foreign savings were attracted by the security implied in Argentina's lucrative customs revenues. In 1913, when primary exports were at their peak, the external debt, including loans floated abroad by the various provinces, was in excess of 3 billion dollars of present-day purchasing power, or about 30 percent of the total long-term investments existing in Argentina that year.

Monetary system

A national budget, however, did not suffice to create altogether satisfactory conditions for capital inflow, especially into government bond issues. A monetary system was also needed that would guarantee currency stability and the regular repayment of the public sector's foreign commitments.[1] Some aspects of the monetary evolution of Argentina during that stage will be discussed later; for the moment, it will only be pointed out that after 1862 the banking system frequently had to use its currency-issue privileges to finance budget deficits, a practice leading to the same kind of monetary expansion often experienced by the province of Buenos Aires after 1822. Such expansion usually occurred when foreign trade had contracted and funds from normal sources, particularly customs receipts, had declined. In these circumstances, the peso depreciated sharply, and the government faced serious difficulties in buying gold with which to service the public debt because it had to pay a higher price in pesos while its peso revenues increased less than proportionately to the external depreciation of the currency. As Ferns has stated: "Argentina's domestic economy operated under a system of inconvertible paper money and a loose credit policy at a time when a high proportion of Argentina's obligations on capital account were payable in gold or gold-backed currencies, principally sterling." [2]

According to the doctrine of that time, a country's money supply had to be closely related to its gold assets. Currency could only be issued against bullion deposits. By authorizing a single agency to convert gold into pesos and vice versa, the government could maintain its exchange rate and place its bond issues on national and foreign markets without having to resort to unwarranted monetary expansion through discounting its securities. Therefore, a strict adjustment of the domestic monetary system to the gold standard served several purposes: it equilibrated the balance of payments; it ensured stability of the peso; it prevented currency issues not backed by bullion; it imposed responsibility on government policy and guaranteed regular service of the public foreign debt. In 1899, the monetary system was finally given a firm basis with the setting up of a conversion office (Caja de Conversión) that centralized the right to issue and established convertibility.[3]

---

[1] Fiscal commitments included not only service on the public foreign debt but also the guaranteed return on foreign investments in railroads and other activities.

[2] H. S. Ferns, *Britain and Argentina in the Nineteenth Century* (London: Oxford University Press, 1960), p. 440.

[3] From the fall of Rosas in 1852 until 1899, when a law was adopted giving the conversion office the exclusive right to issue currency, Argentina's monetary

Another point should be mentioned in connection with the above institutional aspects. Increased exports and capital inflow expanded the country's capacity to purchase goods and services from abroad. But the free-trade policy Argentina chose to follow could be effective only if the national market was unified by eliminating inland customs and restrictions on traffic between provinces. This was accomplished by the first national government in 1862, and will be referred to later in discussion of the ultimate breakdown of inter-regional balance.

---

system was based on foreign coinage which had legal tender in the country, on locally minted gold coins, and on paper currency. Paper currency was at various times either convertible into gold or inconvertible.

From the battle of Monte Caseros until national unity, the gold parity was 17 pesos fuertes per ounce of gold in the Federation and 16 pesos per ounce in the province of Buenos Aires. Given these slightly different parities, modified on one occasion by the Federation, 10 to 10.70 pesos fuertes were worth 10 dollars. These parities were enforced for the coinage of gold but not for paper currency, because no paper money was issued in the Federation and because paper currency was not convertible into gold in the province of Buenos Aires. After consolidation of the Argentine nation in 1866, the province established effective convertibility, but at a parity of 25 paper pesos per peso fuerte. In turn, the National Law of 1881 replaced the peso fuerte with the *peso oro* containing 1.6129 grains fine gold. Later, the Conversion Law of 1899 fixed a new parity of one paper peso per 0.44 gold pesos, that is, 2.27 paper pesos per gold peso.

Until the creation of the National Bank in 1873 and its authorization, together with other banks, to issue bank notes in exchange for gold deposits, the Bank of the Province of Buenos Aires was the sole agency of issue. The 1887 Law of Guaranteed Banks (*ley de bancos garantidos*) confirmed the right to issue of the two official institutions and other specified banks. Bank notes issued by the province bank were convertible into gold (at the rate of 25 paper pesos per peso fuerte) from 1866, when by provincial law its bureau of exchange was set up and authorized to convert gold into pesos and vice versa, until May 1876, when inconvertibility was declared. On the other hand, bank notes issued by the National Bank were convertible only from 1873, when it was created, until 1876. Paper money issued by both banks again became convertible in July, 1883, when all banks of issue were required to withdraw from circulation their old currency and replace it with new "metallic" or gold-backed currency at the rate of 25 paper pesos per new peso. In January, 1885, convertibility of the National Bank's currency was once more suspended, as had occurred the previous year with bank notes issued by the province bank. Convertibility was not re-established until 1899.

Following the Conversion Law in November, 1899, convertibility was maintained until its suspension by the emergency laws of August and September, 1914. It was restored in 1927 and abandoned permanently in December, 1929.

The political and institutional organization of the country provided the necessary guarantees for the inflow of foreign capital and immigrants and made possible an economic policy facilitating integration of the Argentine primary-exports economy into world markets. It is interesting to note that the stage of primary exports, which began at the time of the Mitre administration in 1862 and ended with the fall of Irigoyen in 1930, covered a period of almost seventy years of uninterrupted constitutional government.

The Land-Tenure System

Although livestock and agricultural output increased due to a combination of the "given" factors (expansion of world demand and availability of abundant fertile land in the Pampa region) and "acquired" factors (immigration, railroads, and national organization), the pace of rural development and the resulting social structure were strongly conditioned by the land-tenure system carried over from the transition stage.

As explained in earlier chapters, the extension of the frontier during the nineteenth century was accompanied by the appropriation of huge tracts of land by a small number of owners. When immigration intensified after 1860, the more fertile and better located lands in the Pampa region were already legally occupied. Because the rural workers incorporated into the growing agricultural economy of the Pampa could not easily acquire land, the basic institutional feature of this economy came to be large production units on the one hand and tenant farming on the other.

The following data illustrate this situation. In 1914, farm units of more than 1,000 hectares represented only 8.2 percent of the total number of units, but held 79.4 percent of the total area. Units of over 5,000 hectares accounted for only 1.7 percent of the total number, but held 49.9 percent of the total area. In the Litoral alone, according to data for 1947, farm units of over 1,000 hectares were 3.5 percent of the total number and 52.1 percent of the total area. Nevertheless, 1937 data reveal that 44.3 percent of agricultural units were farmed by tenants.[4]

The land-tenure system affected the development of agriculture

---

[4] G. Germani, *Estructura social de la Argentina* (Buenos Aires, 1955). The data given in the text for the years 1914, 1937, and 1947 may be considered representative of the situation throughout the primary-exports economy stage.

and of the economy as a whole in three different ways: by bringing about social stratification, by limiting the growth of output, and by creating a powerful political group. The high degree of land concentration and the extent of tenant farming were naturally reflected in the social structure of the agricultural sector. According to Germani's estimates based on 1937 data, 94.8 percent of the active population in rural areas consisted of landless workers, small landholders, tenant farmers, and sharecroppers. By contrast, 1 percent of the active rural population owned agricultural properties of at least 2,000 to 3,000 hectares and controlled 70 percent of the total area. The remaining 4.2 percent of the active population owned medium-size properties, ranging from 200 to 2,000 hectares, and controlled 20 percent of the total farming area. Therefore, the land-tenure system prevented the emergence of a strong class of medium producers who would have introduced into their farm units the techniques and agricultural machinery needed for a steady rise in output and income.

Lack of available land also held back rural output by discouraging further immigration from abroad. Not more than 25 percent of foreign immigrants went into farming activities, whereas the remaining 75 percent settled in urban centers and swelled the supply of labor for industry and services. In 1914, although 42.7 percent of Argentina's population was foreign-born, immigrants accounted for only 10 percent of property owners.[5] Furthermore, capital formation in agriculture was limited because tenant farmers had no incentive to make fixed investments on land that did not belong to them and also because large proprietors were prone to spend a substantial part of their income on luxury consumption and on investment outside farming, especially on construction in Buenos Aires and other cities.

Finally, land concentration created a social group that, given the key role played by agriculture and livestock development in Argentina's economic development during the primary-exports stage, was to exercise a decisive influence on the political life of the nation. Mindful of its own interests and those of the foreign circles (particularly the British) to which it was linked, this group advocated a free-trade policy which inhibited the development of the basic industries needed to integrate the national economy and

[5] G. Germani, "El proceso de transición de una democracia de masa en la Argentina," *Política*, no. 16 (Caracas, Venezuela), June–July, 1961.

which, of course, opposed any reform of the land-tenure system. Notwithstanding the pressure of this group, Argentina developed during the primary-exports stage due to the steep growth in external demand and the continued incorporation of new Pampa land into production. However, after 1930, when a radical change in the economic structure became imperative, the economic attitudes and political maneuvers of this group constituted one of the fundamental obstacles to national development.[6]

The Expansion of Farming

In the exceptionally favorable conditions for agricultural development then prevailing, the amount of land farmed in the Pampa region increased rapidly. The total area sown with grain and forage rose from 340,000 hectares in 1875 to 6 million in 1900, 20 million in 1913, and 25 million in 1929. Throughout the period of growth in output and exports of agricultural and livestock products, acreage under cultivation expanded.

Exports soared. In 1875, they were 260 million dollars of present-day purchasing power; by 1900, they had reached 460 million; and by 1929, the peak of the primary-exports stage, 2 billion. The rate of growth in exports was 3.8 percent per year from 1875 to 1900 and almost 5 percent thereafter until 1929. The extent of the integration of the farm economy of the Pampa region into world markets can be measured by recalling that in 1900 agricultural and

---

[6] Argentina's experience with land appropriation differs radically from that of the United States, where the unoccupied lands west of the original thirteen colonies furnished a permanent outlet for population pressure and the possibility of independent employment. Actually, American democracy and equality of opportunity for the common man, as compared with the situation in Europe and the rest of colonial America, was based on expansion of the western frontier. The Homestead Act, adopted in 1862 during Lincoln's administration, clearly defined the government's policy of making land available to anyone willing to work it. In spite of forces tending to concentrate farmland (for example, land grants to the railroad companies), there is little doubt that land could be acquired much more easily in the United States than in Argentina. This was reflected in the American farm sector—its social structure, development possibilities, and political weight in national life. In the nineteenth century, therefore, the United States offered far better opportunities to immigrants than did Argentina after 1860. It is symbolic of the experience of the two countries that while land in the Argentine Pampa was being appropriated by a small number of owners in the 1860's, the United States was approving the Homestead Act of 1862.

livestock exports were 55 percent of the total output and that by 1929 this proportion had climbed to 70 percent.

The outstanding feature of the expansion of farm output from 1870 until the first decade of the present century was the rapid rise in agricultural products, chiefly cereals and flax, as clearly indicated in the pattern of exports. In 1870, agricultural products were less than 1 percent and livestock products were 95 percent of total exports. By 1890, agricultural products had gone up to 20 percent, and during the first five years of the present century, they reached 48 percent, or almost the equivalent of livestock exports. Since then, this ratio has continued, except for short-term fluctuations.

Within exports of livestock products, there were also important changes over the period. First came a rise in exports of wool. Toward the end of the century a rapid expansion in meat exports took place when refrigeration was introduced and meat was exported frozen, chiefly to the United Kingdom.

Capital formation and technical improvements in livestock and agricultural production were an integral part of the process of growth in this sector. At the beginning of the second half of the century, livestock production was still carried out in rather primitive conditions, and agriculture was almost nonexistent. But subsequently, better techniques were adopted, and more capital was employed in production. Barbed-wire fences began to be used instead of ditches to separate livestock properties, and windmills and Australian tanks replaced wells and natural watering places. No data are available on the extent of wire fences set up after their introduction in 1848, but they spread rapidly. As Taylor says: "exceptionally efficient fences must be listed as the first and one of the greatest pieces of mechanization in Argentine agriculture." [7] Windmills and Australian tanks also proliferated. The number of windmills increased a hundred-fold between 1888 and 1904 and had again tripled by 1914. Capital invested in tractors and agricultural machinery, *galpones* [sheds], and various types of constructions and installations, as well as vehicles, rose sharply during this period. Larger herds were another sign of increased investment in the livestock sector.

Livestock productivity also improved with the importation of blooded cattle and the reorganization of estancias by specialized

[7] C. C. Taylor, *Rural Life in Argentina* (Baton Rouge, 1948), p. 143.

personnel from England and Scotland. Agricultural productivity was helped mainly by imported equipment and seed.[8]

Throughout the entire period, the amount of reproducible fixed capital in the farm sector steadily mounted.[9] According to ECLA estimates based on data available after 1900, total fixed capital in agricultural and livestock activity in 1900–1904 was 12,850 million pesos of 1950 purchasing power; it went up to 29,281 million in 1925–1929, which was an increase of 128 percent. Manpower employed in agricultural and livestock production expanded 112 percent during the same period, so that the amount of capital per person employed climbed 16 percent.

Technical improvement, capital formation, and the progressive modernization of the primary-exports system were instrumental in raising the productivity of labor by 21 percent from the beginning of the century to the end of this stage. If data were available for the period from 1860 to 1900, the figures on capital formation and productivity gains might turn out to be similar to those indicated for the last thirty years of the primary-exports economy.

---

[8] "In the cultivation of these crops the use of the most scientifically constructed farm machinery has induced, if not forced, modern methods. These machines are constructed of rigid iron and steel, built to operate in a given way, and farmers automatically learn to practice the methods of planting, cultivating, and harvesting which these machines dictate. Most of the machines were built in response to what scientific agriculture required and those who use them have come to practice a degree of scientific method without knowing science." *Ibid.*, pp. 373–374.

[9] Reproducible fixed capital includes barbed-wire fences, windmills and pumps, housing, sheds, and other constructions and installations, machinery and vehicles.

Development during this stage was strongly conditioned by the high proportion of exports in Argentina's total output and by the country's heavy external indebtedness. These factors, therefore, should be examined.

Exports

Exports over the whole period amounted to 25–30 percent of gross product and 50–70 percent of the agricultural and livestock output of the Pampa region.[1] These figures show the importance of exports in the economic activity of Argentina and the extent to which agriculture and livestock, the key sector of the economy, were integrated into the world market. Both the volume and the price of Argentina's rural exports were determined by foreign demand, which in turn depended on the level of output in the industrialized countries absorbing the bulk of the marketable agricultural products in the world market. At this time, the evolution of capitalism was characterized by a succession of periods of prosperity and depression in production, employment, and income in the more developed countries. Imports of agricultural and livestock products and, in general, of foodstuffs and raw materials were determined by their domestic activity. When the business cycle swung upward, more foodstuffs and raw materials were imported to meet the growing needs of the population and of domestic output. During the downward phase, the contraction in employment and income reduced effective demand and, consequently, imports of foodstuffs and raw materials. Expansion and contraction in imports of primary products not only affected the volume of imports but also the prices paid for them. It should be recalled that primary products have always fluctuated much more in price than have industrial goods. Thus, a fall or rise in the volume of exports of foodstuffs

---

[1] See ECLA, *El desarrollo económico de la Argentina*, Vol. II (United Nations, México, Sales No. 59.II G.3, 1959). This report is the main source of statistical information for the period following 1900.

and raw materials usually has been accompanied by a corresponding deterioration or improvement in the terms of trade of these products. This characteristic behavior of world trade in primary products results from the interaction of a number of factors that need not be discussed here (for example, in the case of agricultural and livestock products, inability to adjust the volume of supply to short-run changes in demand and prices). However, such fluctuations in the terms of trade exerted a strong influence on the functioning of Argentina's primary-exports economy. Briefly, then, the volume, prices, and purchasing power of Argentine exports throughout this period were essentially conditioned by the phase of the business cycle in the industrialized countries importing such products.

Foreign Indebtedness

As already stated, Argentina received a large flow of foreign capital during the second half of the nineteenth century, particularly from Great Britain. According to available data, investments of foreign capital, which had been practically nil in 1860, went up to 2.5 billion dollars at present-day purchasing power in 1900 and reached 10.5 billion dollars in 1913. The importance of foreign investment in capital formation is evidenced by the fact that in 1913, when the inflow was at its height, almost 50 percent of fixed-capital assets in Argentina was foreign-financed. Even in 1929, at the very end of this stage, the proportion was 32 percent.

In 1913, 36 percent of existing capital was invested in railroads, 31 percent in government bonds, and 8 percent in public utilities; that is, three quarters of total foreign investment went into infrastructure capital for transportation and public utilities, and, through the purchase of government bonds, it helped to articulate Argentina politically and economically by financing investment and public expenditures. The remaining 25 percent was absorbed by trade and finance (20 percent) and by agriculture and livestock (5 percent).

Interest and profits earned by foreign capital in Argentina were sent abroad together with repayments. Foreign indebtedness was so great that a large share of the gold and foreign exchange generated by Argentine exports had to be allocated to servicing foreign capital. During this stage, such service often represented 30 to 50 percent of the value of exports. Furthermore, a high proportion—

almost a third of total foreign capital in Argentina—was invested in bonds issued by the national and some of the provincial governments, so that a substantial part of fiscal revenues had to be used to service the public debt. Usually from 30 to 40 percent of the consolidated fiscal revenues of the national and provincial governments was applied to amortization and interest of the external public debt.

The structure of Argentina's external debt made servicing of foreign capital extremely rigid. Interest and amortization were fixed, irrespective of the state of general economic activity and fiscal revenues. Because the external public debt and other foreign investments were liabilities in sterling and other currencies having a fixed gold parity, the service of such foreign capital invested in Argentina was due in gold (or as later designated, in "strong" currencies) and not in paper currency. In terms of gold the latter frequently fluctuated in value during the forty years of inconvertibility in the primary-exports stage. The guaranteed return on certain foreign investments, particularly in railroads, meant additional fiscal commitments whenever the minimum rate of profit was not covered by the earnings of these companies. The only exceptions to the creation of liabilities in gold were mortgage certificates, which were issued, were repayable, and earned interest in national currency, and direct foreign investment in sectors of the economy such as trade, finance, and agriculture and livestock.

In practice, the gold and foreign exchange needed to service foreign capital were supplied not only by income from exports but also by new foreign-capital inflows. Thus, net long-term investment of foreign capital [2] from 1900 to 1930 offset 70 percent of interest and profits on foreign capital already invested. The entrance of new capital from abroad was essential throughout the period, because otherwise the high ratio of the service of foreign capital to the gold and foreign-exchange availabilities and to fiscal revenues invariably caused a crisis in the balance of payments and in public finance.

Nevertheless, new foreign investments were in turn conditioned largely by the direct and indirect effect on Argentine exports of the level of economic activity in the industrialized countries. During periods of prosperity, large amounts of capital were placed abroad,

---

[2] That is, the inflow of foreign capital minus the amortization of existing capital together with capital exports, the latter mainly consisting of repatriated foreign investment.

much of it in Argentina. At the same time, these countries increased their imports of agricultural and livestock products. Argentina, therefore, became more prosperous and was in a position to assume more foreign commitments; fiscal revenues and exchange earnings allowed Argentina to easily service foreign investments already made in the country.

Thus, the level of economic activity in the industrialized countries governed the two principal factors in Argentina's economic development: exports and foreign investment. Clearly, the level of employment and income in Argentina, as well as its balance-of-payments position and its public finance, was extremely vulnerable to changes in the business cycle of the industrialized countries. Certain aspects of this external vulnerability of the Argentine economy will now be discussed.

External Vulnerability

The Argentine economy was vulnerable at three different but interdependent levels: employment and domestic income, balance of payments, and public finance.

Employment and domestic income

The agricultural and livestock sector employed 35 percent of the labor force and 25 percent of existing capital. Wages, rents, profits, and interest (income accruing to workers, proprietors, and rural entrepreneurs) depended directly on the value of exports. About 70 percent of the production of the Pampa region was exported, and as long as sales abroad were high in volume and price, the farmer's income was high. An expansion of exports not only raised the level of employment and income of the population engaged in agriculture but also determined the growth of the economy as a whole through the multiplier effect of the initial increase in income. The higher income of agricultural workers and entrepreneurs was spent partly on imports and partly on consumption and investment in the domestic market. The proportion of income spent in Argentina generated employment of labor and capital in the sectors of activity that supplied the mounting domestic demand. In turn, this new employment meant wages and profits for workers and capital engaged in such domestically oriented sectors. The increase in income was also spent partly on imports, partly on consumer goods and investment in the domestic market, and so on.

Obviously, the stimulus to the national economy provided by the increase in exports depended upon the proportion of total income spent abroad, which consequently did not employ labor and capital in production for the domestic market. The demand for goods and services for consumption and investment was met largely out of imported goods and services. Broadly speaking, about 25 percent of such demand was supplied by imports. The outflow of money to pay for these imports naturally weakened the multiplier effect of the rural sector's income expansion.[3]

Conversely, when exports declined, farm producers received less income and reduced their purchases both of imports and of internally produced goods and services. This led to unemployment of capital and labor in the sectors supplying the domestic market and to a consequent drop in incomes and expenditures in these sectors. Thus, the initial recession started by the contraction of exports tended to spread.

In considering the relation of the servicing of foreign capital and of new foreign investment to the level of employment and domestic income, analysis will be simplified by taking the net effect of both factors, that is, the difference between profits and interest on foreign capital and the net inflow of new capital.[4] From 1900 to 1930, the latter was about 70 percent of gross profits and interest on foreign capital; in other words, 70 percent swelled the amount of foreign investment in the country, and the remaining 30 percent was transferred abroad. Over the entire period, there was net reduction in the income available for expenditure on domestic production and/or imports. A part of the income derived from exports

---

[3] However, this should not be overemphasized. In the final analysis, Argentina exported a substantial part of its output, not to accumulate gold and foreign exchange, but to be able to import and thus increase the total amount of goods and services available for national consumption and investment. In this stage of Argentina's development, the total volume of imports and its relation to domestic demand mattered less in the long run than the composition of imports, because the latter had a decisive influence on the structure of output and through this structure on the possibilities of growth.

[4] In practice, new foreign investment is financed not only out of new capital but through reinvestment of some of the profits and interest generated by existing capital. However, balance-of-payments statistics show as debits all earnings and interest generated by foreign capital, even if a part is reinvested, and as credits all capital inflow, including the part derived from reinvestment.

(approximately 11 percent) was absorbed in this way, thereby diminishing the growth effect of the increased exports on the level of output, employment, and income.

However, it is not enough to compute the difference between profits and interest on foreign capital and new investment from abroad and to point to the effect of this net balance on the level of domestic activity. Both profits and interest and new investment were resources linked to the process of savings and investment rather than to consumption. Profits and interest were the earnings of the foreign capitalist, who applied them almost exclusively to savings and investment and not to consumption. The inflow of foreign capital went into three different lines: financing of imports of machinery and equipment for investment projects (for example, the purchase of locomotives), payment of local costs of investment projects (for example, construction of buildings and sheds for a railroad), and purchase of bonds issued by the government, which in turn employed the money to finance not only current expenditures (administration, defense, and so on) but preferably public investment (buildings, public utilities, and so on). Thus, foreign capital was used principally to finance, directly and indirectly,[5] investment in machinery, equipment, buildings, and so on.

It was therefore natural that capital formation should have slackened or intensified according to whether or not new inflows of foreign capital were in excess of profits and interests. This is clearly shown in the figures compiled by ECLA for the period 1900–1930.

Throughout this period, the rate of capital formation, that is, the share of gross product allocated to investment, fluctuated sharply. In 1907 it reached a peak of 58.8 percent, and in 1918 it fell to a minimum of 10.4 percent. The average for the thirty years was 32 percent. Two different periods may be singled out: first, from 1900 to 1914, when net investment from abroad exceeded profits and interest on existing foreign capital by 10 percent, and second, from

---

[5] Even when the government used the funds it had obtained abroad to finance current expenditures, it conceivably liberated other resources for investment. In order to finance local costs of investment projects, the foreign investor sold foreign currencies in Argentina in exchange for pesos with which he paid wages and made purchases from Argentine suppliers. Although such foreign exchange was ultimately spent on imports of consumer goods, the fact remains that foreign investment financed the employment of manpower and other domestic factors of production.

1915 to 1929, when net investment was 55 percent below the amount of profits and interests. This explains why during the first period the average investment ratio was 38.8 percent and during the second 24.6.

Because investment is one of the main components of aggregate demand, the level of investment largely determines the volume of employment of manpower and other factors of production. By influencing the amount of investment, foreign indebtedness played a significant role in the determination of domestic employment and income.

Balance of payments

Imports tended to adjust to the availability of foreign exchange generated by exports. An increase in exports raised the level of income and, therefore, the demand for imports. On the other hand, the servicing of capital required a fixed sum that did not fluctuate with changes in exports and in the domestic level of income. When exports were high, service on foreign capital was from 20 to 25 percent of the value of exports, and when the latter declined, that ratio soared to 40 or 50 percent.

If Argentina had had to pay in any given year the services on foreign capital with its own resources, it would have been obliged to use up a substantial proportion of the gold and foreign exchange generated by exports and to reduce imports. In other words, it would have needed a large export surplus in order to service foreign investment. Nevertheless, 70 percent of the profits and interest on foreign capital was offset by the net inflow of foreign investment over the period from 1900 to 1930. Although this applies to the average for the entire period, it does not hold true for the short run. From year to year there were sharp changes in the amount of foreign investment. When investment declined or, in extreme cases, when there was disinvestment and Argentina appeared to be exporting capital, the service payments on foreign capital had to be met wholly out of the gold and foreign-exchange reserves and out of current income from exports. As reserves became depleted, there were only two avenues open: to curtail imports to a level that would free foreign exchange for servicing foreign capital, or to suspend payments altogether. The former solution involved serious economic, social, and political problems because it would drastically reduce the amount of goods and services available for consumption and domestic investment, which in turn would severely lower living standards and levels of employment and income. The latter solution would create difficulties abroad, cut off the inflow of new capital, and induce the flight of existing capital. Except in a crisis like that of 1890, disequilibrium was never serious enough to paralyze the functioning of the system and to bring about a moratorium in the servicing of foreign capital; adjustment mechanisms began to operate in time to prevent collapse. In any case, throughout the stage of the primary-exports economy, the balance of payments was extremely susceptible to this type of disequilibrium.

Public finance

National as well as provincial (primarily Buenos Aires) governments resorted on a large scale to foreign loans through the issue of bonds in the international finance markets. The external debt was from two to four times the amount of current fiscal revenues, and its servicing absorbed 30 to 40 percent of such revenues. Amortization and interest commitments on the external public debt were expressed in gold or foreign currencies tied to gold and had to be met whatever the situation of the government's current revenues. When the latter were high, thanks to the country's general prosperity, servicing claimed only 15 to 20 percent; but during times of depression when fiscal revenues declined, the percentage reached 60 percent or more.

Actually, by assuming new loans the government could service its debt more easily, and, taking fiscal revenues and new loans together, it did not spend more than 20 percent of aggregate resources on servicing. However, in the short run, when the issue of public bonds abroad had to be suspended due to a slump in the international capital markets during a downswing in the business cycle of the industrialized countries,[6] servicing of the debt had to be met completely out of current fiscal revenues. This usually happened when such revenues were decreasing because of a drop in foreign trade and domestic activity, which was also the result of a cyclical disturbance in the industrialized countries. Given these

---

[6] Whenever the national and provincial governments had difficulty in meeting their commitments, foreign investors lost confidence and became reluctant to buy their bonds, thereby reinforcing the original cause of their difficulties.

conditions, servicing of the external public debt required an exorbitant proportion of current fiscal revenues. This problem could be solved in two ways: by a sharp curtailment of public expenditures and investment in order to create a current budget surplus out of which to meet servicing of the public debt, or by a suspension of payments. Again, the first solution was very difficult from an economic, social, and political point of view, because any cutback in expenditures during a depression would only intensify the impact of the economic crisis. In any event, the bulk of public expenditures consisted of the salaries of teachers, army personnel, administrative employees, and so on, which could hardly be lowered.[7] The other solution, the suspension of payments, implied damaging the financial relations of Argentina with other countries and closing international financial markets to new issues of Argentine bonds. As in the case of the balance of payments, adjustment mechanisms generally began to operate before breakdown.[8]

The Adjustment Mechanisms

In a primary-exports economy, it is possible to define two types of adjustment mechanisms that operate in conditions of disequilibrium: one, related to world demand for agricultural and livestock products

[7] In these situations, salaries were occasionally reduced, but large-scale dismissal of personnel was and still is politically very difficult.

[8] The most striking exception to this was the crisis of 1890, which had been preceded by a sharp increase in foreign indebtedness and in the servicing of the public debt. Such servicing had been largely met out of new issues. But with the advent of the world depression, the value of exports fell, and the market for new public bonds rapidly disappeared, forcing the government to suspend payments. The disastrous impact of Argentina's financial crisis on the London market was a measure not only of the intensity of the crisis but of the predominance of Argentina's position in international finance. As some observers have remarked, the 1890 depression was not simply a business-cycle slump but an authentic growth crisis. Argentina had exceeded its possibilities of external indebtedness, but the investment thus generated had not yet exerted its full effect on a system in the process of changing into a primary-exports economy. However, the vast natural resources of Argentina and the opening up of new sources of activity in its agricultural and livestock production—the appearance of the packing house and refrigerated meat exports and the swift increase in the output and exports of cereals—in a few years corrected the maladjustment between external indebtedness and the country's payment capacity. Once the crisis was over, Argentina entered its most intense period of growth, which continued until the beginning of World War I.

and to the international flow of long-term capital, that is, to exogenous factors; the other, an endogenous mechanism related to the internal dynamics of the economy itself.

In respect to the exogenous adjustment mechanism, it has been established that Argentina, by expanding area under production in the Pampa region, increased its volume of exports to keep up with rising world demand for agricultural and livestock products. In the long run, the growth of farm output in the Pampa region and the increase in exports continued throughout the period because of a steady rise in world demand. In the short run, the volume and prices of exports were influenced by the business-cycle phase of the industrialized countries and its effect on imports of primary products by those countries. The flow of foreign capital was conditioned in the long run by the growth of the economies of the industrialized countries and by the ability of the primary-producing countries to expand exports, and in the short run by the business-cycle phase of the industrialized countries and its repercussions on all the nations integrated into the world market.

Throughout the period, the business-cycle phase of the industrialized countries governed exports and foreign investment and, consequently, affected levels of employment and income, balance of payments, and public finance in Argentina. Increased exports and new capital inflow expanded employment and income in Argentina at the same time that the balance of payments and public finance improved. A fall in exports and a reduction in capital inflow, or an actual outflow of capital, contracted the level of income and created a critical situation for the balance of payments and public finance. A slump or a boom in the primary-exports economy was adjusted to new positions of temporary equilibrium by a mechanism operating from abroad.

In this stage, Argentina did not adopt compensatory policies to reduce the impact of external factors on either employment and domestic income or the balance of payments and public finance. In any event, before 1930 no theoretical basis had existed for such compensatory policies, and it was not until after the "Great Depression" that the problem was analyzed and policies of this type were adopted.[9] Thus, the Argentine economy was extremely vulnerable

[9] Reference is made here to short-term compensatory policies and not to long-term policies for the purpose of diversifying the structure of output and promoting industrialization, which made the national economy less dependent

to external factors. However, the behavior of the economy must be considered in the light of two different systems: the gold standard and inconvertible paper currency.

As noted before, the gold standard prevailed for thirty of the seventy years of the period, and a system of inconvertible paper currency prevailed for the remaining years. Under the gold standard, paper currency was convertible into gold and vice versa, and the money supply was directly related to the gold and convertible foreign-exchange reserves.[10] Transactions in gold and convertible exchange took place freely, with their volume determined by the net balance of payments.

Theoretically, the gold standard provided an automatic mechanism for stabilizing the balance of payments and the domestic price level. A surplus in transactions with the rest of the world [11] led to a net inflow of gold and foreign exchange which automatically increased the money supply. At the same time, banks expanded credit on the basis of their additional reserves. From a monetary point of view, the expansion of the money supply merely reflected the internal prosperity. Except for emergency situations like World War I, the balance-of-payments surplus indicated that farmers were receiving higher incomes as a result of increased exports, that their domestic expenditures were climbing, and that employment and income in the sectors producing for the domestic market were also rising. At the same time, investment financed out of domestic and foreign savings reached new heights, pushing up employment and activity throughout the economy. The demand for labor tended to raise wage levels and consequently the general price level. Exports

---

on external factors and incorporated into it the dynamic forces of development. There are a number of outstanding analyses of the policies of industrialization and integrated development, including the nineteenth-century studies of Friedrich List and Charles Carey. In practice, these policies involved strong elements of short-term compensation.

[10] The authorized banks of issue (after 1899, the conversion office) delivered paper currency at a fixed gold parity in exchange for gold and delivered gold against the presentation of paper currency. The amount of paper money in circulation therefore fluctuated according to changes in the gold and convertible foreign-exchange holdings of the issuing agencies. For the purposes of this analysis, no distinction is made between the gold standard and the gold-exchange standard.

[11] This occurred when exports plus net inflow of new foreign capital minus imports and profits and interest on existing foreign investments yielded a surplus.

and commodities for domestic consumption became more expensive, which discouraged exports and stimulated imports. The contracting economy eventually wiped out the balance-of-payments surplus. With less money available, the level of employment and domestic activity dropped, lowering wages and the general price level and finally bringing about a new equilibrium of the economy.

If, on the other hand, the initial impulse originated in a payments deficit with the rest of the world, the money supply declined and with it the level of rural income, which led to lower employment and income for the sectors producing for the domestic market. Exports and commodities for the domestic market became cheaper, tending to raise exports and discourage imports and finally re-establishing an equilibrium position.

In practice, this adjustment mechanism under the gold standard did not operate as it was supposed to mainly because the volume of exports was not a function of Argentine prices but of world demand. The volume and prices of exports increased with rising demand, and, even though prices of agricultural and livestock products went up, the higher prices of Argentine exports did not exclude them from world markets. When the general level of activity in the industrialized countries declined, demand for agricultural products shrank and international prices fell, so that Argentine exports did not increase even though they became cheaper through domestic deflation. On the other hand, the adjustment mechanism did operate for imports, which increased with any rise in income and prices in Argentina and fell as domestic prices and income declined.[12]

The adjustment mechanism under the gold standard was subject to difficulties related to external indebtedness. When exports and capital inflow declined, the servicing of foreign capital had to be met totally out of the gold and foreign exchange generated by exports, which intensified the initial impact of the contraction of exports. On the other hand, when exports increased, capital inflow

---

[12] When imports contracted, the adjustment mechanism operated through a reduction in domestic income and in the demand for imports. Although the prices of domestically produced commodities fell in relation to the prices of imports, this change did not lead to an expansion in activities that might have replaced imports, because the domestic structure of output was not flexible enough to enable capital and labor to shift out of other sectors into those able to produce goods normally imported.

rose and swelled the expansion of domestic activity. In this way, the forces of disequilibrium tended to gain strength.

Under the system of inconvertible paper currency, the money supply was not determined by gold and foreign-exchange reserves. Paper currency was not convertible into gold, and banks could issue currency in exchange for public bonds or acceptances. Because of these circumstances, the amount of the money supply was independent of the net balance of transactions with the rest of the world. A decline in exports and/or the inflow of foreign capital could, and usually did, bring about a balance-of-payments deficit followed by a transfer of gold and convertible exchange to pay for this deficit. However, at the same time, the money supply could increase because banks were issuing currency to the government in exchange for the latter's bonds. The rate of foreign exchange was determined by the demand and supply of gold and of inconvertible currency. During periods of inconvertibility, the Argentine peso depreciated in terms of gold, or in the terminology of the time, gold acquired a "premium" in terms of paper currency.

How did the adjustment mechanism operate under the system of inconvertible currency? The depreciation of the peso cheapened exports in terms of gold and convertible foreign exchange, but just as under the gold standard, this did not stimulate Argentine exports, which actually depended on the world market situation. The expanded money supply and bank loans to the government and to the private sector maintained a high level of monetary income,[13] which exerted pressure on the availabilities of gold and foreign exchange to pay for imports. As a consequence of depreciation, imports became more expensive, thereby adjusting the demand for imports to the country's effective capacity to import.

Depreciation of the peso created other problems for national economic development, especially for public finance, because up to 1893 most fiscal revenues, including customs duties, were paid in paper currency, whereas the external debt had to be serviced in gold or in convertible currency. Therefore, the cost in national currency of servicing the public debt became higher precisely at the moment when, as usually occurred, the reduction in exports,

---

[13] Real income declined because the reduction in exports implied a fall in real output in Argentina. The decreased value of exports could originate in a contraction of the volume of exports, or a worsening of the terms of trade, or a combination of both factors.

imports, and the level of domestic activity tended to depress fiscal revenues. The government was obliged to obtain further advances from the banks of issue in exchange for bonds, and the new currency issue again lowered the external value of the peso. On the other hand, whenever paper currency went up in value due to improved transactions with the rest of the world, the peso was once again made convertible into gold.

Under both the system of inconvertible paper currency and the gold standard, the adjustment mechanism to an externally produced disequilibrium was ultimately subject to external factors. The complications peculiar to the situation under inconvertible currency, such as occurred in public finance, do not alter this basic conclusion. In a completely open economy like the Argentine, changes in employment and domestic income, as well as in the balance of payments and public finance, were mainly conditioned by external factors.

Inflation and currency depreciation might have been expected to stimulate industrialization and diversification of domestic output. Depreciation raised the cost of imports, and inflation increased profit margins in business enterprises by lowering real wages, thus setting the stage for import replacement to meet the domestic demand formerly satisfied with imports. In practice, however, the incentive was temporary and uncertain, because as soon as exports recovered and new capital entered the country, the peso tended to appreciate, thereby making imports cheaper. Furthermore, the absence of a systematic protectionist policy for industrial development discouraged investment in sectors that could have produced commodities in competition with imports. Thus, the potential industrializing effect of currency depreciation and domestic inflation was nullified.

Depreciation and its concomitant, monetary expansion, severely affected relative domestic price and wage levels and, therefore, had an important impact on the distribution of income between the different economic and social sectors. By the same token, appreciation of the currency, if carried too far, necessarily shifted the income pattern. The following section will discuss this situation in detail.

Income Distribution

During the primary-exports stage, the allocation of income between different sectors was largely determined by the concentration of land in the Pampa region. To a lesser extent the concentration of capital in industry also affected income distribution, but this influence cannot be appraised because of lack of data.

With no farmland available, the immigrant was obliged to work as a tenant farmer or as a field hand and to accept low wages. The profits, interests, and rent generated by rural output were concentrated in the hands of a small proportion of the population. About 70 percent of the gross income derived from the agricultural sector was held by not more than 5 percent of the active population in that sector; on a national scale, this means that about 2 percent of the population received 20 percent of Argentina's gross income.[14]

Furthermore, land concentration also affected the remuneration of labor in urban activities: first, by swelling the supply of manpower for urban employment, which kept wages down; and second, by establishing poor pay for alternative activities in agriculture. The pressure of cheap manpower in urban centers was reflected in the large ratio of unemployment. Even in times of prosperity when exports were high, as in 1913, more than 5 percent of the labor force was idle. In the war years that succeeded 1914 and during periods of slump, unemployment rose to as much as 20 percent of the labor force. Thus, land concentration was the decisive factor in the level of remuneration of labor in agricultural and urban activities and in the share of labor in net income.

---

[14] Gross income in the agricultural and livestock sector breaks down into wages received by workers, rents collected by landowners, and the income of entrepreneurs plus interest. The last two items correspond to income accruing to capital and enterprise, and during the primary-exports stage, they were 80 percent of gross agricultural and livestock income, including 10 to 15 percent allocated to depreciation of invested capital. The remaining 20 percent was the income of the workers. If it is recalled that, according to the estimates by Germani already cited, landless rural workers were 65 percent of the active population engaged in agricultural and livestock production, and that small proprietors and tenant farmers made up another 30 percent, and that large and medium landowners (who controlled 90 percent of total exploited land) were only 5 percent, it can be calculated that about 90 percent of rents, profits, and interest was paid to no more than 5 percent of the active population engaged in the sector. On the other hand, the sector gave employment throughout the period to about 35 percent of the total labor force and generated about 30 percent of gross national income. It is clear that the pattern of income distribution in the agricultural and livestock sector alone explains why about 20 percent of gross domestic income went to no more than 2 percent of Argentina's active population.

To this should be added other factors which worsened income distribution, namely, fluctuations in the exchange rate, the weakness of rural and urban labor organizations, and fiscal policies. During the forty years of inconvertibility within the primary-exports stage, domestic prices and rural wages were naturally affected by the fluctuations in the exchange rate, and price instability in turn affected income distribution. When the currency depreciated, the export sector increased its peso income roughly in proportion to the depreciation.[15] Depreciation raised domestic prices, first of agricultural and livestock products, which were the major item in the expenditures of lower-income groups,[16] and second of manufactured and intermediate imported commodities, which represented a significant share of total consumption.

Rural wages went up less than the depreciation of the currency and the rise in agricultural and livestock prices, so that profit margins of rural entrepreneurs increased while the share of agricultural workers in the income of this sector declined.[17]

Depreciation had an even greater impact on urban than on rural wages. As Williams says:

> For the rural peasant population the problem of depreciated paper money, in so far as it affected the cost of living, was much less significant than for the city population. The former lived directly upon the fruits of its 'chacras' (small farms), buying but little, either of domestic or imported products. The city population, on the other hand, was dependent for its food on the country, and for virtually everything else upon imports. In the cities, therefore, the problem of debased currency was acute and ever present.[18]

An income transfer to the agricultural and livestock sector was brought about to the extent that the latter purchased goods and

[15] This argument is not invalidated by the transactions of commercial organizations authorized to sell products abroad or by the effect of the depreciation of paper currency on prices expressed in gold or convertible exchange paid by foreign importers.

[16] "This state of things is quite in accordance with expectation, when one remembers the dominating position of the export trade in Argentina, and the insignificance of the home market . . . , a market so small that it could not affect, but merely reflect, the conditions operative in the export market." J. H. Williams, *Argentine International Trade Under Inconvertible Paper Money, 1880–1900* (Cambridge: Harvard University Press, 1920), p. 194.

[17] "Depreciating paper created a gap between selling price and costs, which was equivalent to a bounty on exports." *Ibid.*, p. 200.

[18] *Ibid.*, p. 195.

services from other national sectors where prices did not increase as much as the currency appreciated and farm prices went up.

On the other hand, domestic industries utilizing a substantial amount of imported raw materials and other intermediate products probably raised their prices *pari passu* with currency depreciation. Therefore, the prices of these industries did not fall in relation to agricultural and livestock prices, and no transfer of income took place. Nonetheless, because prices outstripped wages, workers received a smaller share of the income generated by such industries.

This was also the situation in industries such as packing houses and other plants that processed livestock and agricultural products. The higher cost of raw materials pushed up the prices of final products. Although there was no transfer of income to the rural sector through a decline in relative prices, there was an increase in the profit margins of these industries with no corresponding rise in wages.

Consequently, inflation intensified the structural factors that conditioned income distribution and the level of wages. It discouraged the entrance of immigrants into Argentina and even led to the emigration of those who had arrived earlier.[19]

Although currency appreciation was less frequent than depreciation, it also had an effect on income distribution. At those times, the peso income of exporters declined because they received less national currency for the same amount of gold and foreign exchange. Real wages of rural and urban workers increased. When prices fell, entrepreneurs of both sectors tried to protect their position by lowering money wages, but the most rapid and effective defense of their interests consisted in stabilizing the peso in terms of gold. It is a fact that convertibility was re-established in 1866, 1899, and 1927 in order to prevent further appreciation of the national currency.[20]

---

[19] "A sharp cut in real wages had the effect of checking immigration and of reversing the flow of people from one side of the Atlantic to the other." H. S. Ferns, *Britain and Argentina in the Nineteenth Century* (London, 1960), p. 445.

[20] The 1866 stabilization "was not intended to raise the value of the currency, but to prevent the currency from further appreciation, and this was repeated thirty-three years later in the 1899 conversion law." Federico Pinedo, *Siglo y medio de economía argentina* (Mexico City, 1961), p. 95. The forces operating behind Argentina's financial and monetary policy are made clear in the following remark by W. R. Lawson in *The Bankers' Magazine*, 1899, vol. 68,

On the other hand, because the landowning class was heavily indebted in inconvertible national currency to banks and to foreign holders of bonds issued by the National Mortgage Bank, currency depreciation decreased the real value of their debts and of their amortization and interest payments. This was another powerful reason not only to promote policies of monetary expansion but also to resist any trend toward appreciation of the peso.

Given these conditions, it is easy to understand why the landowning class opposed any policy of financial stabilization based on higher revenues and lower expenditures for the purpose of balancing the budget. Instead, they always favored a policy of inflationary financing of the budget through currency issues. They were the sector that would bear most of the burden of higher taxes, whereas inflation would bring them a number of benefits.

Other forces tending to diminish the share of urban and rural labor in the national income were related to the weakness of their organization. Labor sectors could not exert a strong enough pressure to defend their share of national income and to maintain levels of employment and wages. Still more important, they could not achieve structural changes such as land reform, which would have helped to correct basic inequalities. Among other reasons, labor organizations were weak because throughout the stage of the primary-exports economy there was unemployment in urban occupations and little industrial development. Difficulties of organization in rural occupations stemmed from the scattered population pattern.

Finally, the fiscal structure also accentuated income inequality. Indirect taxes, borne by the great mass of consumers, accounted for 70 to 80 percent of current revenues of the national and pro-

---

p. 693, quoted in A. G. Ford, "Argentina and the Baring Crisis of 1890," *Oxford Economic Papers* (June, 1956), vol. 8, no. 2, p. 132, n. 1:

> The great obstacle to sound money in states like the Argentine Republic is, that the classes who benefit, or who suppose they benefit, by a falling exchange are much more influential than the classes who lose by it. The former include all the staple producers and exporters . . . They convert their exports into gold in foreign markets and sell their gold at home for paper dollars. Indirectly they are bulls of gold just as much as if they were speculating in it for the rise on the Bolsa.

The rapid fall in the gold premium was not welcomed, and when it threatened to lead to uncontrolled appreciation of the peso, the alarmed exporters decided to take action. Obviously, the solution was to re-establish convertibility with a fixed gold parity for the peso.

vincial governments. Import duties alone represented 50 percent
and various excise taxes about 20 percent of current revenues. On
the other hand, educational and health expenditures, which benefited the low-income sectors, were not important enough in the
national and provincial budgets to counteract the regressive nature
of the tax system.

The Structure of Output

During the stage of primary exports, a feature of Argentine
development was that although exports and the farm sector played
a dominant role in the economy and in the process of development,
the active population was fairly evenly distributed among the
different sectors of activity. The occupational structure of the
population did not change significantly between 1900 and 1930,
and by the end of that period manufacturing (including mining
and construction) employed about 26 percent of the active population; services (including commerce, finance, personal services, transportation, communications, electricity, and so on) about 38 percent; and the agricultural and livestock sector the remaining 36
percent.[21] The relative diversification of the occupational structure
and the lower proportion of employment in the rural sector than
in manufacturing and the services can be explained by the high
output per person engaged in agriculture and livestock and by the
concentration of land.

In respect to high per capita productivity in agriculture and
livestock, it should be recalled that at the end of the nineteenth
century Argentina's was the typical case of the incorporation of

---

[21] Existing capital was also widely distributed. Of the increase in capital from
1900 to 1930, 36 percent went into housing, 17 percent into transport, and
12 percent into public investment. The remaining 9 percent was allocated to
other sectors, including commerce, finance, mining, construction, electricity,
and communications. Capital accumulation in the farm sector and in transport
—mainly railroads—was related to the sharp expansion in exportable agricultural and livestock output and its transportation to points of embarkation; the
large share of investment in housing was explained primarily by the urbanization that went on throughout the period; and the investment in manufacturing
resulted largely from the growth of the domestic market, import replacement
in certain fields, and the emergence of industries processing exportable agricultural and livestock products. Investment by the public sector was principally to finance part of the economic and social infrastructure deriving from
the process of development itself.

an open space economy into the world market. When the primary-exports stage began, Argentina offered huge stretches of fertile land in the Pampa region, but it was too sparsely populated to properly utilize that area. However, farm output began to increase rapidly due to the arrival of immigrants, the cultivation of new lands, the investment of foreign and national capital in railroads and agriculture, and the improvement in techniques of production. Although extensive agriculture prevailed, a relatively large amount of capital per person was used. As the Argentine agricultural and livestock economy became part of the world market and all significant forms of subsistence production were eliminated, high output per person in agriculture enabled Argentina to feed its population and generate a sizable export surplus while employing only a minor portion of its total labor force.[22]

On the other hand, the land-tenure system prevented the employment of more people in rural activities and the creation of a class of medium landholders who would have made good use of mechanization and modern technology. Inability of the rural sector to absorb a higher share of immigration after 1860 limited its employment of manpower. Clearly, had it been possible to speed up the rise of output and employment in the rural sector, sooner or later increased incomes and diversification of demand would have caused the rural population to shift to urban activities. But given world market conditions in the second half of the nineteenth century, it would have been possible to expand exports even more and to raise even higher the volume of output and level of employment in agriculture and livestock. In this way, the land-tenure system hampered development of the rural sector by restricting its relative importance in over-all employment during that stage.

The distribution of active population and the structure of output were influenced by two other factors: the composition of imports and income distribution. The level of income per capita in the Argentine economy was substantially above minimum subsistence, which meant that demand was diversified and was directed predominantly to manufactured articles and services. However, this

---

[22] This situation actually differs from that of other countries where there is a high ratio of population to available land, but where, on the other hand, the level of capital formation and technical progress is low. In the latter, per capita productivity is so limited that most output is used to meet the consumption needs of the farmers themselves.

did not have a direct impact on the structure of output because about 25 percent of demand was met out of imported commodities. From 1900 to 1930, 40 percent of imports on the average were consumer goods, 30 percent were intermediate goods and fuels, and 30 percent were machinery and equipment for agriculture and transportation as well as construction materials. Thus, imports largely supplied the country's requirements for manufactured consumer goods, including durables, machinery and equipment for capital formation, and even intermediate commodities and fuels deriving from industries of complex technology and high capital intensity.[23] Domestic industry supplied only consumer goods with a lower degree of processing, or capital goods such as construction materials; production of the latter was usually located close to the market. Industries like packing houses, which processed agricultural and livestock products for export, were also important.

The volume of imports did not have a decisive effect on the significance of the manufacturing sector in the national economy because Argentina obviously had to use its foreign exchange to increase the availability of goods and services by importing them from abroad. The composition of imports and the total absence of a development policy in certain sectors of manufacturing limited industrial development to industries that were less capital intensive and used simpler technology, principally the light metallurgical plants and the food and clothing industries. Basic manufacturing such as steel, machinery, and equipment, and some intermediate commodities and fuels either did not exist or were just beginning to develop.

Modern literature on economic development has put special emphasis on the relation between income distribution and the structure of demand. Today, it is recognized that in developing countries with income concentrated in a small section of the population, there is a disproportionate demand for luxury consumption and investment, usually met out of imports, whereas the low income level of the bulk of the population restricts the latter's demand for manufactured commodities and, therefore, is an obstacle to industrial development. Inequality of incomes during all of the

---

[23] During the last five-year period, 1925–1929, imports of consumer goods were 13.3 percent of aggregate consumption; imports of intermediate products were 8 percent of total final demand; and imports of machinery and equipment were 35.3 percent of total investment in machinery and equipment.

primary-exports stage of the Argentine economy followed this pattern and necessarily restricted domestic demand for manufactures produced internally. Briefly, income inequality tended to increase the demand for luxury consumer and investment goods and to hamper the development of activities oriented toward the internal market.

Growth and Dependence of the Primary-Exports Economy

The export economy grew very rapidly. From 1850 to 1900, exports increased from 35 million to 460 million dollars of today's purchasing power, which is a compound rate of more than 5 percent per year. The economy as a whole possibly expanded at a similar rate. After 1900, according to ECLA estimates, gross product rose from 10,756 million pesos in 1900–1904 to 35,181 million pesos (at 1950 prices) in 1925–1928. The rate of growth between the two five-year periods was therefore 4.6 percent per year.

The population also soared, going from 1,737,000 inhabitants in 1869 to 11,600,000 in 1929, or at a rate of 3.2 percent per year. Thus, Argentina's per capita product must have climbed at a rate slightly above 1 percent per year between 1860 and 1929.

ECLA estimates indicate that fixed capital rose from 44,606 million pesos in 1900–1904 to 140,280 million pesos (at 1950 prices) in 1925–1929, which is an annual rate of growth close to 5 percent. Fixed capital per person employed increased from 22,348 to 32,715 pesos (at 1950 prices) during the same period, which is a rate of growth of almost 1.5 percent per year.

Development did not proceed at a steady pace throughout the period. The long-term growth of population, output, and capital varied in intensity according to the changes in the world economy and to the volume and expansion of international demand for Argentina's agricultural and livestock products. The 1890 crisis was followed by a period of swift growth. From 1900 to 1914, population—due largely to immigration—increased at a rate of 4.2 percent per year, gross product at 5.5 percent, and per capita product at 1.3 percent. The amount of fixed capital assets in Argentina more than doubled, implying an annual growth rate of 6 percent. Although interrupted by World War I, the elements of growth maintained their high rate of increase until the last decade of the primary-exports stage. At that time, immigration and its relative importance in over-all population declined, and capital accumulation slackened mainly as a result of reduced foreign investment. Rates of population growth and capital formation fell to 2.7 and 4 percent respectively. Nevertheless, gross product rose at 5 percent and per capital product at 2.3 percent annually, due to the gradual maturing of the investments carried out in previous periods and to the continued stimulus of external demand.

Expansion of the economy was rapid, albeit subject to certain limitations, such as the land-tenure system inherited from the transition stage. However, output and income were directly dependent on a constant increase in the area under cultivation, in exports and in capital inflow.

Clearly, the foundations of economic growth were shaky and vulnerable. Should the external stimulus disappear and/or should the production frontier of the Pampa region be closed with all available land exploited, a crisis was inevitable. When this occurred after 1930, Argentina's economic development entered a new stage. From then on, increase in output and real income was not to be related to the continued growth of agricultural and livestock production and the investment of new capital. Rather, it was to depend on the expansion of internal demand based in turn on the diversification of the structure of output and on increases in the productivity of each sector of the economy due to capital accumulation and the assimilation of technical progress. Domestic savings and investment and an expanded national market were to become the mainstays of Argentina's growth. An economy dependent on external demand was to turn into an economy based on an active development and investment policy in new sectors which produced for the domestic market and helped integrate the country's structure of output. Furthermore, rural output, having lost its dynamic role, was to be raised through higher yields per hectare, which required a reconsideration of the land-tenure system.

At the same time, the change in the structure of output was to modify the composition of Argentina's foreign trade. A mounting proportion of exports was to be industrial commodities, which after 1930 were to become the most dynamic items. The transformation of the structure of output thus was to be essential to growth as well as to expanding trade with world markets. Part IV of this book will deal with the problems that Argentina faced during this stage. The present analysis will conclude with a discussion of how the dynamics of the primary-exports economy led to the ultimate collapse of Argentina's interregional equilibrium and to a subordination of the interior to the Litoral or, more precisely, to the agricultural and livestock economy of the Pampa region.

Population Growth

In the interior provinces, population increased from 889,000 to 2,470,000, or at an annual rate of 2.3 percent, between the census years of 1869 and 1914. On the other hand, population in the Litoral rose from 847,000 to 5,416,000, that is, at a rate of 4.3 percent per year. For the country as a whole, the rate of growth was 3.4 percent during that period. The main reason for the different rates of population growth was that in the middle of the nineteenth century, 90 percent of the immigrants to Argentina remained in the Litoral region.

The interior, which had contained the leading centers of settlement and of economic activity in the regional subsistence economies stage and even into the transition stage, began to lose relative importance. At the end of the eighteenth century, 70 percent of Argentina's population lived in the interior; but by 1869 this had dropped to 50 percent, and by 1914 it was barely 30 percent, while the share of the Litoral increased correspondingly.

The decline of the interior can be traced mainly to the reduced importance of the Northwest in the total population of Argentina. This region accounted for 43 percent in 1800, but for only 26 percent by 1869 and 12.6 per cent by 1914. Meanwhile, regions that had been almost uninhabited like the Northeast and Patagonia, began gradually to absorb population, so that by 1914 they had 2.7 percent of the total.

As Argentina's population increased and concentrated in the Litoral, there was also a rapid growth in urban population. According to the 1869, 1895, and 1914 censuses, urban population in cities of over 2,000 inhabitants rose from 28 percent to 37 percent to 53 percent of the aggregate for the country. At the same time, rural population decreased from 72 percent in 1869 to 47 percent in 1914. The number of people actually living in urban centers went up from 500,000 in 1869 to 4,200,000 in 1914, or by almost eight times in 44 years, which is an annual compound rate of growth of about 5 percent. Because this was a period when total population soared, it was possible for rural population to increase also, in spite of its relative decline. At a growth rate of 2.5 percent per year, rural population almost tripled from 1869, when it was 1,250,000, to 1914, when it reached 3,700,000.

Urbanization was concentrated in the Litoral cities and particularly in Buenos Aires, where there was a heavy demand for manpower in manufacturing and services and an availability of basic social services such as housing, education, and public health. In turn, manufacturing and services were chiefly located in the Litoral because of the advantages of an immediate consumer market; of utilities such as electric power, drainage, and transportation; of proximity to the importing centers of the raw materials and intermediate products used in industries; and of an abundance of skilled labor. Briefly, the series of economic and social factors that determined the initial concentration of services and industry had a cumulative effect, which was to be repeated after 1930 in these same Litoral cities.

The federal capital should have its population increase discussed separately. It went up from 187,000 inhabitants in 1869 to 663,000 in 1895 and 1,576,000 in 1914; and it held 13 percent of Argentina's population in 1869 and 30 percent in 1930. Other Litoral cities such as Rosario, Santa Fe, and Bahía Blanca also showed rapid increases in population, although less so than the capital.

Obviously, urbanization was affected by the same factors that made the Pampa region's agricultural and livestock sector progressively more important within the national economy: high per capital yields and land concentration. The first of these factors determined a high level of income per inhabitant for the economy as a whole, which was reflected in increased consumption of services and industrial commodities. Given the urban nature of these occupations, the process of urbanization intensified. Land concentration prevented the emergence of an authentic class of rural proprietors living on their own land. Extensive agriculture employing little labor was the rule, and this was one of the main reasons most immigrants remained in the cities and joined the urban labor force.

Breakdown of the Old Equilibrium

A series of forces combined to destroy the protectionist barriers that during the transition period had helped to maintain the relative positions of the various interior regions. The fate of the interior was sealed by the vigorous expansion of exportable agricultural and livestock output and its concentration in the Pampa region; by the federal government's free-trade policy; by the spectacular development of the railroad; and by the formation of a national market. The interior became a peripheral zone depending on its dynamic center, the Litoral. Thus culminated the process that had begun in the transition period, when for the first time in Argentina's economic history, external demand began to exert a steady and growing influence on over-all growth.

But the second half of the nineteenth century, which ushered in the integration of world markets together with a dramatic improvement in overseas shipping and railroad transportation, was when Argentina felt the massive impact of external factors on its general growth. While the traditional interior regions remained outside the current of change, the Pampa region was populated, its lands put into production, and its exportable surpluses became greater and more diversified.

It is therefore not surprising that after 1860 the Litoral became the dynamic center of the Argentine economy. As explained earlier, under the continuous stimulus of export expansion, there was sharp increase in employment and income in the Pampa region. Although no data on regional distribution of income are available, it is certain that the Pampa, in the light of the higher productivity of its rural and urban areas, had a concentration of economic activity and income that surpassed its population density.

The free-trade policy followed by the government from the time the country was united had a decisive influence on the development possibilities of the interior. Because the latter was not directly linked to a growing world market, it could only benefit indirectly from the agricultural and livestock expansion of the Pampa region through supplying the rising demand of the Litoral. However, this possibility was frustrated when the Litoral market was opened up to foreign imports. Although there was no question of prohibiting imports, a selective policy could have been adopted in order to protect the development of certain domestic activities that would have helped to integrate and gradually diversify the national economy. A large part of the natural resources necessary for the development of import-replacement industries were located in the interior of the country, so that the protectionist policy would have encouraged the opening up and consolidation of new activities there. Under this initial impulse, the services and manufactures required to supply local markets would also have been established. However, the liberal policy on imports excluded the interior from the dynamic repercussions of the expansion of agricultural and livestock exports from the Pampa region.

Although the formation of a national market created development possibilities in certain provinces in lines of production oriented toward that market, it meant the final subordination of the interior. The railroad, which speeded up communication and ended the isolation of many regions of Argentina, were the crucial factor. From 1857 to 1914, the railroad grid lengthened from 10 kilometers to 33,500 kilometers. Except for Patagonia, all the interior provinces were connected by railroad with Buenos Aires and the Litoral ports. For the first time in Argentina's history, geographical distance ceased to protect the various economic regions. Imports easily reached the interior, and their competition dealt a death blow to the shaky local industries. For example, the production of cloth succumbed completely to imported textiles. Railroads not only enabled imported manufactures to penetrate the regional markets of the interior, but they also doomed the traditional, albeit modest, trade between the regions. With all the railroads leading from the peripheral zone to the Litoral center, the regions remained uncommunicated, and their reciprocal trade declined even further.

By bringing every region of Argentina into the national market, the railroad shattered the system of closed and self-sufficient economies. But at the same time, it led to the possibility of developing in some of these regions new activities producing for domestic demand, which was actually national demand. These possibilities did not, however, offset the interior's loss in relative importance. Among the new activities were sugar cane plantations in Tucumán and Jujuy, vineyards in Cuyo, orchards in the Upper Valley of the Río Negro, cotton in Chaco and Formosa, and maté in Misiones.

As national demand mounted and became more diversified and access to the natural resources of the peripheral regions was growing, the latter were able to expand those activities in which their natural resources gave them a relative advantage. Some of the expanding regional activities, such as sugar production in Tucumán and wine production in Mendoza, had their origins in the colonial economy and were partly oriented toward the limited interregional trade of the time. But from the end of the nineteenth century, these activities changed substantially and became oriented toward the national market. Thus, a clearly capitalistic relationship was established between entrepreneurs and workers, although in the plantations of sugarcane in Tucumán and of yerba maté in the Northeast, certain forms of personal servitude persisted or were still maintained. The experience of the *mensu en Misiones* and the conditions of the sugar cane workers were fairly recent episodes in Argentina's history.

In order to appreciate the rapid growth of activities oriented toward the national market, the following illustrations are useful: sugar production increased from 1,400 tons in 1872 to 336,000 tons in 1914; wine output rose from 57 million liters in 1895 to 500 million in 1914; after World War I, production of cotton in Chaco and Formosa also increased sharply, and a similar expansion of fruit crops took place in the irrigated lands of Mendoza and the Upper Valley of the Río Negro.

Regional economies became specialized and their efficiency improved as they integrated into the national market and established enterprises of high productivity. But provinces like La Rioja, Salta, and Santiago del Estero, which did not follow this pattern of development, declined still more swiftly in relation to the rest of the national economy, and their inhabitants reverted to subsistence activities, thus earning the lowest real incomes in the country.

In any case, the stage of the primary-exports economy left an indelible impression on the geographical distribution of population and production in Argentina. The interior became a clearly peripheral area dependent on the dynamic center of the Litoral, thus breaking up the old economic federalism of the self-sufficient regional economies.

Subordination of the Interior

As previously stated, the federalism espoused by the province of Buenos Aires during the transition stage was based on its possession of the port and the lands that were most fertile and closest to embarkation points. However, under the influence of the Pampa region, the interests of the province of Buenos Aires came to encompass those of the other Litoral provinces and consolidated its key position in the country as a whole. When this happened, the predominance of the Litoral interests ceased to be a struggle vis-à-vis the interior provinces and became a national affair.

National organization was a necessary step in the political and institutional articulation of Argentina; without it, Argentina could not have developed in any way nor could it have become a nation in the broadest sense. However, in view of the forces at work in Argentina's development in the nineteenth century, national organization was bound to strengthen the influence of the export sectors of the Litoral—and thereby the foreign interests in that area—in the economic structure of the whole country.

As the interior economies became relatively weaker, their treasuries became more dependent on subsidies from the federal government and on participation in national tax revenues. Only the Litoral provinces, being the center of economic activity, of agricultural and livestock output, and of urban expansion, were able to maintain a comparatively sound financial position by supplying their own fiscal requirements out of tax collections and the issue of bonds in international capital markets. After customs receipts were nationalized in 1862 and the city of Buenos Aires became a federal district in 1880, the province of Buenos Aires remained prosperous because it could collect other taxes of a local kind, particularly land and real estate taxes, and place its bond issues on both the national and foreign capital markets.

Thus, the stage of the primary-exports economy witnessed the end of the long road of the subordination of the interior, which began with the creation of the Viceroyalty of the Río de la Plata in 1776 and continued with the enactment of the Free Trade Regulation of 1778 and the Litoral's steady development of stock raising for export. The regional economies, with their primitive levels of productivity and development, could no longer remain isolated from the technological revolution of the time, for their narrow local markets and insignificant interregional trade would have smothered any possibility of growth.

The old economic federalism of the subsistence and transition stages was to be replaced by the formation of a national market and the gradual shaping of a policy for the integrated development of the Argentine economy, meaning by this not only geographical integration but diversification of the structure of output, both inseparable aspects of the same process. However, more than thirty years later, Argentina still finds itself in the stage of a nonintegrated industrial economy.

PART IV

THE NONINTEGRATED INDUSTRIAL ECONOMY (1930–   )

13. CHANGES IN THE WORLD ECONOMY SINCE 1930

During the primary-exports stage, Argentina's development was largely induced by the growth in world demand for agricultural and livestock products and was made possible by expanding the frontier of the Pampa region. By 1930, both dynamic elements had disappeared, and Argentina entered a new stage of development.

In that year, no unexploited land remained in the Pampa region, and output could no longer be increased by the traditional expedient of simply incorporating additional acreage. Furthermore, the great depression had intensified certain trends in the world economy which adversely affected trade in agricultural and livestock products. Thus, although Argentina had by no means exhausted its possibilities of economic and social development, it would have to realize them along lines different from the ones it had followed in the primary-exports stage.

The new stage of development that began in 1930 is here defined as the nonintegrated industrial economy. It is industrial because throughout this period Argentina's economic structure displays the characteristics of a diversified and complex economy in which manufacturing is the key sector in employment and a leading sector in growth. It is a nonintegrated industrial economy because manufacturing output consists mainly of final consumer goods and because machinery, equipment, intermediate goods, and fuel have to be imported in order to fully utilize installed capacity and assure a steady growth of the system. This pattern of expansion took shape as Argentina's exports and, consequently, its capacity to import goods and services declined.

An analysis of economic development in this new stage, therefore, is basically a study of the growth limitations imposed on a nonintegrated industrial economy by a bottleneck in imports. It is useful to summarize briefly the changes in the world economy after 1930 that affected Argentina's international position and the course of its development.

Collapse of the Multilateral Trade and Payments System

During the second half of the nineteenth century, technological progress had speeded up the formation and integration of the world market through the expansion of international trade, the international flow of capital, and migration. The multilateral trade and payments system based on the gold standard facilitated an increasing volume of transactions in capital and commodities throughout the world. The 1929 crisis brought this process to an end and initiated a prolonged decline in international economic relations. Only later was technological progress to open new channels of integration at an international level.

The 1929 depression started out in the same way earlier crises had begun. The contraction in output, income, and employment in the industrialized countries led to a reduction in their imports and, consequently, in the volume of international trade. The depression was spread by the same mechanisms that had operated during previous cyclical disturbances; but never before had the rules of the game been generally abandoned, and recovery had always taken place without damage to the normal channels of international trade and finance. However, the 1929 crisis lasted so long and was so profound that the industrialized countries adopted a whole series of protectionist measures: the formation of trade blocs; the substitution of bilateral for multilateral trade arrangements; currency devaluation and suspension of the gold standard; exchange control; import quotas; and a substantial upward revision of tariffs. The purpose of all these measures was to insulate the money supply and the level of domestic activity from balance-of-payments fluctuations, thus enabling compensatory monetary and fiscal policies to counteract the impact of the crisis. At the same time, the restrictions imposed on imports in order to stimulate domestic production diminished world trade even further and intensified the effects of the depression.

From 1929 to 1933, world exports declined 25 percent in volume and more than 30 percent in price, which, taken together, meant that they fell about 50 percent in value. The volume of world exports did not recover its predepression level in the 1930's. There was a slight improvement from the depths of the depression, which were reached in 1932 and 1933; but in 1938, just before World War II, the volume of world exports was still 11 percent below that of

1929. In spite of Great Britain's departure from the gold standard in September, 1931, the consequent depreciation of the pound sterling, and the devaluation of the dollar by more than 40 percent of the old gold parity in January, 1934, prices did not regain their pre-depression levels; in 1938, they were still 20 percent below 1929 prices. Thus, the 3 percent annual growth rate in world exports that had continued from 1870 to 1929 came to a halt in the 1930's.

The international flow of capital was also adversely affected. In addition to reducing international trade, the crisis restricted savings in the capital-exporting countries, made it difficult for the debtor countries to meet service payments on their foreign-capital liabilities, and created a climate of general insecurity. Not only were traditional capital movements interrupted, but the capital-exporting countries even began to repatriate some of their investments. France, Great Britain, and the United States—countries that had exported 3.3 billion dollars in short- and long-term capital between 1928 and 1930—experienced an inflow of 1,589 million dollars of capital in 1931 and 1932. The effects of the crisis were permanent: "it marked the end of the era of plentiful and, on the whole, indiscriminate international lending and equity investment which, only temporarily interrupted by World War I, had lasted for many decades." [1]

After 1929, the behavior of international trade and capital flows particularly affected countries specializing in the production and export of primary products. In Latin America, the purchasing power of exports decreased almost 50 percent between 1928–1929 and 1932 owing to the combined effect of the fall in the volume of exports and the deterioration in the terms of trade.

At the same time, the flow of international capital to the debtor countries specializing in primary production was reversed. As the payments capacity of the primary-exporting countries was weakened by the decline in the purchasing power of exports and the change in the direction of capital movements, the burden of service payments increased appreciably. Argentina is a case in point. During the 1925–1929 period preceding the depression, the servicing of foreign capital represented 21.9 percent of the country's external payments capacity; by 1930–1934, it had risen to an average of 37.4 percent. With certain variations, this was the experience of most debtor countries specializing in the export of primary products.

---

[1] United Nations, *International Capital Movements During the Inter-War Period* (Lake Success, New York, October, 1949), p. 68.

As a consequence, all these countries incurred substantial balance-of-payments deficits, which were at first met out of gold and foreign-exchange reserves. "The use of gold for the balancing of accounts was necessarily an expedient of limited duration." Once they had exhausted their gold, "countries under pressure followed a policy of 'sauve qui peut,' employing exchange controls, quantitative restrictions and other devices which lent themselves to discriminative regulations of external transactions, and the international economy disintegrated rapidly." [2]

Countries specializing in the production and export of primary products now faced conditions radically different from those which had previously determined their participation in the world economy. In the past, their capacity to make external payments had derived from their export surpluses as well as from new capital inflows and reinvestment of profits. Furthermore, under the gold standard and the free transferability of currencies, a debtor country could make payment to any creditor country whether or not it had a favorable balance of trade with that particular country.

The new situation was the direct result of the decline in the purchasing power of exports and of the impossibility of reducing imports at the same rate; of the reversal in the flow of capital; and of the inconvertibility of currencies. The primary-exporting countries, in order to protect their own levels of employment and balance their transactions with the rest of the world, had to take measures which, added to the restrictive policies already adopted by the industrialized countries, meant the end in the 1930's of the pattern of relationships which had constituted the framework of their integration into the world economy during the second half of the nineteenth century.

Trends in the Exports of Primary Products

The world depression accentuated the effect of certain trends which had already appeared at the beginning of the century[3] and which decreased the share of primary products in world production and trade. Such trends are of importance in any analysis of the Argentine experience after 1930 and therefore should be described briefly.[4]

---

[2] *Ibid.*, pp. 37–38.
[3] United Nations, *World Economic Survey, 1955* (New York, 1956).
[4] Data in this section have been taken from: United Nations, *World Economic*

Consumption of foodstuffs tends to grow at a lower rate than increases in income. As living standards rise, the proportion of expenditures on foodstuffs declines within aggregate consumption because a larger part of family income is devoted to purchasing industrial products and services and to savings. Furthermore, the pattern of food consumption shifts from commodities like cereals to meat, fruit, sugar, beverages, and dairy products.

More important forces operate in the case of raw materials. One of them is the increasing use of synthetics to replace natural raw materials. In 1899, for example, 3.2 kilos of coal were used in the United States to produce 1 kilowatt hour of electric energy, whereas by 1950 only 0.5 kilos of coal were required. Furthermore, as the industrial structure alters with changes in the composition of demand and advances in technology, both the aggregate use of raw materials and the relative share of the different raw materials are affected.

The composition of demand is subject to many influences; among them are changes in the pattern of consumption and increases in public expenditures. As regards the former, not all commodities participate equally in the increased share of industrial commodities in aggregate consumption. The demand for nondurable goods such as textiles rises slowly, and the share of these products in aggregate demand for manufactured consumer goods declines. The demand for durables such as automobiles, refrigerators, and television sets increases rapidly, and so does the share of these products in total demand. As regards expansion of public expenditures, the growing participation of government in over-all economic activity—especially through increased military outlays in the industrialized countries—has generated a sharp increase in production by heavy industry. This combination of factors has stimulated expansion of the metallurgical and chemical industries on the one hand, and on the other, has restricted the development of industries producing nondurable consumer goods. Within the industrial structure, the former type of industry is gaining importance at the expense of the latter, which is reflected in the pattern of demand for industrial raw materials. For instance, there has been an intense growth in the use of nonferrous metals as opposed to a stagnation in the demand for natural fibers.

Survey, 1958 (New York, 1959) and ECLA, *Theoretical and Practical Problems of Economic Growth* (Mexico, 1952).

Technological progress is another factor of change in the industrial structure and, consequently, in the demand for industrial raw materials. Advances in internal combustion engineering have led to the widespread use of gasoline and diesel motors in both industry and transportation; other examples are the development and multiplication of synthetic materials, improvements in mining and metallurgical techniques, and new processes for the elaboration and conservation of food and for the production of synthetic rubber. Finally, the composition of the demand for certain industrial raw materials also responds to the relative prices of competitive products, which explains why the use of aluminum has expanded more rapidly than copper and steel.

In the final analysis, the demand for traditional foodstuffs and raw materials rises more slowly than aggregate output and living standards. In the United States, from 1927–1929 to 1955–1957, gross product per inhabitant at constant prices increased 60 percent, whereas per capital consumption of textile fibers declined 25 percent, food and tobacco 3 percent, and natural rubber 1 percent. On the other hand, over the same period, the demand for beverages went up only 22 percent. Again in the United States, from 1927 to 1952, the consumption of raw materials grew only half as fast as the increase in industrial production. And the consumption of foodstuffs rose even less.

Trends in the industrialized countries of Western Europe are broadly the same as those in the United States, although they differ in respect to specific commodities. The trends in the consumption of foodstuffs and raw materials, inherent in the very process of development, have influenced the level of imports of these commodities into the industrialized countries. Other factors must also be taken into account which restrict even more the growth of imports of primary products. As is clearly shown by the data available for the past thirty years, the industrialized countries have followed a policy of self-sufficiency in certain primary products. In the United States, imports of 23 primary products[5] mounted 17 percent from 1927–1929 to 1955–1957; whereas consumption of these products went up 35 percent. In Western Europe, imports of these products

---

[5] Including nonferrous metals (aluminum, copper, lead, tin, and zinc), natural rubber, textile fibers (cotton, wool, silk, jute), beverages (coffee and cacao), foodstuffs (wheat, rice, corn, rye, meat, sugar, copra, coconut oil, and bananas) and tobacco.

increased only 9 percent over the same period, although consumption rose 35 percent. The Western European countries are particularly inclined to be self-sufficient in agricultural and livestock products.

It should be noted that the data on world trade in primary products since the great depression offer eloquent evidence of the effect of these factors: exports of primary products (excluding petroleum) increased 14 percent from 1928 to 1955–1957, but at the same time, exports of manufactured goods climbed 103 percent and aggregate world output expanded 104 percent.

The International Flow of Capital

After 1930, the flow of foreign capital to primary-producing and -exporting countries was subject to two important influences: first, the sharp decline in exports from these countries, which reduced their capacity to make external payments; and second, general currency inconvertibility and restrictions on the free transfer of payments balances. These problems compelled a number of countries to default and, as a consequence, destroyed the confidence of international financial circles.

During the 1930's, there was a reversal of the international flow of capital. Traditional capital-exporting countries like Great Britain, France, and the United States began to repatriate their investments abroad, and continued to do so through the second half of the decade because of the growing insecurity of the political situation in Europe. On the other hand, the capital-importing countries began to export capital partly through the liquidation of existing foreign investment and partly because of the halting of new investment.

In addition to these general trends in capital movements to the primary-producing and -exporting countries, there was also a radical change in the type of foreign investment. For seventy or eighty years before the depression, about 50 percent of long-term foreign investment in the primary-producing countries had gone into public issues and into direct investment in social overhead capital such as railroads. During the crisis, these types of investment almost disappeared because of the growing financial difficulties of the debtor governments and, in many cases, the suspension of service on existing foreign debt, which made it impossible to sell new issues. On the other hand, the decline in traditional exports ended opportunities for investment in the infrastructure intended to provide basic services to the export sector or services necessary to expanding internal activities.[6]

Thus, after 1930, private foreign investment began to take new directions. The capital-exporting countries invested increasingly in the countries within their sphere of influence, where there was more security and no problem of foreign-currency transfer. For example, the United Kingdom oriented its investments toward the Commonwealth countries and the United States toward Canada. Moreover, foreign direct investment became concentrated in a few primary products such as petroleum and nonferrous metals, for which there was still a sizable demand in spite of the depression. These products were exported directly to the investing countries, so that the risks of inconvertibility and transferability of profits were minimized. Some primary-exporting countries (Argentina, Brazil, and Mexico in Latin America) with fairly large domestic markets began to attract direct foreign investment into manufacturing activities. Because they imposed import restrictions on finished goods, such investments could not only take advantage of the unsatisfied domestic demand but at the same time could create a need for semi-finished products from the industrialized countries. Typical of this kind of investment was the setting up of automobile assembly plants. It is easier to restrict the importation of automobiles than of parts for use in factories employing local labor and services.

After World War II, further changes took place in the international movements of capital. For the first time since the nineteenth century, public funds predominated in capital movements. During the 1920's, out of 57 billion dollars (at present-day purchasing power) of long-term international capital flow, 51 billion were private capital and the rest were mainly reparation payments made by Germany as a result of World War I. That is, in the 1920's, private investment came to 90 percent of all long-term capital exports, a ratio which continued through the 1930's. In contrast, during the 1946–1955 period, the international flow of capital was approximately 110 billion dollars (at present-day purchasing power) of which 85 billion were public loans and grants[7] and only 25 billion

---

[6] The official control of public utility rates in the last few decades has restricted the yield of capital invested in those services and, therefore, discouraged such investment.

[7] Two thirds of the public loans and grants went to Europe as a result of the

were private investment. The share of private foreign capital, therefore, decreased from 90 percent before the depression to just over 20 percent after World War II. Since 1956, private capital has recovered a part of its relative position, but public funds still represent more than 50 percent of the long-term international movement of capital.

During the 1945–1955 period, foreign private investment was 50 percent below its predepression level. In recent years, it has begun to recuperate; but given the growth in trade, output, and income throughout the world since 1930, the relative significance of the international flow of private capital has diminished appreciably. Some of the trends already evident in the 1930's have continued. For instance, the amount of portfolio investment, including both public and private issues, remains very low. Before 1930, almost 70 percent of the exports of private capital from the United States was in the form of bonds and other issues purchased by that market. After World War II, direct investment led portfolio investment. Although the latter has gained in recent years, it has not recovered its predepression level.[8]

Direct private foreign investment has gone mostly into the more developed countries, which offer vast markets and investment opportunities. Some investment has also been attracted into the exploitation of natural resources such as petroleum and nonferrous metals. Finally, in countries in the process of industrialization, manufacturing activities have absorbed some direct private investment.[9]

---

financial and economic recovery programs sponsored by the United States. The remainder went to Africa, Asia, and Latin America, mainly out of funds supplied by the United States. During the last few years, more than 50 percent of long-term public capital movements has been toward developing countries in these areas.

[8] "United States portfolio investments have increased by more than $1 billion during the three-year period from 1956 to 1958. Their outstanding value at the end of 1958 was about $6.5 billion, which, although an impressive figure, is still $1 billion below that at the end of 1930, a year when the purchasing power of the dollar was about twice as great as it is today." United Nations, *The International Flow of Private Capital, 1956–1958* (New York, 1960), p. 51.

[9] Between 1951 and 1959, from 54 to 58 percent of net long-term private investment was made in Australia, Austria, Canada, Italy, New Zealand, and Norway, developed countries that are net importers of capital.

As regards allocation by types of activity, since World War II, private foreign investment has tended to concentrate in the rapidly expanding produc-

To conclude this brief analysis of changes in the world economy during the last few decades, it should be stressed that the slow growth in world demand for primary products, the radical alterations in the flow of international capital, and the collapse of the multilateral trade and payments system after 1930, all combined to modify the conditions that had favored Argentina's development from 1860 to 1930.

If it is recalled that toward the latter year, exports were 25 percent of gross domestic product in Argentina, that 32 percent of the country's fixed assets was foreign-financed, that domestic economic stability was subject to a delicate balance between exports, new foreign investment, and service payments on external capital, and that the rise in aggregate demand and the whole process of development depended on a steady increase in agricultural and livestock exports, it can easily be understood why the changes in the world economic situation had such a tremendous impact on the Argentine economy. These changes are relevant, not only to any analysis of Argentina's economy from 1930 to date, but also to an evaluation of the policies that have been followed in recent years in an attempt to lift Argentina out of its economic stagnation.

---

tion of petroleum and nonferrous metals. In 1957, investments in petroleum and in mining and smelting in Latin America accounted for 50 percent of existing United States investment in the region.

An analysis of Argentine development in the stage of the non-integrated industrial economy should begin by studying the changes that occurred in the dynamic behavior of the economic system. This chapter will try to define the nature of those changes and the new problems Argentina would have to overcome in order to ensure its continued development. Certain details and variants are not taken into consideration because they are not essential to an understanding of the central problem.

Changes in the Components of Aggregate Demand

It has been seen that exports were the basic growth factor in Argentina's economic development during the primary-exports stage. Exports conditioned aggregate demand and determined the level of employment of manpower and of installed productive capacity, not only in agriculture and livestock, but also in other sectors of the economy. Exports were therefore an autonomous element in that they did not change in response to other components of aggregate demand, whereas investment and consumption were affected by the level of domestic income and, in the final analysis, by exports.

The economy was able to keep up with the growth of external demand because Argentina had unexploited land available and, having made the necessary internal adjustments (immigration, railroads, and national organization), could put that land into production. In this way, the increase in external demand brought about a higher volume of agricultural and livestock exports. The latter, in turn, generated foreign exchange with which to pay for a part of the goods and services required to satisfy the higher levels of national consumption and investment. The remaining were supplied by domestic output, which was stimulated by the expanding internal market to employ more manpower, attract further investment, and fully utilize existing productive capacity. In short, the supply of goods and services (whether out of domestic output or out of imports) for national consumption and investment responded quickly to any increase in demand deriving from the higher income of the population.

When world trade in agricultural and livestock products came to a standstill in 1930, exports naturally ceased to be the dynamic component of Argentina's aggregate demand. This alone meant a radical change in the conditions of economic development that had prevailed over the previous seventy years. From 1930 on, expansion of demand would have to depend on components other than exports, and, at the same time, output responding to increased demand would be subject to a new set of forces.

Let us glance at the changes in the components (excluding exports) of aggregate demand and at their relation to the supply of goods and services or, in other words, their effect on national production. Take, first of all, the consumption of the private and public sectors. The former is a function of household income, which, in turn, derives from the level of domestic economic activity and the pattern of income distribution. Consequently, private consumption is highly dependent on the general situation and does not condition the level of aggregate demand.[1] Changes in income distribution can affect consumption insofar as the proportion of income spent on consumption varies according to the propensities to consume of the different social groups. But beyond certain limits, this no longer operates as a growth factor in aggregate demand. Consumption by the public sector, on the other hand, is to some extent independent of the level of employment and even of fiscal receipts, because the government can finance an excess of expenditure over revenues—that is, a deficit—by creating means of payment through bank loans, which obviously augments aggregate demand.[2] However, expenditure on consumption, whether by the private or the public sector, does not increase the amount of fixed capital per person employed nor does it improve the technology applied in the different activities. Therefore, consumption does not raise the pro-

---

[1] Assuming that individuals continue to allocate the same proportion of their income to savings and investment, that is, that they do not alter their propensities to consume and to save.

[2] No account is taken of deficit financing with resources transferred from the private sector through the issue of bonds because, other things being equal, this would restrict consumption or private investment and, consequently, aggregate demand, thereby counteracting the expansion effect of the fiscal deficit.

ductivity of labor or the capacity of the economy to produce more goods and services.[3]

The other component of aggregate demand is investment, which conditions both the actual level of aggregate demand and the economy's capacity to increase output. Investment can be independent of the level of income and of domestic activity because, in the case of private investment, it can be financed not only by the savings of that sector[4] but also by means of bank credit, always provided that profit expectations are sufficient to induce entrepreneurs to invest; in the case of public investment, because it can be financed not only out of public savings (the difference between current expenditures and revenues) but also through bank loans obtained by the government. On the other hand, both public and private investment, by increasing the stock of capital in the economy as a whole as well as in each of its sectors, helps raise the productivity of labor and expand production of goods and services. Of course, investment may not raise productive capacity if it is concentrated in public buildings and similar enterprises that do not increase labor productivity. But apart from such special cases, investment is the only component of aggregate demand that can be independent of the level of income of an economy and bring about an expansion of aggregate demand and of output.

To summarize and conclude this brief analysis, the following should be stressed: after 1930, exports ceased to be the dynamic element in Argentine development, and public and private investment became the autonomous factor that was to raise the level of aggregate demand and at the same time increase the economy's capacity to produce more goods and services for consumption and

---

[3] This statement needs to be elaborated. As far as consumption in the public sector is concerned, it is conceivable that an increase in expenditure on education and health may raise the productivity of labor through the attainment of higher cultural levels and better sanitary conditions. This kind of investment can be broadly considered an income-yielding investment as distinct from the public sector's typical expenditures on administration, defense, public security, and so on. In respect to private consumption, if individuals begin to spend a higher proportion of their income on education, it can be argued that the productivity of labor will rise. But such autonomous changes in the pattern of private consumption do not normally take place and, therefore, cannot be taken into account as significant factors in an increase in the productivity of the economy.

[4] In the absence of any change in the propensity to save, private savings are determined by the level of income of the private sector.

for capital formation. As long as Argentina was mainly a primary-producing and -exporting country, its steady growth was ensured by exports. After 1930, it could only maintain growth through increased investment channeled into certain activities.

Alternative Paths of Industrialization

In an economy where the level of employment, activity, and income depends on exports, a decline in the latter in the absence of any compensatory measures leads to unemployment of a part of the labor force and of a part of the available productive capacity, as well as to a fall in the level of income and in living standards. If there is a prolonged slump in exports, the economy is bound to grow more slowly and, in extreme cases, may stagnate or even retrogress to lower levels of employment, income, and forms of organization.

In this situation, the government may adopt compensatory measures such as financing the fiscal deficit and part of private investment through increases in the money supply, in order to uphold the level of aggregate demand by expanding consumption in the public sector and investment in both the public and private sectors. It would thus be possible to maintain employment and income in spite of a contraction in exports.

But given these circumstances, there will necessarily be a maladjustment between the demand for imports and the capacity to import, the latter having fallen because of the decline in the supply of foreign exchange generated by exports.[5] Such a maladjustment can only be corrected by decreasing imports to the level permitted by the capacity to import. There are many ways to accomplish this. Owing to the imbalance between supply and demand for foreign exchange, the currency may depreciate, thereby raising the price of imports in local currency, that is, making imports more expensive to the local consumer. Alternatively, imports may be deliberately restricted through exchange control and through the

[5] The following example will serve to elucidate this problem. Let us assume that in Year I income is 100, of which 20 units are spent on imports and 20 units are provided by exports. Thus, exports supply enough foreign exchange to pay for imports. If in Year II exports decline to 10 units but income is maintained at 100 through a compensatory policy, the demand for imports will continue to be 20 even though the capacity to import has fallen to 10.

allocation of foreign exchange solely to persons authorized to carry out imports; import duties may be raised; import quotas may be established; or many kinds of imports may be prohibited altogether; or a combination of all these measures may be used. A purposeful reduction in imports may cause less depreciation of the currency than if the rate of exchange were allowed to fluctuate freely according to the supply and demand of foreign exchange. In extreme cases, fixed rates of exchange may be adopted. Whatever the method used to prevent a decline in the value of the national currency to the point where supply and demand of foreign currency would be equated, a fixed rate of exchange would imply an overvaluation of the national currency.

In any event, as imports decline and the level of domestic income is maintained, the prices of imports in the domestic market will rise. At the same time, wages and certain prices necessary to produce goods internally are likely to lag behind the prices of imports, that is, the depreciation of the national currency. Therefore, the profit margin becomes larger for domestic enterprises able to produce commodities previously imported, which attracts investment, if such stimulus continues, into the establishment and expansion of that kind of enterprise. In this way, a part of national consumption and investment that was formerly met out of imports is now supplied out of domestic output. In other words, imports have been replaced.

But import replacement does not refer only to domestic production of commodities previously imported. Income expansion and technological progress lead to further increases in the demand for goods and services and to further changes in the pattern of demand. Import replacement, therefore, is dynamic because it is not limited to the internal production of a given number of commodities formerly imported but keeps pace with a progressively broader and more diversified demand that is part of the very process of development.

Let us consider this case a little more closely. Assuming that the economy is capable of growing in spite of the contraction of exports, a gradual and permanent change will occur in the composition of demand for consumer and investment goods. On the one hand, as their incomes rise, consumers will demand a larger proportion of industrial commodities (for example, refrigerators and television sets) and a smaller proportion of foodstuffs. On the other hand, as technology improves, machinery, equipment, and the process of production itself becomes increasingly complex. The demand for commodities produced by industries of greater technical complexity and cost, such as the electrometallurgical and the petrochemical industries, expands at a very rapid rate, whereas the demand for food grows slowly. Furthermore, the demand for services such as advertising, entertainment, and education also rises steeply under the impulse of higher living standards and higher technical and cultural levels.

Thus, import replacement in the broadest sense of domestic output, not only of goods and services previously imported but of other services and commodities required by the growth of the economy, begins to exercise a strong influence on the volume and the allocation of investment. Although in a system of private enterprise, it is mainly private investment that is affected, public investment also reacts. As a country diversifies its domestic structure to carry out import replacement, new needs arise for certain basic services that can be provided only by the nation's infrastructure. Diversified development requires more energy, communications, transportation, and, to the extent that it stimulates urbanization, more housing, waterworks, urban transport, and so on. Likewise, a number of basic services like education and public health must be expanded. In fact, if the social overhead capital and basic services provided by the government do not increase swiftly enough to meet the needs of the over-all development of the economy, serious bottlenecks may be created which will stand in the way of development.

The weakening of exports on the one hand and the replacement of imports on the other bring about profound changes in the structure of output. In the economy as a whole, there is certain to be a shift from export activities to activities producing for the domestic market. Among the latter, domestic industry undergoes the most radical transformation, because it must grow very quickly and play a leading role in the process of development. Industry must adjust the supply of manufactured goods to imports and satisfy the demand for new ones generated in the process of development. Industry must, in the final analysis, supply an increasing amount of machinery, equipment, and other investment goods for capital formation and expansion of the economy's productive capacity. Therefore, it is legitimate to identify the process of national development with industrialization.

To conclude this analysis, we should also consider the paths industrialization may follow in a country that can no longer rely exclusively on the production and export of primary products and that must diversify its economic structure and produce principally for the domestic market. The path chosen can determine whether a country will grow steadily and become self-sustaining or will stagnate. Argentina's experience after 1930 and its stagnation after 1948 cannot be properly understood without a careful study of the course of its industrialization.

Industry is a complex sector (one of "indirect methods of production") characterized by a heavy interdependence of enterprises and types of activities. From the extraction of a raw material like iron ore until its conversion into a final consumer good like a refrigerator or a tractor, there are many intermediate stages. Such stages increase in number and complexity, the more advanced the country and the more developed its technology.

Consequently, several courses are open to the country, whatever the original cause of its industrialization. It can develop only the final stage of industry (automobile assembly), or it can attempt parallel development of the prior stages, that is, the basic industries, which include the production of steel and metals, machinery and equipment, and heavy chemicals and fuels.

The type of industrialization chosen[6] determines the degree of capital formation and of technological assimilation that the country must undertake. In general, basic industries are technically more complex, larger, and more capital intensive per person employed than are industries producing final goods. The next section will deal with these characteristics and how they influence the possibilities of developing basic industry.

If the first type of industrialization is chosen, manufacturing will require importation of the intermediate goods—raw materials and fuels—that are not produced internally. For example, the manufacture of a refrigerator uses steel plate not produced in the country. At the same time, in order to convert savings into investment, it is necessary to import machinery and equipment. Full employment

---

[6] Perhaps "chosen" is overly optimistic in view of the forces that drive industrialization toward the manufacture of final goods.

of the capacity of the industry producing final goods—"light industry"—and the amount of investment in the different sectors of activity depend on the capacity to import. If the latter is not sufficient to bring into the country all the commodities needed to fully utilize the installed capacity of light industry and to purchase the machinery and equipment needed for domestic investment, part of the industry's capacity will be wasted, and capital formation will be impeded. Therefore, the development not only of industry but of the whole economy (insofar as it depends on the expansion of capital assets and the assimilation of technology) is conditioned by the capacity to import or, more precisely, in the absence of adequate capital inflow, by the level of exports. In an economy oriented toward the development of light industry, that is, a nonintegrated industrial economy, if exports stagnate or contract, serious internal pressures are bound to build up, and the available factors of production will not be properly used.

Argentina offers conclusive proof of this experience. Furthermore, two important features of a nonintegrated industrial economy must be pointed out. In the first place, when it is impossible to import the machinery and equipment necessary to capital accumulation, the latter tends to be carried out in projects of low import content. Private investment is channeled into projects having a higher proportion of locally produced machinery and equipment than of imported capital goods. Investment thus yields less income,[7] that is, it generates a smaller increase in the productivity of labor and of the economy than it would if equipment and machinery could be imported. The limited growth possibilities of the economy mean that in certain sectors, although employment rises, productivity

---

[7] In countries where industries producing machinery and equipment have not sufficiently developed, investment projects require a fairly large proportion of imported capital goods. In Argentina, during the 1925–1929 period, imported machinery and equipment accounted for 35 percent of investment in such capital formation. Because the importation of capital goods has been one of the traditional ways of incorporating technical progress and raising labor productivity, a decrease in the import component of investment implies a fall in the productivity of the economy. On the other hand, investment in basic industries has a high import component of expensive and complex machinery and equipment, so that a decline in the capacity to import has a particularly adverse effect on investment in this type of industry where development is more dynamic. In short, in a nonintegrated industrial economy, a lowering of the import component of investment due to a reduction in the capacity to import limits the increase in output brought about by capital formation.

per employed person decreases. Furthermore, other sources of employment are created, generally in the public sector and often non-essential.[8] This, in turn, attracts investment into projects like public buildings to house the expanded administration, which yield little or no income. By constricting the growth possibilities of a non-integrated industrial economy, a standstill or a decline in the capacity to import leads to an inefficient utilization of available manpower and capital, thereby retarding development or, in extreme cases like Argentina's, resulting in long periods of stagnation.

In the second place, insufficient import capacity, by creating obstacles to capital formation and to the development of basic industry, prevents the economy from assimilating or generating technical and scientific advances. In this way, a nonintegrated industrial economy is unable to incorporate modern society's autonomous, dynamic, elements of development: increased capital per person employed, and technical and scientific progress.

When industrialization is oriented toward not only industries producing final goods but also basic industries, the result is an integrated industrial structure. Given these conditions, although a contraction in the capacity to import may create some difficulties, it will not paralyze development, because the economy will be able to produce the capital goods essential to expansion of the country's productivity and will also be able to assimilate and generate technical and scientific advances. At the same time, an integrated industrial economy is in a better position to export manufactured products, for which there has been a substantial rise in demand since 1930. Thus, even if there is a decline in primary exports, an integrated industrial economy is capable of autonomous growth as well as active participation in the international division of labor and of world trade.

Obstacles to Integrated Industrial Development

Having discussed the alternative paths industrialization may take, either toward an integrated or a nonintegrated industrial structure, it should be noted that an economy in transition from primary exports is subject to certain forces that tend to drive it in the direction

---

[8] This type of employment of manpower is usually called "disguised unemployment."

of a nonintegrated industrial structure.[9] Unless decisive measures are taken to channel investment into the development of basic industry and social overhead capital, the bottleneck in the flow of imports may lead to general stagnation.

Industries producing consumer goods—foodstuffs, beverages, tobacco, textiles, clothing, and durable commodities—and industries manufacturing simple machinery and equipment do not require high levels of technology and organization. They employ relatively small amounts of capital per worker and yield fairly rapid returns on investment inasmuch as they do not take long to be put into operation. Furthermore, large sums of money do not have to be spent on installation, because small and medium-sized plants are able to reach a reasonable level of efficiency. In countries that are in the early stages of industrialization, this combination of advantages attracts private investment.

On the other hand, basic industries manufacturing machinery and equipment, electrometallurgical and electrochemical products, as well as fuels and petrochemicals, are extremely complex in technology and organization, require a sizable investment per worker, must operate on a large scale in order to be efficient, and involve a long period of construction. All these considerations tend to discourage private investment: first, because the capital markets in countries just beginning industrialization are not sufficiently developed to meet the financial needs of large enterprises; second, because foreign technology is not easily introduced into this kind of industry owing not only to its complexity but also to the restriction placed by such enterprises in the more advanced countries on the flow of technology to countries that are normally their export market; third, because there are other investment possibilities where yields are higher and recovery of investment more rapid and certain; and fourth, because political and economic insecurity deters private investment in enterprises that cannot be readily sold out in times of emergency.

An additional problem is that infrastructure capital for transportation, communications, energy, and other basic fields must be financed almost exclusively by the public sector. Although essential

---

[9] The obstacles to integrated industrial development described in this section are further analyzed in my article, "Los problemas de la transición: el caso argentino" ["The Problems of Transition: The Case of Argentina"], *El Trimestre Económico,* January–March, 1963.

to the functioning and development of the economy, this kind of investment is of more benefit to the economy as a whole than to the enterprise undertaking it. For example, a highway may not generate enough income to recover its maintenance costs, amortize its investment, and yield a reasonable profit; but it can open up natural resources that were previously inaccessible, thereby increasing the output and income of the entire community. In any case, this tends to prevent infrastructure investment from being financed by private capital, which naturally expects to receive an adequate return (private benefit) on its investment. After 1930, it became all but impossible to obtain foreign capital to finance infrastructure development[10] and, therefore, the savings of the public sector had to assume this burden. They have usually been insufficient because, on the one hand, current expenditures use up most of public revenue[11] and, on the other hand, the domestic capital market cannot furnish funds to the public sector. In some cases, such markets are insignificant, and in others, inflation has made it unfeasible to issue low-yield bonds expressed in rapidly depreciating national currency. In addition to the inadequacy of its savings, the public sector sometimes orients its investment toward low priority projects

[10] Foreign private capital has played a changing role in the development of the infrastructure in most of the primary-producing countries that integrated into the world market in the second half of the nineteenth century. It made a fundamental contribution to those countries by financing their transportation systems, communications, public utilities, and other basic installations so that they could participate in the growth of the world economy. In Argentina, for example, in 1913, 75 percent of foreign capital was invested in infrastructure either directly or indirectly through the purchase of public issues which enabled the government to finance public investment. After the world depression, foreign private investment in social overhead capital declined precipitously, and each country had to rely on its own resources in that field. Since the end of World War II, there has been a new and significant current of foreign public capital, but it still assumes only a very small part of the role played by foreign private capital in the expansion of infrastructure before 1930.

[11] In the case of Argentina, this trend has been strongly influenced by the growth of employment in government and in nationalized utilities as a consequence of the incapacity of the economy to absorb, in activities of growing productivity, not only the increases in the labor force but also the manpower displaced from rural occupations. In this sense, the growth of employment in the public sector has been both cause—by reducing public savings available for infrastructure investment—and effect of the stagnation of the national economy.

having a negligible impact on the capacity of the economy. To summarize, the free play of economic forces tends to direct the process of industrialization toward the expansion of manufacturing branches that produce final goods, whereas basic industries and infrastructure capital tend to lag.

The Role of the Public Sector

When a compensatory policy (the financing of the fiscal deficit and of part of private investment through an increase in the money supply) is adopted in the face of a sharp and prolonged decline in exports, it induces import replacement and industrial development even if these are not its objectives.[12] On the other hand, when the aim of an economic policy is to redistribute income in favor of the lower social classes, as occurred during the Perón regime, manufacturing is further stimulated. The demand for consumer goods soars as the income of workers rises above the subsistence levels necessary for food, clothing, and housing. This is because these items represent a greater share of expenditure in the groups benefiting from income redistribution than in the higher income groups which are adversely affected—in the case of Argentina, principally the owners of rural and urban property and the large farmers.

If economic policy is confined essentially to maintenance of the

---

[12] W. M. Beveraggi-Allende, *El servicio del capital extranjero y el control de cambios* (México: Fondo de Cultura Económica, 1954), p. 214:

The landowners and exporters, who traditionally dominated Argentine politics, tended to favor imports of manufactures rather than imports of raw materials that could be used to produce those manufactures in Argentina. The result was a curious situation in which Argentine customs legislation imposed duties in order to discourage the importation of raw materials, a policy which has been properly termed "protectionism in reverse." But, even more interesting, exchange control was used to inhibit rather than to encourage the country's industrialization.

In the same work, the author quotes the following opinion of F. J. Weil: "The Argentine official attitude towards growing industry was remarkable in its outright hostility or, at least, 'malevolent neutrality.' Though industrialization was not prohibited, it was, with few exceptions, discriminated against by the customs tariff. Once the exchange control was instituted in 1932, this discrimination often extended to foreign exchange matters also." Felix J. Weil, *Argentine Riddle* (New York, 1944), p. 135.

level of domestic income, import restrictions, and income distribution, it will tend to concentrate industrialization in the manufacture of final goods, that is, in light industry. Given the nature of the obstacles to development of basic industry and infrastructure capital, indirect incentives will not suffice to channel private savings into basic industries, nor will the savings of the public sector increase and be used to finance infrastructure investments that are not clearly defined as part of the country's development objectives.

The development of basic industry and social overhead capital requires a *direct policy of encouragement* or, more precisely, an *investment policy*. Using more than indirect incentives, such a policy should try to channel an adequate proportion of private investment into basic industry. There are many ways to accomplish this, such as by bank credit or by special budget appropriations. If, despite these incentives, the private sector is not ready to undertake the expansion of some basic industries, the public sector can directly undertake their development. Infrastructure investment requires adoption of a program and priorities for basic projects and the financing of these projects out of resources available to the government. The latter can obtain such funds through savings derived from the surplus of its revenues over its current expenditures, through the issue of its bonds in domestic and foreign capital markets, or, in the absence of genuine savings possibilities, through loans from the banking system.

A direct policy of industrial development, that is, an investment policy, is imperative if the level of domestic employment and income is to be maintained and industrialization is gradually to integrate the economic structure and establish the foundations of sustained growth. The vital importance of indirect and direct development policies in the transition of an economy from primary exports to an integrated industrial structure throws new light on the matter of state intervention in development,[13] both in its general aspects and in its application to the case of Argentina.

To the extent that, in the modern state, management of economic policy falls within the competence of the public sector, the latter determines, one way or another, the orientation of industry and shapes the development process. The question is not whether an

---

[13] For an analysis of other aspects of this problem, see my *El estado y el desarrollo económico* (Buenos Aires: Raigal, 1956).

economy like Argentina's can achieve sustained growth under a system of private enterprise, but whether the free play of economic forces can be left alone to bring about the changes in the structure of output necessary to sustained growth, mainly a sufficient expansion of basic industry and social overhead capital. It is argued in this study that only through the timely adoption of direct and indirect policies of development can the economy grow with no more limitations than those existing in the highly complex and industrialized economies of the Western democracies.

The longer suitable direct and indirect policies of industrial development are delayed, the greater the intervention that will be required to adjust the functioning of the economy. Continued stagnation makes it increasingly difficult to reallocate resources and heightens political and social tensions, thereby diminishing the possibilities of applying a gradual and effective policy of development. This has been the situation in Argentina.

The problems faced by Argentina in the new stage are relevant to the role of the public sector. During the stage of regional subsistence economies, the narrow framework of development with insignificant external demand and low cultural and technical levels prevented the public sector from acting positively to promote economic development. Whatever the government did, it could not overcome the stagnation of the regional economies. During the transition stage, with a growing stimulus from external demand for hides and other livestock products, the problem was to increase the amount of land available for grazing. This was achieved by expanding the frontier of the Pampa and expelling the Indian. During the primary-exports stage, the rapid rise of foreign demand focused attention on the vast supply of fertile land in the Pampa region and led to the adoption of policies favoring immigration, railway construction, and national organization. These policies were induced by the massive impact of external factors and by their relationship to the social groups in Argentina who would most benefit from integration into world markets.

However, after 1930, the public sector ceased to play a passive role, subject to outside influences. On the contrary, it became the conditioning factor in the growth of the Argentine economy. The country's experience after that date indicates to what extent the action of the public sector coincided with national needs and contributed to establishing the bases for sustained growth.

New Conditions for Agricultural and
Livestock Development

Because of the conditions prevailing after 1930, what happened to the rural sector? During the primary-exports stage, it was the dynamic nucleus of growth because it supplied foreign demand. After 1930 the rural sector lost its predominance owing to two concurrent sets of circumstances. First and foremost was the stagnation of external demand, which had been the main growth factor as late as 1929 when 70 percent of the output of the Pampa region was exported. The second was the growth of domestic demand for agricultural and livestock products at a rate below that of the economy as a whole because of changes in the pattern of demand.

After 1930, the domestic market began to absorb progressively higher proportions of the Pampa's output. At present, only 30 percent of that output is exported, which means that development of the rural sector depends largely on the expansion of the domestic market. This is a radical change from the situation before 1930 when rural output was not only independent of domestic demand but even conditioned the level of the demand.

Before 1930, there was a "seller's market" in agricultural and livestock products. After that date, the decline in world demand for certain agricultural and livestock products, together with protectionist policies and the formation of trade blocs, reversed this situation and made it necessary to actively pursue market opportunities. Therefore, agricultural development became heavily dependent on the government's commercial policy.

The foregoing does not imply that the rural sector was to decline in absolute terms after 1930, but simply that because its growth lagged behind that of other activities, it was to lose importance in the economy as a whole. Nevertheless, if agriculture was to continue to develop in the new conditions, at least two aspects of development policy had to be revised: the composition of agricultural output and the land-tenure system.

In respect to agricultural output, its increasing dependence on the domestic market compelled its diversification. There were comparatively few exports: meat, hides, wool, cereals, and oilseeds. But domestic demand, which reflected the requirements of industries processing agricultural products as well as general consumption needs, had to be supplied with not only the traditional export products but also with industrial fibers, fruit, wine grapes, and so on. That this actually happened is shown in the relative increase of agriculture in irrigated and subtropical areas outside of the Pampa region.

In respect to the land-tenure system, it will be recalled that until 1930, agricultural output was expanded largely by exploiting new lands within the Pampa region. By about that time, however, most available land had been put into production, and output could only be increased by raising yields per hectare. Because rural Argentina was sparsely inhabited and, in view of the agricultural sector's loss of dynamism, not likely to gain population, higher yields would have to be effected through mechanization, soil conservation, and more efficient farming methods. It may be questioned whether Argentina's system of huge estancias and tenant farming is consistent with what has been called "the technical revolution in agriculture." Judging by the patterns of behavior of tenant farmers and large property owners, the answer appears to be negative.

To the extent that an increase in yields per hectare requires fixed improvements (windmills, pumps, wire fences, housing, silos, sheds, and other constructions and installations), the temporary user of the land, who is the tenant farmer, certainly would not be inclined to make an investment that would benefit him only during his period of occupancy. This is also true of investment in soil conservation and the purchase of heavy machinery and equipment. The basic insecurity of the tenant farmer was not solved by the freezing of rents under the Perón regime. In fact, the tenant farmer is interested in carrying out only those improvements on his farm that yield immediate results not extending beyond his occupancy. Schickele has described the similar behavior of tenant farmers in the United States.[14]

Large landowners do not seem to have followed the pattern of behavior characteristic of the entrepreneur in the capitalist system.[15]

---

[14] Rainer Schickele, "Effect of Tenure Systems on Agricultural Efficiency," *Journal of Farm Economics*, XXIII (February, 1941).

[15] Investment in land is altogether different from capital invested in other sectors of activity, for example, machinery in an industrial plant. The owner of the plant must renew his capital and maintain efficiency levels because, otherwise, competition from other entrepreneurs would displace him from the market and reduce the value of his investment. Land is not subject to this process of competition, and, consequently, capital invested in it may be immobilized. Far from losing its value, this capital becomes a protection against

Frequently, land is held for prestige or social status and as a hedge against inflation, rather than as capital that should be turned to yielding a maximum profit through the use of manpower and investment.[16] This is a serious obstacle to any increase in agricultural productivity and, consequently, to the ability to generate the savings needed to finance the construction of improvements and the mechanization of farms. Furthermore, it is doubtful that large farming units necessarily lead to a more efficient administration of manpower and capital.

The system of large landowners and tenant farmers for the most part explains the continued low yields per hectare of the main products of the Pampa region. It also explains the failure of price-incentive policies followed after 1950 for the purpose of raising agricultural output in the Pampa region. Moreover, the increased yields per hectare obtained on medium-sized holdings farmed by their owners in Mendoza, the Upper Valley of the Río Negro, and Chaco corroborate this conclusion.

---

inflation and may even increase in value as a result of the construction of new roads and other public investments that improve the use and location of the land.

[16] Even though a tract of land may be undercultivated, it can provide enough income to permit the owner to maintain a high level of consumption. Because this situation satisfies their needs, many large landholders are not interested in achieving maximum yields.

15. DEVELOPMENT OF THE ECONOMY
AND ITS LIMITATIONS

Weakening of the External Factors

Although the world trade crisis affected the volume of Argentine exports, it had a much greater impact on the terms of trade. From 1925–1929 to 1930–1934, the deterioration of its terms of trade caused Argentina a loss of over 600 million dollars per year. Because the decline in international prices for agricultural and livestock products was more intense than for manufactures and other commodities imported by Argentina, the purchasing power of exports fell from an annual average of 2 billion dollars in 1925–1929 to 1.2 billion dollars in 1930–1934, that is, by about 40 percent. Furthermore, the net inflow of foreign capital also decreased, while profits and interest on existing investment surpassed the high levels reached before the depression. These circumstances combined to reduce Argentina's capacity to import to only 46 percent of what it had been in 1925–1929.

The steep decline in the purchasing power of exports and in the capacity to import severely affected the level of domestic employment and income, the balance of payments, and public finance. Under the theoretical functioning of the gold standard, the fall in domestic employment, wages, and prices would have made Argentine exports more competitive in the world market, thereby stimulating domestic economic activity. However, during the 1929 depression period and during previous world depressions, this so-called endogenous adjustment mechanism did not bring about a recovery of Argentine exports because, as has been explained, the drop in Argentina's domestic export prices was offset by the drop in international prices for agricultural and livestock products. The balance of payments might have become stabilized eventually through the contraction of domestic economic activity and its effect on the volume of imports as a result of the decline in effective demand. At the same time, a sharp reduction of public expenditures, particularly investment, might have liberated resources with which to pay the service on the public debt. However, this method of balancing international payments and public finance would have caused employment and income to fall well below their predepression levels.

In practice, a compensatory policy was followed. In December, 1929, the peso became inconvertible and depreciated rapidly, owing to the balance-of-payments disequilibrium. At the same time, a budget deficit developed which was financed largely by bond issues purchased by the banking system, that is, by increases in the money supply. The conversion office was later authorized to exchange commercial paper for bank notes. Finally, in October, 1931, exchange control was imposed chiefly in order to prevent further depreciation of the peso as a result of the domestic monetary expansion and the balance-of-payments disequilibrium. By insulating domestic monetary expansion from balance-of-payments fluctuations, the government could purchase foreign exchange at a fixed rate, thereby stabilizing the cost of servicing the foreign debt. The policy followed during the depression arose more from a need to find an immediate solution to very serious and urgent problems than from a clear understanding of the compensatory effect of the policy itself: "the monetary authorities believed that sooner or later conditions would return to normal and that, therefore, the problems of structural and temporary disequilibrium would all disappear." [1]

In spite of the compensatory effect of fiscal and monetary policy during the depression, unemployment increased substantially, and capital formation contracted. In 1925–1929, the investment ratio was 34.1 percent, but by 1930–1934, it had fallen to 22.4 percent. Gross income[2] per inhabitant declined almost 20 percent between those two periods and did not regain its predepression level until 1946.

---

[1] W. M. Beveraggi-Allende, *El servicio del capital extranjero y el control de cambios* (México: Fondo de Cultura Económica, 1954), p. 167. During the 1930's, several important changes were made in the administrative structure and in the economic policy of Argentina. In addition to exchange control, an income tax was adopted, a central bank was established, and a number of special agencies called Juntas Reguladoras or marketing boards were set up to regulate activities in different sectors. All this new machinery enabled the state to intervene to a greater extent in the functioning of the economy, and it considerably improved the management of economic policy.

[2] Including the effect of the change in the terms of trade.

The weakening of external factors was to be a long-term process and not the immediate result of circumstances as had occurred in earlier depressions. In particular, the terms of trade continued to deteriorate. From 1925–1929 to the present, Argentina has lost roughly 12 billion dollars because of the decline in its terms of trade. The purchasing power of exports has never recovered its 1925–1929 level, and after 1950 it fell to less than 1 billion dollars, or to 50 percent below its peak period. From 1956 to 1961, the situation only changed for the worse. Exports, which were 25 percent of gross product in 1925–1929, since 1950 have amounted to under 7 percent.

After 1930–1934, the inflow of foreign capital ceased to be a significant item in Argentina's foreign transactions. In 1945–1949, there was a strong outflow of capital due to nationalization of the railroads and other public utilities and to repatriation of the external public debt. These net movements of long-term capital have reduced foreign investment from 32 percent of existing capital in 1929 to its present level of just over 5 percent.

As external indebtedness declined, there was a sharp decrease, intensified in part by restrictions on financial transfers abroad, in the remittance of profits and interest. This helped to offset the fall in the purchasing power of exports and in the inflow of new foreign capital as well as to stabilize the rate of capital formation, which before 1930 had fluctuated appreciably owing to changes in those remittances. On the other hand, the capacity to import continued to decline and after 1950 was only 50 percent of its 1925–1929 level.

It was not only a, question of the diminished importance of these external factors but also of the insulation of the domestic money supply and income from balance-of-payments fluctuations. In other words, the level of aggregate demand was determined by public-sector expenditures and by private investment rather than by the volume and prices of exports. The dynamic significance of this change has been discussed in previous chapters. The present chapter will examine the effect on Argentina's economic structure of the weakening of external factors.

Expansion of Industry and Subsequent Stagnation

From 1930 to the end of the 1940's, Argentina's industry expanded steadily under the stimulus of the declining capacity to import, the rising price of imports, the growth and diversification of internal demand, and, finally, the incorporation of technical advances. After 1946, an additional spur to industrial development was the rapid increase in the demand for consumer goods, including durables, due to labor's higher share in the national income.

Employment in industry went up 68 percent between 1925–1929 and 1945–1949, and it accounted for 20.8 percent of Argentina's active population in the first of these periods and for 23.9 percent in the second. In the same periods, manufacturing generated 17.7 percent and 23.5 percent of gross product.

The development of industry led to the replacement of imports of consumer goods, intermediate products, and machinery and equipment. In 1925–1929, imports of consumer goods were 13.3 percent of aggregate consumption; imports of intermediate products were 8 percent of total demand; and imports of machinery and equipment were 35.5 percent of total investment in these items. By 1955, these ratios had declined to 1 percent, 5.1 percent, and 15.8 percent respectively. However, industrial development was concentrated in the replacement of imports of consumer goods, intermediate commodities, and simple machinery and equipment, all of which were supplied by industries of little technical complexity. The production of steel and highly complex and costly capital goods, as well as the output of fuels and intermediate goods like heavy chemicals and petrochemicals, were hardly developed.

The insufficient development of heavy industry at the same time that the capacity to import was declining forced the consumption of steel per inhabitant down from 130 kilograms in 1929 to about 80 kilograms in the 1950's. Furthermore, imports of fuel doubled between 1929 and 1955 as the economy's requirements outstripped the development of domestic petroleum production. Thus, domestic manufacturing had to rely on increasing imports of raw materials and intermediate goods while the industry as a whole, together with agriculture, electric power generation, petroleum production, communications and transport, also became progressively more dependent on imports of heavy capital goods for further expansion.

The process of industrialization gradually changed the composition of imports. The relative significance of imports of durable and nondurable consumer goods dropped swiftly, whereas that of fuels, metallic intermediate products, pulp and paper, lumber and its products, and other intermediate commodities soared. Imports of capital goods remained high, although subject to violent short-term fluctuations as the capacity to import varied.[3] Imports of consumer goods, which had accounted for almost 40 percent of total imports before 1930, shrank to about 10 percent in the 1950's. On the other hand, the share of intermediate products increased from 30 percent to 60 percent and that of capital goods remained in the neighborhood of 30 percent both before and after 1930.

At the end of the 1940's, nevertheless, most of the substitution of domestic production for imports of consumer goods and simple intermediate commodities and capital goods had been achieved. From then on, imports of fuels and commodities produced by heavy industry and other complex industries would have to be replaced. Toward the end of the 1940's, Argentina's capacity to import again fell and remained at a level of about 1 billion dollars per year. Meanwhile, social overhead capital needs had accumulated particularly in transport, electric power generation, and communications, thus holding back industrial development.

As indicated in the preceding chapter, the obstacles to solving these problems were formidable. The indirect policy of industrial development based on import restrictions, the maintenance of domestic levels of employment and income, and even income redistribution to expand mass consumption were necessary measures, but inadequate to ensure growth of basic industry and expansion of the infrastructure.

Because a vigorous *direct* policy of industrial expansion, that is, an investment policy, was not laid down in the 1940's, the deficiencies of Argentina's economic structure were not overcome. This explains why the process of industrialization has regressed in recent years. In 1959–1961, employment in manufacturing was similar to that in 1945–1949 and below the level of 1955. The increase in the economically active population means that manufacturing now absorbs less than 20 percent of the labor force, compared to 24 percent in 1945–1949.[4]

---

[3] Within a structure of imports like Argentina's, when the capacity to import declines, the first items to be eliminated are machinery and equipment. This is natural because other imports such as fuels and raw materials are essential to keep the economy going. The long-term downward trend in the capacity to import is immediately accentuated, and foreign exchange to pay for the necessary imports of capital goods becomes scarcer.

[4] Since this book was completed (1962), new official statistics have been published on the distribution of the labor force and of gross product between the various activities. According to the new series, manufacturing employed

The Structure of Output

At the beginning of the stage of the nonintegrated industrial economy, there was a relatively diversified distribution of manpower, and labor employed in agriculture and livestock production came to 35 percent of the total active population. The reason for this has already been discussed in chapter 11.

During the stage now under consideration, important changes took place in the structure of output. Within this stage, two periods need to be distinguished: the first from 1930 to 1950, and the second from 1950 to date.

Let us now examine the forces operating to diversify the pattern of employment in the first two decades of the present stage. In the first place, industrial development and import replacement attracted a substantial part of the increase in the labor force. Second, owing to the changes in both external and internal demand for agricultural and livestock products and to the nature of the land-tenure system, the share of rural employment declined. Third, expansion in public expenditures became an important new source of employment. From 1925–1929 to 1945–1949, agriculture, industry, mining, and construction, as well as the basic services (transport, electricity, and communications), absorbed 60 percent of the growth in the labor force, while activities not producing commodities (government, commerce, finance, and personal services) accounted for the remaining 40 percent.

After 1950, the stagnation of industrial development radically modified the trends in the allocation of the gainfully employed population among the different sectors of the economy. In 1961, industrial employment did not exceed the 1945–1949 level of about 1.5 million people, so that obviously industry could not absorb any part of the approximately 800,000 people that had been added to the labor force between those two periods. On the other hand, the persistence of conditions adversely affecting agricultural development meant

about 25 percent of total manpower at the beginning of the present decade. From 1945–1949 to 1960, industrial product per inhabitant grew at an annual rate of 1.5 percent. Although the new statistics do not show as marked a stagnation in employment and industrial development as the series used for this book, there can be no question that my basic conclusions are still valid; that is, after 1945–1949, industry lagged behind and developed even more slowly than it had in the first years of the stage of the nonintegrated industrial economy.

that this sector could only occupy a negligible part of the increase in the labor force. Most of the latter found employment in activities that did not produce commodities, such as railroads and construction; but because output in these sectors did not go up proportionately, the rise in employment was accompanied by a decline in productivity.

The reasons for these trends in the allocation of manpower after 1950 are clear. Stagnation in industry prevented this sector from absorbing further manpower, and agriculture could not offer any new employment opportunities. Therefore, labor shifted gradually into activities that did not produce commodities, principally government services and nationalized public utilities.[5] This is reflected in the real level of remuneration of public employees, which, except for 1949, has remained for the last twenty-seven years permanently below the 1935 level. Had there been alternative employment opportunities at higher levels of remuneration, the public sector would not have attracted such a large proportion of the increment in the labor force. Employment in other activities not producing commodities (commerce, finance, and public services) also went up appreciably after 1950. The growing urbanization and the stagnation of industrial development meant that the increase in manpower in the city went chiefly into nonproductive activities, even though the real level of remuneration in these activities also remained unchanged or even fell.

In countries where living standards and the levels of production are rising, employment grows steadily in nonproductive activities because of expansion in the demand for education, health, advertising, commerce, entertainment, and miscellaneous public-sector services. In Argentina, however, growth of employment in these activities results from other causes. Per capita income and living standards today are barely equal to or are below the levels reached in 1948. The allocation of manpower between the different activities is

---

[5] The new statistical series referred to in the preceding footnote reveals significant changes in the factors that influence the distribution of labor between the various sectors of activity after 1950. In fact, there was a massive shift of labor out of the agricultural and livestock sector, of which 75 percent went into industry, mining and construction, and the basic services (transportation, electric energy, and communications). Consequently, commerce and other services (government and personal services and finance) not only absorbed the total increase in active population but also part of the manpower displaced from agriculture.

not so much explained by the changes in the composition of demand due to increases in income as by the stagnation of industrial output. People could not find employment in manufacturing, so they were forced to work in other sectors. Because the stagnation of industry slowed down the whole process of development, there were hardly any possibilities after 1950 of expanding employment in other sectors at rising levels of productivity.

Argentina's experience is in this sense similar to that of countries where a high proportion of the population is engaged at low levels of productivity in agriculture. As this population moves into urban centers, it does not find employment in industry and adds to the manpower in nonproductive activities defined as disguised unemployment.

In the final analysis, this process is a waste of a large part of the labor force and, consequently, limits development possibilities. In any case, the growth of employment in nonproductive activities, including the government, is an effect and not a cause of stagnation. But employment in the public sector increases current public expenditures, thereby diminishing the amount of savings available to the government to finance investment. Between 1925–1929 and 1955, aggregate public expenditure went up from 15.6 percent to 28.2 percent of gross product. However, most of the increase was in current expenditures; whereas public investment, although it fluctuated throughout the period, did not rise appreciably above the 1925–1929 level. Here we have another case of the vicious circle of stagnation: the slowdown in development leads to higher employment in government, which in turn prevents the public sector from carrying out infrastructure investment and leads to further stagnation.

Therefore, this stage marked the consolidation of the typical structure of a nonintegrated industrial economy. The diversification of the occupational structure is similar to that in countries with high levels of income and rapid rates of growth. But this diversification is largely the result of the stagnation of the basic sectors and of the economy as a whole and actually implies a waste of a high and rising proportion of the country's real resources.

Income Distribution

During this stage, a number of frequently contradictory forces affected the distribution of income between workers and capital and enterprise. In this respect, it is advisable to distinguish structural factors from short-term factors related to the management of economic policy. Among structural factors, the concentration of land and of capital invested in industry continued to be significant. In the long run, the effect of the former on income distribution tended to decline as income generated by the agricultural sector became relatively less important. On the other hand, the growing importance of industry meant that until 1950 the concentration of capital in this sector exerted an increasing influence on income distribution.[6]

Other structural factors tended to expand the share of labor in total domestic income; among them were changes in the structure of employment and the strengthening of labor unions. It should be recalled that the respective share of labor and of capital and enterprise in total income varies substantially according to the activity. For example, in agricultural and livestock production, the share of labor is about 25 percent of net income generated by the sector, with the remainder going to capital and enterprise. In industry and the services, the share of labor is about 55 percent and that of capital and enterprise about 45 percent of net income generated by those sectors. With such differences in the distribution of the income generated by each activity, any change in the occupational structure naturally affects the distribution of income in the economy as a whole. A shift in the labor force from agriculture to industry and the services raises the share of labor in the country's net domestic income, and vice versa. A significant increase occurred after 1930. Employment in agricultural and livestock activities declined from 36 percent of the total labor force in 1929 to 26 percent at present; and employment in industry and the services rose from 64 percent to 74 percent over the same period.

The strengthening of labor unions has also tended to raise the share of labor in total income. In countries now at a higher level of development, pressure brought by organized labor has been decisive in maintaining and even expanding the worker's share in total income and in ensuring his participation in the increases in productivity that accompany development. In other countries, particularly

---

[6] According to estimates made by Germani from industrial census data, the proprietors of large manufacturing enterprises employing an average of 200 workers were 0.4 percent of the active population engaged in industry and controlled from 60 percent to 65 percent of total manufacturing output.

the underdeveloped countries with an elastic labor supply and limited employment opportunities, the unemployed and underemployed mass pushes down wages and weakens the position of labor unions in their attempts to protect the share of the worker in total income. In Argentina, increased employment in industry and the services and the concomitant process of urbanization reinforced the labor unions and enabled workers to more effectively defend their share of total income. However, political circumstances largely conditioned the activity of unions. The government was much more receptive between 1945 and 1955 than afterwards to union demands for higher wages, ceiling prices on primary necessities, rent control, and so on. The trends in labor's share in total net income reflect to some extent the changes in government policy toward labor unions from 1945 on.

The short-term factors affecting income distribution during the stage of the nonintegrated industrial economy were mainly related to the management of economic policy, and they can be grouped under two headings: the transfer of income from agriculture to other sectors of the economy, and urban rent control. If income from a sector in which the remuneration of labor is a small part of total income generated is transferred to another sector in which the share of income is higher, there must be an increase in the aggregate share of labor. If the transfer is reversed, it has the opposite effect. This actually happened when income was transferred from one sector to another as a result of government measures affecting relative prices, and it must be discussed in greater detail.

During the period of exchange control subsequent to December, 1931, and particularly between 1946 and 1955, the peso was artificially overvalued. The rate of exchange on, let us say, the dollar, was maintained at a level higher than would have been set by the supply and demand of foreign exchange. For instance, in 1950 exporters had to sell their exchange proceeds at 5 pesos to 1 dollar, although the equilibrium rate for foreign exchange was probably above 15 pesos. As almost all exports originated in the agricultural sector, the latter's income was obviously reduced.[7] In turn, the

---

[7] The prices at which exportable commodities are sold on the domestic market are strongly influenced by the prices of exports. On the other hand, ceiling prices on basic commodities from the agricultural and livestock sector during the early years helped keep down the prices of products from the Pampa region. Agricultural and livestock output from outside the region was not

foreign exchange purchased by the central bank was sold at the official rate, which was well below the equilibrium rate, to industrial and other users of imported raw materials, intermediate products, fuels, and machinery and equipment. Thus, buyers of foreign exchange profited by the income loss of the agricultural producers, and, insofar as lower production costs resulted from cheaper imports by those to whom foreign exchange was allocated, the whole Argentine population benefited from the transfer of income. On the other hand, because the agricultural sector had to purchase in the domestic market a mounting proportion of commodities for its consumption and investment, it suffered a further loss of income when these goods cost more than the imports they replaced.

As a consequence of government intervention in the price system, real prices in the agricultural sector (according to available data) declined steadily from 1937 to 1949, with the exception of 1946. While real prices in that sector descended 20 percent and in the services 6 percent, in industry they improved 42 percent.

The situation changed after 1950. Because the government adopted a policy of encouraging agriculture, farm prices rose much more swiftly than industrial prices and the general price level. The 1955 devaluation, followed by total liberalization of exchange transactions and another currency devaluation in December, 1958, intensified this trend. In April, 1962, the peso depreciated again and has continued to fall in value, thereby once more boosting the relative prices of agricultural and livestock products.

The magnitude of the changes in relative prices for the rural sector during the 1950–1960 decade and the impact of these changes on income transfers between the agricultural sector and the rest of the national economy have been analyzed in a study that the author, together with a group of experts, prepared on the evolution of prices and income in Argentine agriculture.[8] This still unpublished study shows that in 1950–1959 prices of agricultural and livestock products multiplied 13 times, whereas in the industrial sector and similarly in the services they went up only 8 times.

---

affected by exchange control because it was mainly for domestic consumption, but it was affected in some cases by ceiling prices. Broadly speaking, prices for this output tended to increase at the same rate as the general price level.
[8] *La producción, ingresos y capitalización del sector agropecuario en el período 1950–1960.* Study prepared by CAFADE (Comisión Nacional de Administración del Fondo de Apoyo del Desarrollo Económico), Buenos Aires, April, 1961.

The general price level rose 9 times during the same period. If these increases are deflated by a general price index for the whole economy, it will be found that real prices in the agricultural sector went up 40 percent, while those in manufacturing and the services declined 10 percent. Such an improvement in the relative prices of the rural sector implies a substantial transfer of income from the rest of the economy to agriculture and livestock raising. In 1950–1960, the transfer amounted to some 19 billion pesos at 1950 prices and to 210 billion pesos at 1960 prices. This would be equivalent to about 2.5 billion dollars at present-day purchasing power.

The report just cited also shows how income increases in the agricultural and livestock sector were distributed between profits and wages. In the short run, profits absorbed most of the increment in income. In 1958–1960, when agricultural income went up appreciably because of the improvement in relative prices, the share of profits in total income of the sector (including interest received) climbed from 53.7 percent in 1958 to 61.9 percent in 1959 and 60.2 percent in 1960. Wages and salaries did not at first share in the income increases of the sector, and, therefore, their relative position worsened. In 1958, wages and salaries were 29 percent of gross income of the sector; in 1959, 21.8 percent; and in 1960, 20.5 percent. This trend also helped raise the share of remuneration of capital and enterprise in aggregate domestic income.

The other short-term factor that affected income distribution during this stage was urban rent control. Insofar as it reduced prices received by owners of property, it restricted the earnings of capital in aggregate domestic income. This would appear to have been the case for the most part, although unfortunately paucity of data does not permit a precise measure of the income transfer effected.

Actually, the forces involved, often conflicting, were bound to have as much influence on long-term trends as on short-term fluctuations in income distribution. According to available data,[9] the remuneration of labor (wages and salaries, including business and personal contributions to social security) came to about 46 percent of net domestic income in the 1935–1939 period before World War II. The remuneration of capital and enterprise (net business income, property owners, independent professions, interest, and

---

[9] *Producto e ingreso de la República Argentina en el período 1935–1954*, published by the former Ministry of Economic Affairs, 1955; and *Boletines Estadísticos*, published by the Central Bank of Argentina.

so on) accounts for the remaining 54 percent. These relative shares remained more or less unchanged until 1946, but beginning in that year, the share of labor rose steadily until it reached a peak of 56.9 percent in 1952. From that year to 1958, it stayed at a level of about 52 percent. But between 1958 and 1959, it declined from 53.1 percent to 45.8 percent; and in 1960, the last year for which there are figures, it was 45.9 percent. The appreciable decline in the share of labor in net domestic income after 1958 is directly related to the economic and financial policy of the time, and especially to the massive transfers of income to the rural sector after that year. This policy will be discussed in a later chapter.

Growth and Stagnation of the Economy

Between 1930 and 1962, Argentina's population increased from 12 million to 21 million inhabitants, that is, at an annual rate of 1.8 percent or little over one half of the rate growth during the primary-exports stage. The main reason for the fall in the rate of growth was the decline in immigration. Whereas in 1914 foreign population was 30 percent of the total, in 1930 it was 16 percent.

On the other hand, capital accumulation in the sectors producing commodities (agriculture and livestock, manufacturing and mining, and construction) and in the basic services (electric energy, communications, and transport) progressed very slowly after 1930. Available data indicate that fixed capital in the 1925–1929 period was 68,849 million pesos at 1950 prices and by 1955 had risen 44 percent to 98,886 pesos. But because population increased almost 75 percent during the same period, existing capital per inhabitant in those basic sectors diminished about 18 percent.

Investment in basic services, that is, in social overhead capital, was singularly low. Capital stock expanded only 29 percent from 1925–1929 to 1955, which, in the light of population growth, meant an actual decline of more than 26 percent. Installed electric-power capacity has risen less than one third of the growth in consumption. Existing capital in railroads in 1955 was one half of what it had been in 1925–1929.

It is worth pointing out that the weak growth in the stock of capital in the basic sectors of the economy was accompanied by a much more rapid accumulation in sectors not producing commodities (government services, housing, commerce, finance, and personal services). Whereas capital in the basic sectors increased 44 percent during the period referred to, it went up in the sectors not producing commodities as much as 86 percent. Of the total accumulation of capital during this period, only 32.8 percent went into the basic sectors. This explains why capital in the basic sectors was 49.1 percent of total capital in 1925–1929 and only 42.7 percent in 1955. In any case, aggregate capital per inhabitant was 5 percent less in 1955 than in 1925–1929.

Although no data are available for the period after 1955, it may be assumed that these trends, far from changing, have become more marked.[10] This slow and distorted accumulation of capital can be understood in terms of the same causes that determined the evolution of the nonintegrated industrial economy. At the same time, insufficient capital formation in basic productive sectors and in infrastructure led to a stagnation of the economy. Here again is the vicious circle typical of economic stagnation.

It is natural that with a lower rate of population growth and a decline in the amount of capital per inhabitant, particularly in the basic sectors of the national economy, income should increase slowly during the entire stage and, of course, at a pace far below that of the primary-exports stage. From 1925–1929 to 1962, gross product expanded almost 2.5 percent per year, as compared with about 5 percent in the preceding stage. On a per capita basis, these figures are 0.6 percent and 1.2 percent respectively.

The situation from 1925–1929 to 1945–1949 should be distinguished from that of more recent periods. During the former, import replacement and industrialization, in spite of a weakening of external factors, permitted gross product to increase 2.8 percent per year and per capita product about 0.8 percent. After 1945–1949, on the other hand, with industrial development at a standstill and the economy stagnating, the increase in gross product hardly kept up with population growth. Gross product per inhabitant remained below the 1948 peak and by 1961 had barely regained this level.

---

[10] From more recent information, it appears that during 1960–1962 a large volume of investment was made in various basic activities, principally the iron and steel, petroleum, and automobile industries, as well as in transportation and electric energy. During that period, there was a substantial increase in imports of capital goods for use in the foregoing sectors and to replace equipment in other branches of industry. On the other hand, the rise in imports of capital goods created a heavy deficit in the balance of trade, equal to 20 percent of the imports of that period.

A further decline was expected in 1962. In other words, as far as gross product per capita is concerned, the Argentine economy has not advanced since 1948.[11]

After 1945–1949, the country's capacity to import again fell and has remained at levels about 50 percent below those of the 1925–1929 period. Moreover, by the end of the 1940's, replacement of imports of final consumer goods and simple intermediate and capital goods could go no farther. Almost all of Argentina's imports from then on were raw materials, intermediate products and fuels needed to keep the economy functioning, and complex machinery and equipment indispensable to capital formation in electric-energy generation, transportation, industry, and other sectors.

Under the combined effect of the fall in the capacity to import and the exhaustion of import-replacement possibilities in light industry, the process of development came to a halt. Shortages of essential materials immobilized a large proportion of installed capacity in industry and prevented new expansion. The establishment of new activities like the automobile industry does not make this statement less valid for industry as a whole. In any case, the new activities were subject to the same kind of limitations. Lack of machinery and basic equipment to augment capital stock in productive activities and the infrastructure meant that as population increased, the existing amount of capital per inhabitant in those sectors declined, which in turn lowered the over-all efficiency of the economy. Moreover, the structural weaknesses of agricultural and livestock production, the mounting inadequacy of the basic services (in particular, transportation and electric energy), and the very slow rise in internal and external demand restricted the growth possibilities of the rural sector, especially of the Pampa region. With opportunities for industrial development blocked and in the absence of a policy for expanding public investment in the infrastructure, capital and manpower came to be used increasingly in sectors not producing commodities and in the nonessential services.

The external vulnerability of the Argentine economy, as analyzed in the ECLA study, underwent a complete transformation. The economy ceased to be vulnerable to external factors insofar as they

---

[11] The new series of gross product shows that between 1945–1949 and 1960 there was a slight increase in gross product per inhabitant, but at a rate still lower than the one recorded in the early years of the stage of the nonintegrated industrial economy.

conditioned the level of aggregate demand. Having insulated the money supply and public expenditures from the impact of foreign transactions, the government was in a better position to maintain the levels of employment and domestic income through monetary and fiscal policy. At the end of the 1940's, on the other hand, the economy became vulnerable to external factors because the use of installed capacity in industry, as well as capital formation and a large part of the assimilation of technology, became dependent on Argentina's capacity to import all the intermediate products, raw materials, fuels, and machinery and equipment necessary for normal development.

Owing to the limited possibilities of its industrial development and the inefficiency of its economy, Argentina has not been able to diversify exports through manufactures, for which there is a growing world demand. Thus, it has been helpless to reverse the downward trend of exports, which is derived basically from the trends of world trade in agricultural and livestock products; and the country has been forced to become self-sufficient to an extent that conspires against its progressive participation in the international division of labor.

In the conditions of stagnation of recent decades, temporary measures to encourage industrial growth (maintenance of the level of domestic income, increase in the price of imports, and short-term redistribution of income) have not sufficed to expand the basic industrial sectors and social overhead capital. At present, the policy of transferring income to the rural sector and of restricting the volume of credit available to the public and private sectors is leading to a sharp contraction in employment and real income accompanied by the closing down of many industries. This point will be taken up in a later chapter. Meanwhile, it should be stressed that in order to overcome the limitations of nonintegrated industrial development and to achieve a transition toward an integrated structure, a direct policy of development, that is, an investment policy should be carried out for the express purpose of expanding basic industries and the country's infrastructure. Argentina has no choice in this matter because it has only one means of ensuring its economic and social development: the integration of its economic structure. Given the changes in the behavior of external factors and the new set of forces acting on the economic and social reality of the country, it would be impossible to return to the stage of primary exports.

To conclude the discussion of the stage of the nonintegrated industrial economy, chapter 17 will deal with the policy followed after 1950 to combat the country's stagnation. But first, some remarks should be made about regional development after 1930.

16. CONSOLIDATION OF THE INTERREGIONAL IMBALANCE

Growth and Distribution of Population

The concentration of population in the Federal District and its environs has been the most striking feature of Argentina's population distribution in recent decades. The large metropolitan area known as Greater Buenos Aires comprises 3,600 square kilometers, that is, 1.3 percent of national territory. In 1914, 25.8 percent of Argentina's population lived in that area; in 1947, 29.7 percent; and in 1960, 38.8 percent. In 1960, the population of Greater Buenos Aires was almost 7 million inhabitants. From 1914 to 1960, it increased 232 percent, whereas the country's total population went up 126 percent. The difference between the growth rates became more pronounced after 1947, when the population of Greater Buenos Aires expanded 43 percent as compared to the country's over-all rate of only 12 percent. It is interesting to note that while the population of the whole metropolitan area increased rapidly, that of the Federal District increased slowly and even declined slightly from 1947 to 1960. This was the result of the process of suburbanization typical of large cities in the United States.

From 1914 to 1960, population in towns of over 2,000 inhabitants rose from 52.7 percent to 65 percent of total population. On the other hand, two thirds of the urbanization that has taken place in Argentina in the last forty-six years is explained by the expansion of Greater Buenos Aires.

Although this pattern of demographic growth is by no means new in Argentina in view of the growth of population in Greater Buenos Aires from 11 percent of the total in 1869 to 25.8 percent in 1914, the reasons for such concentration changed after 1914. Until that date, a large part of the immigrants entering the country remained in the Federal District and surrounding areas. The census of that year showed that 49 percent of the total population of Greater Buenos Aires was of foreign extraction. The subsequent slowing down of immigration reduced the proportion of foreign population in Greater Buenos Aires to only 36 percent in 1936. In that year a new force emerged that was to have a profound influence on the distribution of population in the country as a whole and on the social and political characteristics of Argentina's development: the massive migration from the countryside to Greater Buenos Aires. From 1936 to 1960, about 2 million people from the interior of the country settled in the metropolitan area, raising the proportion of this sector of inhabitants from 12 percent to 40 percent of total population in Greater Buenos Aires.

Most of the migration to Greater Buenos Aires between 1936 and 1960 originated in the provinces of the Pampa region. The provinces of the Northwest (Santiago del Estero, Tucumán, Catamarca, Jujuy, La Rioja, and Salta) were net exporters of population, but in absolute amounts they contributed relatively little because in 1914 these provinces contained only 13 percent of the country's total population. The province of Córdoba maintained its relative share of total population from 1914 to 1947 at about 9.3 percent; however, in spite of its recent industrial development, its share fell to 8.8 percent in 1960. Apart from Greater Buenos Aires, the only regions to increase their relative share were Cuyo (provinces of Mendoza and San Juan), Patagonia (provinces of Santa Cruz, Chabut, Neuquen, Río Negro, and Tierra del Fuego) and the Northeast (provinces of Chaco, Formosa, and Misiones). Cuyo's population ascended from 5 percent of the total in 1914, to 5.3 percent in 1947, and to 5.9 percent in 1960; the share of Patagonia in total population rose from 1.4 percent in 1914, to 2.2 percent in 1947, and to 2.5 percent in 1960; the Northeast's share went up from 1.5 percent in 1914, to 5 percent in 1947, and to 5.5 percent in 1960. The circumstances affecting the relative shares of the various regions will be discussed later, but in any case the combined population of these three regions is only 13.9 percent of the total, which means that its upward trend could not counteract the general imbalance between regional populations.

Concentration in Greater Buenos Aires

After 1930, the concentration of population in Greater Buenos Aires, which had begun in the primary-exports period, was intensified. Industry and services began to absorb an increasing share of the country's labor force and, at the same time, urbanization was accelerated because such activities were carried out in urban centers. In the last few decades, Greater Buenos Aires has been the focal point of the establishment of industry and the expansion of services by virtue of the following attractions: a greater availability of basic utilities and services such as water and sewage disposal, urban transport, electric energy, schools, and hospitals; the location of most of the national market in an area which by 1930 contained 30 percent of Argentina's population representing the sector with the highest income level; the city of Buenos Aires as port of entry for a large proportion of the raw materials, intermediate products, machinery and equipment, and fuels needed for many industrial activities; an abundant supply of labor with an above-average level of training; the employment and income afforded by a vastly expanded program of public expenditures in that area, especially after 1945.

Most of these forces were already operating by 1930 and were decisive in the subsequent location of economic activity and population. This is typical of the cumulative nature of the development process, in which certain original causes become self-reinforcing and strengthen the pre-established trends.

At the same time that Greater Buenos Aires attracted population, the latter was actually expelled from other parts of the country. The stagnation of agricultural and livestock output in the Pampa region and the concentration of land in the hands of a few property owners limited employment opportunities and reduced relative income levels. The settlement of most immigrants in urban centers, especially Greater Buenos Aires, was largely the result of the land-tenure system, which also prevented the emergence of a class of medium landholders. After 1930, the shift of rural population to urban centers was more rapid than it would have been if the producer had had a more stable relationship with the land he was cultivating.

The "expulsion" effect of the land-tenure system in Argentina after 1930 was especially important in the Litoral and the Pampa. The share of these provinces in the country's total population decreased from 44.3 percent in 1914 to 37 percent in 1947, and by 1960 it had fallen to 32.4 percent. Thus, the land-tenure system hastened the decline in the relative importance of the agricultural and livestock sector which was implicit in the process of development. It not only drove away labor but hindered the adoption of higher levels of technology which would have offset this loss. Unlike the United States and the more advanced countries of Europe, in Argentina the shift from farm to city did not coincide with but preceded the technological revolution in agriculture, and this helps to explain the stagnation in output over the last thirty years. The problem must be solved by improving agricultural techniques and mechanizing rural activity rather than by redirecting the urban population to the countryside.

Changes in the Interior Regions

Elements existed which, although they were not sufficient to offset the concentration of population and economic activity in Greater Buenos Aires, enabled some provinces to maintain their share in the country's total population and, in the case of Cuyo, Patagonia, and the Northeast, even to improve it.

Industrialization and the decline in imports, due to the fall in Argentina's capacity to import, opened up a domestic market for lines of production that had not figured in the over-all economy or had scarcely developed. For example, output of certain farm products for domestic consumption increased as follows: cotton, 432 percent; sugar, 64 percent; wine grapes, 108 percent; and yerba maté, 495 percent.[1] Most of these crops, for ecological reasons, are grown outside the Pampa region, so that agricultural and livestock output in the rest of the country (including those crops and others for domestic consumption) expanded its share in total agricultural and livestock output from 22 percent in 1925–1929 to 32 percent in 1955–1957.

On the other hand, the development of mining and of petroleum production, although never very important in this stage, did attract economic activity to areas distant from Greater Buenos Aires, for example, Patagonia.

Provinces like Cuyo, where output for the domestic market increased, were able to diversify their economic structure on the basis of the dynamic nucleus of their exports to the national market. Industries were established to supply the regional markets insofar as the availability of natural resources, manpower, and the basic services, together with growth in local demand, made this feasible.

---

[1] The numbers indicate the increase in output of these crops between 1925–1929 and 1955–1957.

A substantial part of the income generated by these export activities spilled over into the region itself and led to economic diversification, new activities and investment opportunities, and a general rise in employment and income.

In other provinces, where basic conditions for the "take-off" of industrial activities and services for the regional markets were not present, the increased income generated by the dynamic export activities was spent on imports from the rest of the economy. This prevented the increment in income from having an impact on the internal economic structure of the regions and kept them as essentially primary-producing areas.

Some provinces had an appreciable expansion, particularly in recent years, of industries producing for the national market, for example, the metallurgical industries in Córdoba. But in several provinces of the Northwest, no activity producing for the national market was established, and the consequent stagnation completed the decline of that region which had begun in the colonial period.

In any event, although some regions of the country have developed to a certain extent in the last thirty years, they are dependent and increasingly so on Greater Buenos Aires as the dynamic center of the domestic market for their exported output. Furthermore, most of the industrial commodities they import from the rest of the economy are supplied by industries within Greater Buenos Aires. There continues to be little communication between the various Argentine regions because the transport system still fans out from the port of Buenos Aires. It was inherited from the primary-exports stage, and is one of the fundamental obstacles to the geographical integration of Argentina.

In each province, fiscal resources are closely linked to the development trend. In the traditionally dynamic provinces like Buenos Aires, Santa Fe, and Córdoba, or in those like Mendoza where some development has occurred, the local government can draw on a substantial volume of revenues to implement its policy. Furthermore, given their relative importance, these provinces are entitled to the largest shares in federal-tax proceeds. An analysis of local budgets and investment programs reveals that a sizable percentage of public investment, as well as the basic services of education, health, social security, and so on, is financed out of local resources.

The relatively stagnant provinces, on the other hand, have to rely on grants from the federal government to finance their administrative expenses and to carry out their public works. The performance of the public sector in the dynamic provinces as contrasted with its performance in the stagnant provinces testifies once again to the cumulative effects typical of economic and social development.

Therefore, the nonintegrated industrial economy which began in 1930 has sealed the doom of the old "economic federalism" and has decisively strengthened the role of Greater Buenos Aires as the focus of economic and social development in Argentina. This process of centralization, however, seems to have reached its saturation point owing to population expansion and the accumulation of shortages in housing, sanitary facilities, schools, hospitals, urban transport, and other general services. It is no accident that the stagnation of the national economy after the late 1940's coincided with exhaustion of the capacities of Greater Buenos Aires. Clearly, the present structure of the national economy is incompatible with realizing the development potentialities of Argentina.

17. INFLATION AND STAGNATION: ECONOMIC POLICY AFTER 1950

Around 1950, a number of trends became evident that clearly indicated the disequilibrium and paralysis of the development of the nonintegrated industrial economy.[1] Insufficient import capacity led to a shortage of essential supplies for the development of economic activity and to a persistent balance-of-payments disequilibrium; in addition, this same deficiency, which actually became more acute between 1945–1949 and 1950–1954, brought the process of industrialization and import replacement to a halt.

In preceding years, 1946–1948, fiscal and monetary policy had resulted in a sharp increase in prices as well as in domestic income and, consequently, imports. The government had also decided to repatriate certain foreign investments, namely, railroads and other public services. The heavy demand for imports and the foreign disinvestment could be met, thanks to the reserves accumulated by Argentina during World War II and the high purchasing power of its exports during the postwar period.

On the other hand, capital formation in industry was facilitated, at the expense of the export sector, by means of imported machinery and equipment at overvalued rates of exchange. Furthermore, industrial costs were kept low by the purchase of raw materials, fuels, and intermediate products at those same rates of exchange.

Finally, the change in the structure of employment, the general increase in wages, the fixing of ceiling prices on staple commodities, and the freezing of urban and rural rents, all contributed to raise the share of labor in domestic income. This in itself was a new spur to industrial output, which had been strongly stimulated by the growth in domestic income, the low prices of imported inputs, and the heavier protection given to industrial production.

This policy, by creating very favorable conditions for the expan-

---

[1] Although, in reality, 1948 was the peak year of development in this stage, it was from 1948 to 1950 that the problems of stagnation became evident and the policies dealt with in this chapter took shape. For purposes of exposition, 1950 will be taken as the starting point of the events discussed here.

sion of industries producing final goods, fully exploited the development possibilities of the nonintegrated industrial economy.[2] However, growth of the economy still depended on capacity to import.
Given the behavior of imports around 1950, the growth possibilities
of the nonintegrated industrial economy were exhausted.

At that time, government policy was revised and a number of
measures were adopted which, in the light of their objectives and
of the assumptions underlying them, can be said to follow a single
line of thought.[3] The objectives of policy after 1950 were basically
three: first, to restore the external factors (exports and foreign
capital) to the dynamic role they had played in the primary-exports
economy; second, to balance public finances by reducing state intervention in the economy, restricting credit to the private sector, and
stabilizing the general price level; and third, to limit the share of
labor in national income as a means of inducing a higher rate of
investment, especially in the private sector.

Exports and Foreign Capital

Discussion of this topic requires a distinction between the policy
followed and the results obtained in respect to agricultural and
livestock production and exports on the one hand, and foreign
capital on the other.

Agricultural and livestock production and exports

Farm production and exports were encouraged by transferring
income to the rural sector through an improvement in their relative

---

[2] In practice, with domestic currency overvalued, cheap imports of machinery
and equipment, petroleum, intermediate products, and other inputs discouraged the development of basic industries in Argentina. Petroleum is a case in
point. Domestic output had to compete with petroleum imported at rates of
exchange below the market ones, which reduced the income of the government
petroleum corporation and, therefore, curtailed its scale of operations. Other
basic industries had to compete in equally disadvantageous conditions with
foreign suppliers.

[3] During the period after 1950, the objectives of the policy did not always
appear to be as clearly defined as is indicated in the text. It is also possible
that the intentions of the government may not have been those attributed to it.
However, it is not the purpose of this discussion to examine the intentions of
those in power, but to point out the main features of the policy, which in its
broad outlines corresponds to the analysis given in this chapter.

prices. This policy underwent various modifications. Up to 1955, the foreign marketing of agricultural and livestock products was managed by the state, and the producers received whatever price the latter chose to pay them. When international prices of farm products started declining steadily after 1950–1951, the government agency paid the producers prices above the export prices and absorbed the marketing losses. Even though the overvaluation of the peso tended to increase marketing losses, the higher prices paid the producer permitted an improvement in the agricultural and livestock sector.[4]

After 1955, the income transfer was brought about increasingly through devaluation of the peso. The first important devaluation took place in October of that year, when the rate of exchange for exports was increased from 5 to 18 pesos per dollar. In January, 1959, there was a new devaluation, and the exchange system was modified in order to adopt a single, free and fluctuating rate of exchange determined by supply and demand; and all financial transactions with the rest of the world were liberalized.[5] After the 1959 devaluation, the exchange rate was pegged at about 83 pesos per dollar through the operations of the central bank in the exchange market. In April, 1962, a new devaluation was authorized which at the time of writing in November, 1962, had lowered the currency to 140 pesos per dollar.

The exchange adjustments of January, 1959, finally brought satisfaction to Argentine exporters. Under the exchange control system in force after October, 1931, the exchange rate was frequently over-

---

[4] From 1950 to 1955, real prices for the agricultural and livestock sector were on the average and for the whole five-year period 12 percent above the 1950 level, whereas real prices for manufactures were 4 percent below it.

[5] From 1955 on, agricultural and livestock exports were gradually shifted from the official exchange market, with a basic rate of 18 pesos to the dollar, to the free market, where the rate was above 35 pesos per dollar. This was done by means of a complicated system of export values whereby exporters were obliged to sell a part of their exchange earnings at the official rate and could place the remainder in the free market. The proportion of export proceeds that had to be sold in the official market was steadily reduced until in January, 1959, a single rate of exchange was adopted at which all exchange earnings from exports could be sold freely. In practice, the system of withholding a proportion of the value of exports (and of imposing a surcharge on imports) meant that Argentina's foreign trade continued to be subject to multiple exchange rates, but this does not invalidate the transfer effect of devaluation on income to the agricultural and livestock sector.

valued, and therefore the income of the agricultural and livestock producers was penalized. From 1959 on, with the freeing of the exchange rate, export prices automatically increased *pari passu* with devaluation, and income was transferred from the rest of the economy to the rural sector in the manner already described.[6]

Furthermore, after 1955, the system of price controls for the domestic marketing of primary necessities was gradually dismantled, so that the internal prices of agricultural and livestock products could rise freely as a result of devaluation and of the increase in export prices. Thanks to devaluation, the relative improvement in farm prices continued; that is, the prices of industrial commodities and services increased relatively less.

Income transfer to the rural sector from 1950 to 1960 amounted to roughly 19 billion pesos (at 1950 prices) or 2.5 billion dollars. The policy objective was to encourage farm producers to raise their output and thereby make available larger exportable surpluses. However, this objective was not achieved. As the CAFADE report says, "the volume of agricultural and livestock output climbed 22.3 percent from 1950 to 1960. But in view of the increase of 23.1 percent from 1950 to 1953, production apparently did not rise during the remainder of the decade. If account is taken of population growth, it is clear that from 1953 to 1960 per capita output declined almost 13 percent." [7] Furthermore, "the stagnation in the volume of output shows that farm production is not responsive to the increases in real prices obtained by that sector." [8] Exports followed a course similar to that of agricultural and livestock output. Although they increased somewhat in volume thanks to restrictions on domestic consumption, they could not rise in purchasing power because of steady deterioration in the terms of trade.

In spite of the incentives adopted, agricultural and livestock output remained unchanged after 1950 for a number of reasons, some of which have been discussed. First, price incentives were ineffective as a means of expanding output because the conditions of tenant farming on the one hand, and the large estate on the other, discouraged the capital investment and up-to-date farming

---

[6] See chap. 11, section on "Income Distribution."
[7] The increase during 1950–1953 reflected agriculture's recovery from the 1950 drought. CAFADE, *La produccion, ingresos y capitalización del sector agropecuario en el periódo 1950–1960* (Buenos Aires, April, 1961).
[8] *Ibid.*

methods needed to increase yields per hectare.[9] Second, the relative improvement in rural prices was not a constant stimulus because of the pressure exerted by urban sectors to keep their share of income and in view of the steady rise in wages and prices of industrial goods and services. This uncertainty also made the farm producer reluctant to expand his activities. Third, the absence of a systematic extension of modern technology in rural areas and the growing need for infrastructure capital, particularly transport and energy, also counteracted the improvement in rural prices and prevented a rise in yields per hectare and, consequently, in output. Finally, the monopolistic practices prevalent in an important part of Argentina's exports, mainly the meat industry, depressed export prices and limited the scope of an effective commercial policy that could have protected export prices and expanded the market.[10] Given these conditions, any improvement in the real prices of agricultural and livestock products could not result in a substantial increase in output or in export earnings.

To summarize, the policy followed after 1950 to restore exports to their dynamic and autonomous role in the growth of aggregate demand and aggregate output could not succeed because not only did world demand for agricultural and livestock products grow very slowly but international trade in these products became increasingly restricted. In addition, given the conditions in Argentina affecting agricultural and livestock products, price incentives could not bring about a rise in output. Thus, a large part of agricultural income was spent outside the rural sector, frequently in unproductive investment such as luxury housing in Buenos Aires and in resorts like Mar del Plata.

On the other hand, this policy, although intended to raise the country's import capacity, defeated its own purpose. By hampering industrial development and the integration of the economic struc-

---

[9] See chap. 14, section on "New Conditions for Agricultural and Livestock Development."

[10] It will be recalled that imports of Argentine meat into the United Kingdom are regulated by a cartel of importers, the so-called "Freight Committee," which prevents the participation of any other seller and fixes the price of Argentine meat in the Smithfield market through control of the volume of sales. Importers of Argentine meat in the United Kingdom actually represent the same interests as the packing plants in Argentina. Official policy and domestic enterprise in Argentina have traditionally respected the arrangements made by the foreign interests that control trade in meat.

ture, it blocked the best avenue open to Argentina to participate in the international division of labor and the expansion of world trade: the manufacture and export of industrial commodities.

Foreign capital

Various measures were adopted after 1950 to attract long-term foreign capital. These measures usually consisted in allowing the free entry (without import duties or exchange restrictions) of machinery and equipment and other materials related to specific capital investment; another means was to free the transfer abroad of profits and interest; and yet another was to guarantee recovery of the investment in case of nationalization. At the same time, a "favorable climate" for long-term foreign capital was supposed to be created through an over-all policy aimed at reducing government intervention in the economy and stabilizing the balance of payments and the price level.

These measures had very little success. From 1951 to 1961, the average annual net inflow of private long-term capital was 95 million dollars. During 1958–1961, the average rose to above 160 million dollars per year.[11] These figures are appreciably lower than those for several periods of the primary-exports stage. For instance, in 1910–1914, the average annual net inflow of foreign capital was 850 million dollars at present-day value. From 1900 to 1930, the annual average was close to 400 million dollars. If account is taken of the increase in population, in the volume of output, and in capital formation, it becomes apparent that after 1950 the inflow of long-term foreign private capital was only a fraction of what it had been before 1930.

Not only has the absolute and relative importance of the foreign-capital inflow declined, but the composition of the inflow has changed. Whereas in 1930, 21 percent of all foreign capital in Argentina was in public issues and 40 percent was in social overhead capital, chiefly railroads, since 1950 foreign investment has been

---

[11] Most of the foreign capital investment was in the automobile industry and in petroleum production, both of which offered exceptional opportunities that owed little to over-all policy. As a matter of fact, a good part of the investment in petroleum took place before the adoption of the stabilization plan in January, 1959.

concentrated almost exclusively in industries offering special advantages to foreign investment. Outstanding examples are recent investments in the automobile industry and in petroleum production. Thus, foreign private capital has ceased to be a significant source of funds for public investment and for the growth of social overhead capital.

The trends in the inflow of foreign capital are typical of the changes in international capital movements after 1930. As we have already seen in chapter 13, since the great depression long-term foreign private capital has gone mainly into the exploitation of natural resources, such as petroleum and nonferrous metals in strong demand abroad, and into industrial activities with a sizable and rapidly expanding domestic market. Favorable legal and administrative conditions are not enough; the general economy must be attractive to capital inflow. In the light of Argentina's economic stagnation after 1948, no amount of official measures could have induced foreign investment on a large scale.

On the other hand, Argentina did not make a serious effort to take advantage of the greater volume of international public funds provided by international agencies and by developed countries, principally the United States, after 1950. It thereby neglected the opportunity of obtaining precisely those external resources most suitable for financing infrastructure investment. The bias in favor of long-term foreign private capital restricted the actual flow of international and foreign public funds, which since World War II have been the main component of international capital movements.

In any case, the policy drawn up was basically wrong because capital formation in Argentina today is dependent on the proper utilization of the country's own resources and only marginally on the inflow of foreign capital. The essential reason for the disinvestment and stagnation after 1948 was the failure to formulate a development policy that would have systematically channeled domestic investment into the key sectors of the national economy. The stress placed on the inflow of foreign capital dates back to the country's experience in the primary-exports stage, which is no longer relevant to present-day conditions. By withdrawing from active participation in development, the state contributed to the country's stagnation and in the final analysis made the Argentine economy less attractive to foreign private funds.

The Sources of Inflationary Pressure

In order to discuss the anti-inflationary policies followed since 1950 and to evaluate their results, it is necessary first to define the nature of Argentina's inflationary process. This will be done by using the "structuralist" approach, which permits a methodical identification of the underlying causes of inflation.[12] In Argentina, there are three types of inflationary pressures: basic inflationary pressures, exogenous inflationary pressures, and propagation mechanisms.

Basic inflationary pressures

These originate in the inability of supply to adjust to increases in aggregate demand and to changes in the composition of demand. Such increases and changes, far from stimulating an expansion in supply, bring about a rise in the general price levels. Supply rigidity may be due to growth limitations in one or more of the key sectors. In Argentina, the underlying inflationary pressures can be identified as follows:

(1) Rigidity in agricultural and livestock output. Because the rural sector does not react to price incentives, its efficiency remains low and its costs high. Thus, real prices of agricultural and livestock products can increase indefinitely without any corresponding increase in that sector's output.

(2) Rigidity in the capacity to import. Argentina's capacity to import has steadily contracted over the last few decades owing to the decline in the purchasing power of its farm exports as a result of trends in world demand and international prices, to the stagnation of its rural output, to the almost complete absence of alternative exports, and to the very reduced amount of its net capital inflow. This implies a decrease in imports of the raw materials, intermediate products, and machinery and equipment necessary for the development and expansion of the economy. Because of these conditions, higher demand for such commodities leads to a rise in their domestic prices instead of to an expansion in their real supply.

---

[12] See especially: Osvaldo Sunkel, "Inflation in Chile: An Unorthodox Approach," *International Economic Papers,* No. 10 (London, 1961), pp. 107–131. See also Horacio Flores de la Peña, *Los obstáculos al desarrollo enconómico* (Mexico City: Escuela de Economía, U.N.A.M., 1955).

(3) Insufficient development of basic industries. Given a decline in the capacity to import, the slow development of basic industries creates supply shortages of certain materials needed for domestic activities as well as the costly and complex machinery and equipment needed for manufacturing, agriculture, transportation, electric power generation, petroleum production, and so on. The expansion of domestic demand for these materials leads to higher prices rather than to an increase in real supply.

(4) Insufficient social overhead capital. The cumulative shortages in the infrastructure, principally in transportation and electric power generation, have already been noted. As these services become more and more inadequate, the production costs of enterprises requires them to go up to the extent that the latter cannot fully utilize their installed capacity. Therefore, rigidity in social overhead capital is an important element in the general rise in prices because it prevents the economy from expanding output of goods and services to meet growing demand.

(5) Structural origin of the budget deficit. Increased employment in the public sector, including the nationalized public utilities, is mainly due to the inability of the economy's basic sectors to absorb the growing labor force at ever-rising levels of productivity. But higher employment in the public sector is to a large extent a waste of available factors of production, and has kept the economy inefficient and unable to respond to the stimulus of expanding demand through an increase in real output.

(6) Inefficient use of the available factors of production and the persistence of institutional rigidities. In the final analysis, rigidities in agricultural and livestock output, in the capacity to import, in the basic industries and in social overhead capital, as well as the excessive growth of employment in the public sector, are the result of the inefficient use of the available factors of production and of the persistence of institutional rigidities.[18] As already seen, in a country in transition from a primary-exports to an integrated in-

---

[18] In Sunkel's analysis, the distortions in the price system brought about by inflation are largely responsible for the inefficient use of available economic resources. These distortions in the price system and in the allocation of resources are part of the "cumulative inflationary pressures." In Argentina, such distortions have occurred as a result of inflation and have led to further inflationary pressures. But in the final analysis, insufficient capital formation and meager development of basic industries can be traced to the economic policy of the government.

dustrial economy, the public sector should channel investment into basic industries and eliminate institutional obstacles to development. Argentina's failure to formulate such a policy from the time it entered the stage of the nonintegrated industrial economy has been a major cause of its stagnation and of the inflationary process itself.

Exogenous inflationary pressures

In Argentina, these are directly linked to economic policy measures such as an increase in public expenditures and in the budget deficit, an expansion of the money supply, higher wage levels, and transfer of income to the rural sector from the rest of the economy. Each of these will be considered separately.[14]

(1) Autonomous increase in public expenditures. From the end of World War II to 1948, the national government followed a policy of increasing public expenditures. The budget deficit was financed by expanding the money supply. The inability of the economy to respond immediately to the sharp rise in money income led to rapid depletion of foreign-exchange reserves and to a sizable balance-of-payments deficit. As a consequence, the cost of living went up 98 percent between 1946 and 1949. The authorities decided to increase public expenditures in order to stimulate demand and to broaden the scope of government action, including nationalization of public utilities and other enterprises.

(2) Autonomous expansion of credit to the private sector. After 1946, the monetary authorities followed a deliberate policy of expanding credit to the private sector in order to encourage economic development, particularly industrial growth.

(3) General rise in wage levels. The social objective of the Perón regime between 1946 and 1949 was a continuous increase in money wages, and this was accomplished by government decree. Furthermore, collective wage contracts were renegotiated annually. The wage policy naturally exerted an upward pressure on the level of costs as well as on effective demand.

---

[14] A distinction that will be examined later should be made between exogenous inflationary pressures and propagation mechanisms. The former are autonomous in the sense that they originate in economic policy decisions that are not the inevitable result of other inflationary forces, whereas propagation mechanisms merely transmit inflationary impulses originating in other points of the system.

As a result of the expansionist policy followed in the early years of the Perón regime, prices soared, foreign-exchange reserves shrank, and the trade deficit grew steadily. After 1948, this policy was revised and measures adopted expressing ideas that still govern economic policy. Anti-inflationary measures were accompanied by an improvement in the relative prices of agricultural and livestock products aimed at stimulating output of the farms. The consequent transfer of income from the rest of the economy to the rural sector has been almost the only exogenous inflationary pressure present since 1948.[15]

(4) Transfer of income to the rural sector. In his excellent study of the Argentine inflation, Julio Olivera analyzes this problem. He writes: "the correlation between relative prices of agricultural products and the general level of prices during the 1950–1960 decade can be seen from the available statistics . . . changes in farm prices relative to those of industry correspond exactly to the speeding up or slowing down of the rate of general price increase." [16] This correlation can be explained by the resistance of urban sectors to the loss of real income implied in the transfer of income to the rural sector. Workers are able to resist, but not to void, such income losses through their unions, which coordinate their efforts in central labor federations. Because of the concentration of ownership in industry, manufacturers were able not only to shift wage increases onto sales prices but also to protect their profit margins. Therefore, any attempt to modify the structure of output through price incentives to the rural sector had to cope with the opposition of the urban sectors plus two other circumstances pointed out by Olivera. First, because of the rigidity of its output, the rural sector was unable to respond to the stimulus of better prices and, given the policy of the time, received new transfers of income at the expense of industry and the services whenever its initial advantage diminished. Second, because per capita product did not increase, any loss of income by the urban sectors was absolute rather than merely relative within a general increase for all sectors. Stagnation made it more difficult to adjust the structure of output, and the income-

---

[15] There are some exceptions to this general statement, for example, the brief financial expansion that followed adoption of the second five-year plan in 1952 as well as the general wage increase ordered in 1958.

[16] Julio Olivera, "El caso de la Argentina" in "Inflación y desarrollo" (Santiago, Chile: ECLA, 1962). Unpublished paper.

transfer policy constantly pushed up the general price level. From 1958 to 1962,[17] when this policy was at its height, the cost of living rose 322.6 percent.

The propagation mechanisms

Although they do not play an autonomous role in the inflationary process, they do transmit inflationary impulses from other points in the system. In Argentina, inflationary pressures are propagated by three means: wages, insufficient public revenues, and devaluation.

(1) Wages. In the face of rising costs, workers try to maintain their real incomes by demanding higher wages. Their effectiveness depends on the strength of their labor unions, which in Argentina are highly organized. Such wage increases, however, are entirely induced by inflation originating in other points of the system, as is shown by the fall in real wages and the declining share of labor in national income after 1956.

(2) Public sector deficit. Higher prices require an expansion of public expenditures; but fiscal revenues tend to lag behind such expenditures, and the gap is progressively widened. The principal reasons for the public sector deficit are tax evasion and the fixing of public utility rates below operating costs. These problems are aggravated by inflationary pressures from other points of the system, and they feed the propagation mechanisms.

(3) Devaluation. Inflationary pressures bring about an increasing imbalance between the country's capacity to import and the demand for imports. Under a freely fluctuating exchange rate, adjustment takes place through devaluation. Devaluation of the peso raises the prices of imports and, consequently, costs in industries using such imports. Furthermore, each devaluation implies a new transfer of income to the export sector, which is the agricultural and livestock sector, and this in turn leads to further exogenous inflationary pressure, as described above.[18]

---

[17] As of August, 1962.

[18] Thanks to stabilization credits obtained abroad at the beginning of 1959, the central bank was able to support the peso on the exchange market. Continued inflationary pressures arising from the devaluation of January, 1959, and the operation of propagation mechanisms, rapidly depleted exchange reserves and brought about a new devaluation in April, 1962. The net result of the stabilization effort was an increase in Argentina's external indebtedness and a reinforcement of the inflationary pressures.

Evaluation of the Stabilization Policy[19]

The measures adopted after 1950 to contain inflation were of three types: reduction of public expenditures and elimination of the budget deficit; restriction of credit to the private sector; and limitations on wage increases.

After the policy of autonomous expansion of public expenditures was abandoned in the second half of 1948, the budget deficit continued because of difficulties in lowering employment in the government and in improving the finances of public utilities.[20]

The "easy money" policy was revised toward the end of 1948 and monetary authorities assumed a passive attitude permitting credit to private borrowers to the extent that the level of costs and prices required an increase in the means of payment available to the private sector.

In 1949 the policy of promoting general wage increases was also discarded, and steps were taken to maintain labor contracts in force and to ensure an "equilibrium" between prices and wages. According to the official interpretation, the main source of inflation was the pressure of wages on costs, so that equilibrium implied limiting wage increases even though the rise in prices reduced real wages. Later on, the authorities tried to divide and weaken the labor movement in order to diminish the latter's bargaining power, and monetary measures were applied to discourage business enterprises from granting wage increases. For example, in 1959 it was announced that loans would not be granted to finance payment of higher wages.

All these measures combined to contain the exogenous inflationary pressures that had been at work from 1946 to 1948. In subsequent years, especially after adoption of the stabilization plan in January, 1959, the anti-inflationary policy was applied to the propagation mechanisms, and attempts were made to reduce the budget deficit drastically and to curtail both credit to the private sector

---

[19] Data used in this section and the following one have been taken from the monthly bulletins of the National Statistical Bureau and the Central Bank of Argentina.

[20] In 1952, when the second five-year plan of the Perón regime went into effect, there was a new autonomous increase in public expenditures. This exception does not modify the general statement made in the text. The losses in grain marketing were eliminated as soon as management of the export trade was restored to the private sector in 1955.

and wage increases. As long as the measures were applied to exogenous pressures, they inhibited increases in public expenditures, credit, and wages. But the money supply continued to expand in order to meet the higher price level, which had its origin in other points in the economic system. After 1959, monetary policy became even more restrictive, severely limiting public as well as private credit. The steady ascent of the general price level meant that during the second quarter of 1962 it became impossible to meet payments in the public sector and in many private businesses. Wages were not as strictly controlled, owing to the strong pressure of labor unions; however, the recent rise in unemployment has tended to weaken union influence.[21]

At the same time that policies were followed to eliminate exogenous inflationary pressures and restrain propagation mechanisms another source of exogenous inflationary pressure, the transfer of income to the agricultural and livestock sector, was created; and this has been the most important inflationary pressure since 1950. It has contributed to inflation much more than the autonomous increases in public expenditures, credit to the private sector, and general wages. From 1946 to 1949, when the government's monetary, fiscal, and wage policy was clearly expansive, the cost of living went up 98 percent, whereas from 1958 to 1962, when the government carried out a stabilization program that coincided with a sizable transfer of income to the rural sector, the cost of living rose 323 percent.

Inasmuch as the anti-inflationary policy involved transfers of income to the rural sector, the inflationary process was bound to continue and to worsen. But even had there not existed this contradiction in policy, the anti-inflationary measures would have had little success because they were only directed at the exogenous pressures and propagation mechanisms and did not attack the basic inflationary pressures, which were the rigidities of the economic structure. Actually, by restricting credit indiscriminately to both the

---

[21] In 1961, because of the lifting of credit restrictions on the private sector and the purchase of public debt issues by the central bank, there was a slight recovery from the 1959–1960 contraction induced by the stabilization plan. Therefore, a rise in the level of employment was actually made possible by suspending application of the restraints laid down by the stabilization plan. On the other hand, there was a large balance-of-payments deficit of 470 million dollars, due to the maintenance of a liberal exchange system and the continued upward pressure of inflation on the demand for imports.

public and private sectors, the policy followed has intensified the rigidities of the economic system. With the present allocation of resources frozen, no increase has been possible in investment in critical points in the system—namely, basic industries and social overhead capital. In addition, by not taking into account problems of land tenure, the policy has strengthened institutional rigidities in the rural sector.

The behavior of public investment is a good example of how an indiscriminate policy of restriction of public expenditures can have an adverse effect on allocation of resources. In drastically reducing the financing available to the public sector, it was easier to suspend public works than to dismiss an equivalent number of employees. Consequently, in practice, the policy led to a new distortion in public expenditures to the detriment of precisely the type of expenditure—properly channeled and expanded—needed to overcome the stagnation of the economy.

So radical a policy of restriction of the money supply has created serious short-term problems. The budget deficit has not been eliminated because its origin is structural and because large-scale dismissal of government and public utilities employees is not possible. On the other hand, the rise in prices has forced the government to raise the wages and salaries of its personnel, although not proportionately. Lowered domestic activity and a decline in the taxable capacity of the population have hurt fiscal revenues.[22] During the first half of the 1961 fiscal year, the deficit was three times that of the previous three fiscal years. Although the restriction of credit to finance the cash needs of the government has failed to reduce the deficit, it has compelled the government to suspend payments and to increase its floating debt, because the treasury has not been able to meet its liabilities to personnel and suppliers.

The delay in wage and salary payments to public employees, the lag in payments to suppliers, the payment of part of the public sector's debt with bond issues that are sold on the market below par, all have decreased the purchasing power of important segments of the population. Furthermore, the restriction of credit to the private sector while general costs and prices are rising has imposed

---

[22] During the first half of the fiscal year—from November, 1961, to April, 1962—the government's tax revenues were 40 percent below projected revenues and were also lower than those of the previous fiscal year in spite of an increase in prices.

severe hardships on private business enterprises, particularly in industry. The fall in the population's purchasing power, due to the reduction in real wages and the declining share of labor in domestic income, has also meant a sharp contraction in effective demand.[23] Thus, a cumulative process of unemployment of labor and under-utilization of installed capacity is underway, especially in manu-facturing.

In spite of this real deflation, the peso has continued to devalue as a result of the steady transfer of income to the rural sector, which is caused by the devaluation itself and by the increase in the domestic prices of agricultural and livestock prices. The devalua-tion, then, becomes a self-generating inflationary mechanism.

Nevertheless, the prices of domestically manufactured products do not go down because, as Olivera points out, in activities where there is a great deal of concentration, "the adjustment to contrac-tion in demand comes about through the volume of output rather than through prices." In the final analysis, the reduction in employ-ment and in the utilization of capacity means that the economy be-comes less efficient and produces fewer goods and services, which is in turn a new source of disequilibrium.

As a specific result of the policy followed, the cost of living in-creased 1700 percent between 1950 and August, 1962. The peso was devalued more than twenty times during that period. The infla-tionary process has become more acute since the stabilization plan was adopted in January, 1959. From 1958 to August, 1962, the cost of living shot up 323 percent, and further devaluations of the peso occurred; the exchange rate went from 28 pesos to 140 pesos per dollar.[24] All the inflationary pressures that the authorities have been trying to eliminate since 1950 still exist, only they are deeper and more serious.

Furthermore, Argentina has incurred considerable foreign in-debtedness in the last few years, especially short- and medium-term, amounting to more than 2 billion dollars. The service of this debt is so large that in 1964, if the present level of exports continues, debt service will absorb 40 percent of the country's foreign-

---

[23] From 1958 to 1959, as a result of the decline in domestic net income com-bined with the decrease in labor's share in total income, the aggregate wage bill went down almost 20 percent, in real terms.

[24] Effective rate of exchange. See International Monetary Fund, *International Financial Statistics*, 1958.

exchange earnings. This heavy indebtedness is proof that the policy followed has been incapable of adjusting Argentina's imports to its effective capacity to import. Insofar as it has not helped to strengthen the economic structure and to diversify and expand Argentina's exports, external credit lessens the likelihood that in the near future the economic structure can be readjusted and an effective policy of economic development carried out.

The acceleration of inflation, the sharp devaluations of the peso, and the growing disequilibrium in the balance of payments are the logical consequences of a policy that has ignored the underlying causes of inflation in Argentina. The policy followed since 1950 has assumed that inflationary pressures originated exclusively in increases in public expenditures, credit to the private sector, and wages. It has not recognized that the inflationary process and the stagnation of the economy have the same source: the insufficient integration of the structure of output; the meager development of basic industries and social overhead capital; and the persistence of institutional obstacles in the rural sector.[25]

Recent experience shows that inflation has caused significant changes in the distribution of national income between the different social sectors. At the beginning of the Perón regime, there was a steady rise in the share of the government, of urban activities, and of the workers. After 1950, and especially in more recent years, inflation radically altered that trend. Now, the agricultural sector and the entrepreneurial class are augmenting their shares. The stagnation in output per inhabitant during the last fifteen years has heightened the conflict between the different social sectors trying to protect or increase their share of the domestic income. This struggle basically involves the allocation of real resources among the various activities. Argentina's stagnation is due mainly to the lack of investment in strategic sectors of the economy, the growing lag in the development of the interior, and the prevalence of a land-tenure system that impedes agricultural growth. Inflation, far from helping to solve these problems of the Argentine economy, has aggravated them. Thus, an anti-inflationary policy must also take into account the reallocation of real resources and economic development; otherwise, it will only worsen the conditions of stagnation and intensify the inflationary process itself.

---

[25] In addition to the effects of the exogenous inflationary pressures already described.

The Redistribution of Income

The third and last objective of the economic policy followed after 1955 was to reduce the share of labor in the national income in order to free resources for investment. The transfer of income to the rural sector and the impact of a number of official measures designed to keep wage demands down in the face of rising prices have been, since 1950, the principal determinants of the share of labor in net domestic income. As indicated before, this share reached a maximum of 56.9 percent in 1952 and declined to 52 percent in 1958. But from 1958 to 1959, the share fell precipitously from 53.1 percent to 45.8 percent, and in 1960 it was still only 45.9 percent. Inasmuch as net domestic income declined more than 5 percent in 1959, the total wage bill decreased almost 20 percent in that year.

Furthermore, there was a sharp reduction in real wage rates. In 1955 they were 23 percent below the 1948 level. Real wages have continued their downward trend and at present are 40 percent below the 1948 average. The contraction was especially severe from 1958 on. In 1959 wages dropped 20 percent, and they have not recovered this loss.

In his study, Dr. Olivera brings up an interesting point in connection with the remuneration of labor and capital. He states that in some branches of production there has been a fall in real wages per man-hour; on the other hand, the income of capital and entrepreneurs (profits, interest, and rent) maintained a comparatively stable ratio to the stock of capital in the period 1949–1959. In other words, whereas the earnings of capital remained constant and even increased toward the end of the period, the remuneration of labor plummeted. To quote Olivera: "Relative factor prices moved against labor during the last decade." The remuneration of capital undoubtedly was affected by the higher income accruing to capital invested in agriculture and livestock.

The ratio of gross domestic investment to product in a five-year period when labor's share of income was rising may be compared with a more recent period when the opposite occurred. It will be seen that between 1947 and 1952, 23.7 percent of gross product went into capital investment (including replacement of existing capital) and that between 1958 and 1961 the percentage declined slightly to 23.3. Irrespective of the allocation of capital between the different sectors of activity, there is no evidence of any correlation, unless an inverse one,[26] between the share of capital in national income and the proportion of gross product used for capital formation.

Continued Stagnation and the Present Crisis

The policy followed since 1950 to overcome the stagnation of the Argentine economy has not been successful. Per capita product has not gone up and during most of the period has remained below the 1948 level. The basic structural problems of the economy, far from being solved, have gradually become worse. Recently, a more restrictive monetary policy and the uninterrupted transfer of income to the rural sector through devaluation have brought about an increasing underutilization of installed capacity and unemployment of labor and have worsened the living conditions of the urban masses.

At the same time that real deflation takes place through growing unemployment of productive factors, the inflationary process is speeded up by continued depreciation of the peso and transfer of income to the export sector. In fact, the worst of all possible worlds has been reached: real deflation with monetary inflation.

The Argentine experience is a logical consequence of a policy that has disregarded the prevailing conditions of the economic and social reality of the country and of the international economy. Before concluding the analysis of the stage of a nonintegrated industrial economy, those conditions may be briefly recapitulated.

---

[26] This has been pointed out by Dr. Antonio Caffiero in *Cinco años después* . . . (Buenos Aires, 1961). In any event, further empirical research on this question is indicated. Investment is conditioned not only by the level of savings but by aggregate demand. To the extent that a decline in the share of labor in income constricts demand, there are fewer incentives for private investment. On the other hand, it should be ascertained to what degree the increased savings that result from a regressive redistribution of income remain in sectors where the propensity to invest is high and where investment is channeled into high-priority activities of development. In Argentina, rural entrepreneurs, especially large landowners, do not seem to respond to a suitable orientation of investment. An analysis is also needed of the evolution of the prices of investment goods relative to the prices of other goods and services. Even though the ratio of investment to net domestic income may rise, the higher prices of investment goods may act as a deterrent to actual investment. On the latter point, see Rolf Hayn, "Capital Formation and Argentina's Price-Cost Structure, 1935–1958" in *Review of Economics and Statistics,* August, 1962.

First, since 1930 the demand for agricultural and livestock products has been at a standstill, partly because of the trend in the demand for these commodities and partly because of the protectionist policies of the countries that are traditional importers of primary products, particularly Western Europe and countries like the United States that are competitors of Argentina. Second, the international flow of private capital has shifted to investments totally different from those it entered before the great depression; foreign capital from public sources is replacing private capital in certain sectors, especially in social overhead investment. Third, the land-tenure system sterilizes price incentives to the agricultural and livestock sector and limits the possibility of expanding farm output through higher yields. Fourth, the increase in employment in the public sector is mainly the result of the inability of the basic sectors of the economy to absorb the increment in the labor force. As long as alternative occupations do not exist, the public payroll cannot be cut without depressing the level of employment and domestic income. Fifth, inflationary pressures actually stem from the inability of the economy to expand the supply of goods and services in order to meet rising demand; and monetary expansion, in conditions of full employment, may accentuate this structural rigidity. Sixth, the transfer of income to the rural sector as an incentive to agricultural output leads to strong inflationary pressures that cannot be alleviated by merely limiting the money supply and wages. Seventh, the economic system cannot automatically make the necessary adjustments for steady growth.

The contradiction between the policy described above and the prevailing objective conditions proves the impossibility of regressing to the primary-exports economy.

It can easily be understood that in a country in which 75 percent of the population lives in urban areas and in which almost all of the manpower is employed in industries and services, this type of readjustment of the structure of output would inevitably run into serious difficulties. Urban population will not return to the countryside merely because of a worsening of living conditions; not only is the rural sector structurally incapable of absorbing a higher share of the labor force, but also it is well known that population that migrates to the cities never returns to rural activities.

The solution to the long stagnation of the Argentine economy is not to be found in a return to the old economic model, but in the integration of the various economic sectors by means of the development of basic industries, the expansion of social overhead capital, and a correction of the geographical imbalance in the distribution of output. In fact, any economic policy must be judged by its effects on the process of integrating the economic structure of Argentina.

PART V

THE PRECONDITIONS OF AN INTEGRATED INDUSTRIAL ECONOMY

As seen in the preceding chapters, Argentina has been stagnating since the late 1940's. Gross per capita product has only recently regained its 1948 level, after having been actually below it in the intervening years. The living conditions of the urban masses, who make up 75 percent of the total population, have declined. Real wages are today 40 percent below those of 1948, and there has been a steady deterioration in transportation, services, housing, sanitary works, education, and public health, particularly in Greater Buenos Aires where 35 percent of the population lives. The geographical imbalance in Argentine development has become more acute in recent years, and the interior regions have fallen far behind the rest of the country. Furthermore, economic disequilibrium and social tensions have heightened, and, even worse, large segments of the population feel that their country offers them no clear course of action or common purpose.

This experience sharply contrasts with that of rapidly developing countries where social relationships and prevailing patterns of culture continuously evolve. For example, in the United States and Western Europe, technological progress and constant improvement in living standards and cultural levels broaden the horizons of society as a whole and of the various groups within it. In fact, social mobility and the prospect of achieving a better individual and collective future are rooted in the structural changes in output and in the opening up of new and better paid opportunities. In this sense, technological progress and capital accumulation, inasmuch as they are the prime movers of economic development, are also the basic factors in social mobility and in steady improvement in the material and cultural conditions of modern society.

Contemporary observers have been puzzled by the fact that Argentina's relatively diversified social and economic structure more closely resembles that of the developed dynamic countries than that of the underdeveloped stagnant countries. Its agricultural and live-stock activities, which are completely integrated into the market and have reached a level of productivity approaching the country's over-all level, only employ one fourth of the labor force.[1] Even after

---

[1] Unlike Argentina, the underdeveloped economies in general and the stagnant ones in particular are characterized by a concentration of population in agricultural and livestock activity. This population lives outside the market economy

fifteen years of stagnation, per capita income in Argentina is still almost twice the average for Latin America. Moreover, its cultural levels and patterns of social behavior belong to a modern society. Finally, for many decades Argentina has had the institutional, political, and administrative machinery necessary for achieving reasonable fluidity in the use of available resources and for channeling those resources into a dynamic development process.

The above conditions have led some observers, such as Professor W. W. Rostow, to place Argentina among the countries having autonomous development possibilities. Rostow, in fact, considers that Argentina has already "taken off" into sustained growth.[2] However, with the exception of special cases like Haiti, Bolivia, and Paraguay, Argentina is the only country in Latin America to have remained at a standstill during the last fifteen years. From a general, theoretical point of view, the Argentine experience is interesting as an outstanding case of the stagnation of a nonintegrated industrial structure conditioned by a breakdown in the country's capacity to import.

It has been argued in this study that the cause of stagnation has been essentially the mistaken economic policy followed since 1930, when Argentina entered a new stage of development.[3] Neither the representatives of the great landed interests that have traditionally governed the country nor the social sectors that came into power during the Perón regime had a clear understanding of the profound currents affecting the economic and social development of Argentina. The first group operated and continues to operate on the assumption that the bases of the primary-exports economy must be restored. The Perón forces limited their actions to the redistribution

---

and barely produces enough for its own subsistence. Furthermore, productivity in that kind of rural pursuit is several times lower than that of the economy as a whole and much lower than that of the more advanced sectors such as manufacturing.

[2] W. W. Rostow, *The Stages of Economic Growth* (Cambridge, England: Cambridge University Press, 1960).

[3] Of course, Argentina's economic structure could have been integrated gradually before 1930, and this, together with a change in the land-tenure system, would have enabled the country to have developed much more rapidly than it did during the primary-exports stage. But the exceptional conditions of the world market before 1930 and the unlimited expanse of land in the Pampa region made it possible for Argentina to grow anyway. After 1930, when both factors disappeared, development at whatever rate became directly dependent on the conduct of economic policy.

of income in favor of the masses and to the nationalization of certain investments like the railroads, symbolizing foreign influence.

Neither group was able to grasp the new realities of Argentine development and thereby shape a suitable economic policy. The primary-exports experience, favored by the exceptional conditions of the Pampa land, gave rise to the conviction that the main impulse of development was external and capable by itself of generating development. Therefore, as the income level rose, Argentina concerned itself with how to distribute those increments of income and not how to guide the forces responsible for it. This explains why monetary policy, as the principal means of redistributing income, has always been so important in the evolution of the country's economy. It also explains why the representatives of the traditional interests have recently made such a determined effort to bring monetary policy back into prominence.

Not even the concentration of rural property, which excluded 90 percent of the population engaged in agricultural activities from landownership, created the pressures needed to alter the tenure system carried over from the transition stage. Because of the abundance of land in relation to rural population and to the early diversification of output, the rural areas of Argentina did not breed social tensions that would have forced a change.

The history of a development conditioned from abroad accounts for the intrinsic weakness of the policy followed after 1930 and especially after 1950, when the nonintegrated industrial economy reached a definite crisis. Unable to understand that the driving force of development in the primary-exports stage no longer existed after 1930, Argentina did not frame an economic policy that would exploit the country's many potentials and lead to its sustained growth. Thus, even today, those in power continue to deal with the more conspicuous aspects of stagnation, such as the budget deficit, inflation, and external disequilibrium, rather than with its underlying causes.[4]

---

[4] Here a few remarks are relevant concerning the experience after 1958. During the administration of President Frondizi—from his inauguration in May, 1958, until he was deposed in March, 1962—the government directed attention to some of the basic obstacles to development and specified the fields in which production would have to be expanded in order to integrate the country's economic structure. The increase in petroleum production since 1958 is a direct result of this concern.

At the provincial level, there were also some interesting experiences after

Argentina can no longer operate in the belief that it will magically receive dynamic impulses from outside. It has to recognize that in reality the solutions lie in a correct interpretation of the problems and in adoption of the measures required to overcome them. It is no longer enough to utilize the analytical tools available for study of the short-term and obvious problems. The economist must employ the deeper, concealed causes of the present stagnation in the Argentine economy and clearly express his opinion, whatever it may be, on the source of these problems and how they should be solved. My own tentative interpretation of the process of growth in the Argentine economy would not be complete or sincere if I did not try to define the origin of the present situation and to set forth the preconditions that would enable Argentina to achieve sustained growth thereby giving its people their long-delayed share in the fruits of progress. They are the preconditions of an integrated industrial economy because in the modern world sustained growth can only be achieved through the assimilation of technological and scientific progress and a steady expansion of productive capital throughout the economic and social system.

Orientation of Economic Policy

A detailed analysis of the various aspects of an economic policy to promote growth is beyond the scope of this study. However, some of the basic concepts and provisions of such a policy will be described.

1958. For instance, in the province of Buenos Aires, where the author had occasion to participate directly in the conduct of economic policy, a program was undertaken based on expansion of social overhead capital (roads and electric energy), a change in the land-tenure system, the promotion of regional development (establishment of autonomous development agencies for the underdeveloped parts of the province such as Lower Río Colorado and the Paraná Delta), and the expansion of social services (education, public health, housing). The provincial program was subsidized under the fiscal reform adopted in 1958, and it was coordinated through the Economic Planning Board of the province of Buenos Aires, the first of its kind in Argentina. The latter was in charge of carrying out basic research on the economic and social structure of the province and of formulating the development plan. In order to coordinate this program with development in other provinces and the country as a whole, the Federal Investment Council was set up at the request of the province of Buenos Aires, and this body is now a powerful tool for the programming of development.

A policy of development and planning

In order to integrate Argentina's economic structure, it is necessary to expand basic industry, to further investment in social overhead capital, to correct regional imbalances, and to overcome institutional rigidities, particularly the land-tenure system, in the economy. This is what is meant by a direct policy of development.

A development program permits the adoption of mutually consistent growth targets, the anticipation of future bottlenecks and the elimination of existing ones, and the coordination of all policy measures that affect economic development. Given the prevailing conditions and the specified objectives, programming is aimed at a more efficient utilization of available resources and the attainment of a higher growth rate. Planning is a fundamental tool of a development policy. Although it does not by itself determine the extent of government intervention in the economic system, it does coordinate the activities of the public sector and gears them to the activities of the private sector within a framework of dynamic growth. Argentina needs to make use of this basic instrument of the government in order to facilitate transition from the present stage into that of an integrated industrial economy.

Structural readjustment with full employment

Integration of the Argentine economy implies that some sectors, even within industry, will grow more swiftly than others and that during this period of readjustment their relative importance will shift. A change in the structure of output and employment is one of the features of development, and it becomes more pronounced as the economy advances and accelerates its rate of growth. Once Argentina achieves sustained growth, such readjustments will take place naturally. Now, however, it is necessary to force the pace of structural integration in order to overcome the present stagnation.

Structural readjustment does not mean that unemployment is inevitable in the lagging sectors of the economy.[5] A transfer of un-

---

[5] This is the essential difference between the type of readjustment necessary to integrate the economic structure and the readjustment to return the economy to the primary-exports stage. In the latter policy, industrial unemployment and lower living standards for the urban masses are necessary conditions to induce manpower to go to the countryside and to channel investment into agricultural and livestock production.

productive manpower employed in the government and certain public utilities to dynamic and essential activities can be accomplished by means of a gradual process of incentives provided by the expansion of the latter activities. In other words, if the Argentine economy is to undergo a structural adjustment with a minimum of social and political tension, there must be full employment of installed productive capacity and of the labor force. A sound development policy will ensure that industries are converted to basic manufacturing, that investment in the latter is promoted, and that capital formation takes place in the infrastructure. The transfer of unproductively employed manpower to essential activities will thus be a direct consequence of the development policy and of the expansion of employment opportunities.

Fiscal policy and the public sector

In the readjustment process, fiscal policy is a key instrument in determining Argentina's ability to finance investment in transportation, energy, communication, and other services indispensable to development. The public sector includes not only social overhead capital but also enterprises that need to be assigned to that sector because their development requires exceptional conditions. Therefore, the fiscal and price policies of public enterprises contribute to development by helping to reallocate resources to essential activities.

Monetary policy as a tool of development

Within a framework of dynamic growth, monetary policy is only one of the tools of a development program. There are other means of channeling resources into activities requiring expansion. For example, an electric power development plan can be financed by raising rates and thereby increasing the profit margin of the utilities, by reallocating budget resources that have been collected through taxes, by obtaining internal and external credits, by long-term borrowing from the banking system, and so on. Price and exchange stability in a free market is not an objective per se of economic policy. The sole objective is to achieve an adequate rate of growth and an equitable distribution of income among the various social groups. When there is runaway inflation, the process of readjustment is impeded because price distortions lead to an undesirable allocation of resources; on the other hand, stability facilitates an economic policy aimed at channeling increasing resources into the development of basic sectors. But an expanding money supply is only one of a series of circumstances that determine the extent of stability possible under a development program. An attempt to do away with inflation by restricting the money supply, while at the same time other exogenous inflationary pressures are introduced and the basic inflationary pressures still operate, may result—as in Argentina—in what we have called the worst of all possible worlds: real deflation with monetary inflation.

A precondition for an effective development policy is the abandonment of a purely monetary approach to Argentine inflation. Controlling inflation by an indiscriminate reduction of credit to both the public and private sectors means hardening the present economic structure to the detriment of precisely those activities which, although essential to development, are least likely to receive available financial resources. If this policy is accompanied by the appearance of a strong exogenous inflationary pressure such as transfer of income away from industrial and urban activity, monetary measures for stability generate not only serious social and economic tensions but further distortions in the utilization of resources and, consequently, postponement of expansion in key sectors.

In Argentina, the price level and exchange rate cannot be effectively stabilized without first overcoming the basic inflationary pressures that originate in the structural rigidities also responsible for the development paralysis. Once full employment of manpower and full utilization of productive capacity are achieved, monetary policy has a legitimate function in preventing an unbridled expansion of domestic demand. A reckless issuing of money, as occurred between 1946 and 1949, is actually a way of avoiding structural readjustment and retarding the growth of key sectors of the economy. Thus, a policy of stability cannot be separated from a policy of development.

The foundations of agricultural development

The role of the agricultural and livestock sector has changed since the primary-exports stage when it was the dynamic sector and the agent for transmitting growth impulses from abroad. The agricultural and livestock sector is now part of the national economy, and its future development is contingent on the growth of that economy. This is because its market will continue to be largely internal and because most of the materials, consumer goods, and machinery and equipment it uses will continue to be supplied domestically. Future growth of the agricultural and livestock sector is closely linked to an expansion of the national market and to a rise in the levels of efficiency throughout the economy, especially in industry. Although farm exports will continue to be significant in the growth of the rural sector and of the country as a whole, the stage of primary exports is definitely over. An increase in agricultural and livestock exports will depend not only on greater diversification of farm output and on the production of exportable surpluses but also on elimination of the monopoly combinations that are strangling the growth possibilities of certain exports, particularly frozen meat.

Future agricultural development is related also to other basic factors—mainly expansion of social overhead capital, revision of the land-tenure system, and diffusion of rural technology. The first factor is important because efficiency in the rural sector depends largely on infrastructure services, particularly transport and energy. The second factor is important because the system of tenant farming, together with huge, undercultivated properties, imposes severe limitations on yields per hectare, as has been shown elsewhere in this book. The diffusion of modern technology through active extension work completes the series of measures that agrarian policy should adopt in order to increase agricultural output, especially in the Pampa region.

Argentina's changing economic relations

Argentina's dependence on exports of agricultural and livestock products has meant a decline in its share in world trade and in the international division of labor. The decrease in exportable surpluses, due to stagnation of output in the Pampa region, intensified a trend that, in view of the behavior of world trade in agricultural products, was inevitable. At the same time, the effect of technology on international relations at all levels, particularly in trade and finance, has continued to promote world integration very rapidly. It should be recalled that after World War II, world trade and international capital movements increased substantially.

Since the breakdown of the multilateral trade and payments system during the great depression, however, economic integration has been compartmental rather than universal. The principal division of the world economy is between two great social systems that coexist in the contemporary world. But within the Western world, subdivisions have been formed that permit a channeling and speeding up of the process of integration. The most notable case in recent times is the formation of the European Common Market and also the communities of interest established between the old metropolitan powers and their former colonies. This trend toward "compartmentalization" in the world economy is an obstacle, at least in the short run, to the integrating effect of technology on a really universal scale.

In spite of the above, there are signs that the barriers dividing the world economy will fall slowly but surely and open up broader horizons, conceivably with the continued coexistence of different social systems. The most significant result of the eventual universalization of the world economy will probably be general disarmament and the liberalization of vast resources that today are spent on arms and defense.[6] Within the framework of the new international situation created by disarmament, this freeing of resources will have a stunning impact on international economic relations. A large part of these resources will go to developing countries in Latin America, Asia, and Africa; and once the impossibility of war is accepted, these areas will become the most important sphere of activities and the chief concern of the great powers.

These possible trends in the world economy will undoubtedly influence Argentina's development. Active participation in the international division of labor and in the process of worldwide economic integration will benefit the country by permitting it to rapidly assimilate technological and scientific innovations and thereby raise its levels of efficiency and income. But if these prospects

---

[6] See the United Nations report, *Economic and Social Consequences of Disarmament* (United Nations, Sales No. 62.IX.1.), prepared by a group of experts. This report states that total world expenditures on armaments and defense is of the order of 120 billion dollars per year, which is about two thirds of the total annual production of all underdeveloped countries comprising nearly 70 percent of world population. The 120 billion dollars spent on armaments is also equal to total world exports, and to 8 to 9 percent of annual world output, and finally to one half of the world's annual capital formation.

are to be realized, Argentina must find a new approach that will revitalize its relations with the rest of the world.

In order to increase its exports, Argentina must diversify them by including increasing proportions of manufactured goods. This can only be achieved through development and through integration of the national economy. The policy followed since 1950 of trying *autonomously* to expand agricultural and livestock exports cannot counter the decline in exports and in the capacity to import, and it only postpones solution of the over-all problems of Argentine development. An increase in exports and in the capacity to import is not a prerequisite; rather, it will be a consequence of Argentina's emergence from stagnation. As the country integrates its economic structure and improves its efficiency, new export opportunities will arise in manufactures at the same time that agriculture will continue to develop and the export of agricultural products will increase and become more diversified. In turn, this expansion in exports and in import capacity will be a further stimulus to economic growth. This is a new approach to the problem posed by the bottleneck in the supply of imports, and it differs radically from the interpretation accepted since 1950. It also implies a possibility that profound changes may take place in economic policy.

In respect to the flow of foreign capital into Argentina, it should be remembered that most of the country's capital formation is carried out with domestic funds. In view of the conditions affecting international capital movements and taking into account the type of integrated development Argentina requires, the future role of foreign capital cannot be expected to approach even remotely the role it played during the primary-exports stage. Within the framework of development, however, it will be advisable to obtain the largest possible amount of external resources to supplement the domestic funds available for capital formation. Funds from public sources will be particularly needed in the present stage for a concerted effort to expand the amount of capital invested in transportation, communication, electric energy, and other infrastructure services.[7]

A country's ability to attract foreign private capital is dependent ultimately on the process of development itself. (An exception is traditional foreign investment in export products such as nonferrous

_____
[7] Subject, of course, to policy decisions that may be taken in the matter of external indebtedness within the framework of a development program.

metals and petroleum, which is negligible in Argentina). International capital flows since World War II show that private capital moves primarily toward the more advanced countries and toward those that are developing most rapidly. This fundamental condition cannot be altered simply by changing the regulations governing investment of foreign private capital. Therefore, any policy aimed at creating a "suitable climate" for foreign private capital by dismantling the instruments of state participation in the economic process and abandoning a policy of development is self-defeating. If these facts are understood, private foreign capital can play a useful role in capital formation within a development program to integrate and reinforce the economic structure.

Participation in the integration of Latin America

Although the economic formation of Argentina differs from that of other Latin American countries, particularly Brazil and Mexico, it is nonetheless part of the general Latin American context.[8] Like the rest of Latin America, Argentina is engaged in modifying and integrating its economic structure. There are well-defined bases for Latin American integration resulting from similar experiences and from cultural and historical affinities.

Regional integration offers immense possibilities for facilitating the growth of each country and of the region as a whole. The expansion of markets and the multiplicity of resources afforded by integration will help effect the necessary structural change within a much broader framework and with a more efficient utilization of available resources. Furthermore, regional integration is the immediate answer to the problem of stagnation brought about by the deterioration of trade in traditional exports.

Latin American integration is not inconsistent with national integration, especially in the larger countries, which are in a better position to achieve it. The more each country develops, the more prospects there will be of integration through joint enterprises.

---

[8] Historically, Argentina, like the rest of Latin America, became integrated into an expanding world market during the second half of the nineteenth century as a producer and exporter of primary products. Argentina evolved differently because of its particular complex of natural resources, which conditioned the manner in which external factors penetrated its economy and largely shaped its later economic and social development.

The strength of the European Common Market rests precisely on the high degree of national integration in the participating countries, and the weakness of the Latin American effort derives from the meager development in its countries.

The foregoing observation is of the greatest practical importance. Argentina and the other Latin American countries must not wait for regional integration before promoting their own development and changes in structure. They must advance as rapidly as possible within their own borders and at the same time support regional integration. More than trade liberalization, regional integration requires a common investment and development policy.[9] A basic condition for the development of the Latin American countries, individually and as a region, is active participation in the process of regional integration.

Role of Social Forces

The behavior of the various social groups is the final and fundamental determinant of a country's growth. In turn, material and cultural progress in these sectors results largely from economic development. Because labor and enterprise are the mainsprings of production, it is especially important to analyze their behavior. In fact, only if these sectors vigorously support a development policy, can an integrated industrial economy be created. And it can also be said that only if the other social sectors—including the armed forces, which are so influential in political, social, and economic life—cooperate, is it possible to alter the economic structure and lay the bases for sustained growth.

Role of labor organizations

In the last fifteen years, the labor movement has been significant in the economic and social development of Argentina. The level of organization attained by the movement is the logical consequence of the country s urbanization and of the high proportion of employment in manufacturing and services. Labor's gains are irreversible unless it is assumed that Argentina can regress to the primary-

---

[9] On this subject, see my article, "Remarks on Industrial Integration in Latin America" in *Política*, no. 24 (Caracas, Venezuela), January-March, 1963.

exports stage and to simpler and less concentrated social relations. However, the belief in some circles is that the labor movement is an obstacle to the country's progress.

In the dynamic and high-income economies of Western Europe and the United States, the labor movement, far from retarding growth, has historically been a strong stimulus to economic and social development. The constant effort of workers to obtain a larger share in the national income and to participate in the productivity increases generated by development has not only expanded the domestic market but has raised cultural and technical levels. This unremitting pressure has been one of the main forces behind the steady improvement of production methods and behind the accumulation of capital in the private sector.[10]

But the role of the labor movement in Argentina has been less positive. Economic stagnation and the limited prospects for the working population have forced the labor movement into a position where its sole concern has been to protect its real wages and to prevent its share of income from falling. As shown by the data on real wages from 1948 to 1962, this struggle has not been successful. Real wages declined 40 percent, and the share of labor in the national income dropped from 57 percent to 46 percent. Other social groups, particularly the powerful landowners of the Pampa region, have influenced monetary policy and have raised their own share in national income.

In spite of its strong bargaining position and political pressure,

---

[10] In the capitalist economy, private investment is one of the main determinants of aggregate demand, employment, and income. Together with public investment, it is also an important stimulus to economic development. The level of private investment is in turn conditioned by the demand for consumer goods (durables and nondurables, including housing); and the demand for consumer goods depends ultimately on the level of income of the population. Wages received by the working population are one of the chief components of the community's income and of expenditure and consumption and, consequently, one of the determinants of the level of private investment. Thus, the capitalist economy is governed by market forces. On the other hand, in the socialist system aggregate demand, employment, domestic income, and economic growth are independent of the level of wages and of the level of expenditures of private individuals. The allocation of resources between consumption and investment is decided by the planning authority. Irrespective of the level of wages and the share of labor in total income, the system can function at full capacity and can grow. Thus, the socialist economy is conditioned not by market forces but by the decisions of the planning authority.

since 1950 the labor movement has done no more than propagate the inflation originating in the rigidity of the economic structure and in the continuous and increasing transfer of income to the rural sector. Inasmuch as monetary policy has been directed by the traditional interests who have always benefited from devaluation of the peso, income transfers at the expense of labor have occurred automatically, and wage increases have been delayed and have only partially offset losses in real income.

It is not the labor movement but a nonintegrated industrial economy in severe crisis and a misguided economic policy that are responsible for inflation and the stagnation of the Argentine economy. A strong labor movement is not a disruptive element in Argentine life; on the contrary, it is potentially one of the mainsprings of an authentic process of national development. To be precise, the problem is not the Argentine Confederation of Labor (C.G.T.) but stagnation.

Recent experience also provides some lessons for the labor movement and for union policy. The first of these lessons is that the only way to continuously improve living conditions for workers is through economic development. The last fifteen years have proven that if there is stagnation, conditions for labor not only do not get better but they actually worsen. Development means the worker's material and cultural expansion, whereas stagnation means the reverse. The second lesson is that increases in money wages alone do not suffice to protect real wages or the share of labor in national income. The obvious conclusion is that labor should be concerned more with the management of economic policy, particularly monetary policy, than merely with measures to raise money wages.

These considerations throw new light on the strategy of the labor movement in the process of national development and in its relations with other social groups. The first objective of labor should be to support and promote a policy of development aimed at integrating the economic structure and at creating conditions for sustained growth. Furthermore, defense of the worker should not be limited to wage increases, but should be extended to a systematic effort to influence the nation's economic policy. There is no doubt that if the unions muster their forces in support of a development program with as much energy as when they demand higher wages, they will be a decisive factor in the policy of change and, therefore, in improving the worker's living conditions.

Role of the entrepreneur

The relationship between private enterprise and the economic system is still not properly understood. Argentine entrepreneurs, particularly in industry, operate under the assumption that state intervention stunts individual initiative. Nevertheless, the country's recent experience refutes this belief. With appreciable state intervention in the economy, especially during the early years of the Perón regime, private enterprise and above all industry flourished, although subject to important restrictions; but these restrictions arose not so much from intervention as from the way the latter was oriented. In the last few years, however, under a policy of nonintervention, industrial activity has gone through one of its worst and most protracted crises.

Argentina's business community has committed a fundamental error in not recognizing that the future of private enterprise in Argentina is indissolubly linked to the development of the economy as a whole.[11] We have seen already that economic development can only be achieved if the economic structure is integrated, which requires clearly defined state intervention in the economy. Otherwise, natural growth of the economy leads to a nonintegrated industrial structure and eventually, as in the case of Argentina, to prolonged stagnation.

In this manner, a policy of liberalization that indiscriminately limits state intervention in the economy, thereby precluding a development program, hinders expansion and the opening up of new opportunities for private enterprise.

Events since 1930 also hold a number of lessons for Argentina's private enterprise. In the first place, they leave no doubt that the interests of the business sector are inseparable from the process of economic growth and, therefore, from an effective development program. In the second place, they demonstrate, particularly to industrial enterprises, that it is not enough to protect money prices

---

[11] Opposition by the entrepreneurial class to state intervention is not due simply to a lack of understanding of the fundamental forces behind the economic process. During the Perón regime, state intervention not only either failed to take measures that were essential to development or took many quite useless ones, but in many cases it applied a real interventionist *sadism*, namely, detailed regulations and altogether unnecessary and maddening red tape which interfered with the operation of business enterprises. This partly explains why later on business groups were so opposed to state intervention.

of manufactures; as long as economic policy is managed by other interests, there will be a transfer of income away from industry and a consequent diminishing of the latter's development possibilities.

The Political Bases of Development

The crisis of the nonintegrated industrial economy has affected every aspect of Argentine life. Argentine politics are strongly conditioned by the stagnation of the national economy and by the severe deterioration in living standards of most of the population over the last fifteen years.

From this point of view, it is clearly impossible to carry out an effective development program unless the people are allowed to participate actively and unrestrictedly in the political process. This is not merely because support from the masses is a basic precondition of growth in modern times, but because only those sectors of the population in favor of transforming Argentina socially and economically can destroy the old political patterns of the primary-exports economy. Therefore, an authentically democratic solution that would ensure the unrestricted participation of the population in political life is indispensable, not only to the reestablishment of democratic legality, but to the process of development itself and the future political organization of the country.

APPENDIX

TABLE 1

GROWTH OF ARGENTINE POPULATION

Year	Source	Estimated or Recorded Population	Increase Over Preceding Date Numbers	Percentage Increase	Average Annual Rate of Growth per Thousand
1797	Azara	311,000			
1809	De la Fuente	406,000	95,000	30.5	22.1
1819	De la Fuente	527,000	121,000	29.8	25.9
1837	Parish	675,000	148,000	28.1	13.7
1860	De Moussy	1,210,000	535,000	79.3	24.7
1869	1st National Census	1,737,076	527,076	43.6	39.7
1895	2nd National Census	3,954,911	2,217,835	127.7	30.0
1914	3rd National Census	7,885,237	3,930,326	99.4	34.9
1947	4th National Census	15,897,127	8,011,890	101.6	20.4
1960	5th National Census	20,008,945	4,111,818	25.9	17.6

SOURCE: National Population Census for 1960.

TABLE 2

URBAN AND RURAL POPULATION, 1869–1947

Census Years	Number of Inhabitants Urban	Rural	Percentage Shares Urban	Rural	Average Annual Increase per Thousand Urban	Rural
1869	492,600	1,224,300	28	72		
					46.3	23.0
1895	1,448,200	2,466,700	37	63		
					55.5	21.8
1914	4,152,400	3,727,900	53	47		
					26.7	14.3
1947	9,932,100	5,961,700	62	38		

SOURCE: National Population Censuses.

TABLE 3

EXPANSION OF ARGENTINE RAILROADS
(in kilometers)

Year	Length of Railroads	Increase
1860	39	
1870	732	693
1880	2,516	1,784
1890	9,432	6,916
1900	16,563	7,131
1910	27,993	11,430
1920	33,884	5,891
1930	38,122	4,238
1940	41,283	3,161
1950	42,865	1,582
1960	43,923	1,058

SOURCE: Ministry of Works and Public Services, *Transportes argentinos: plan de largo alcance*, Buenos Aires, 1962.

TABLE 4

RATIO OF IMPORTS TO GROSS PRODUCT, 1900–1955

Periods Averages)	Gross Product	Imports	Imports as Percentage of Gross Product
	(Millions of Pesos at 1950 Prices)		
1900–04	10,756	2,806	26.1
1905–09	15,890	4,544	28.6
1910–14	19,896	5,719	28.7
1915–19	19,131	3,345	17.5
1920–24	25,491	5,395	21.2
1925–29	33,184	8,214	24.8
1930–34	33,863	4,985	14.7
1935–39	39,754	5,884	14.8
1940–44	45,908	2,956	6.4
1945–49	57,009	5,605	9.8
1950–54	63,150	4,614	7.3
1955	68,769	5,186	7.5

SOURCE: U. N., Economic Commission for Latin America, *El desarrollo económico de la Argentina*, México, 1959.

TABLE 5

AGRICULTURAL AND LIVESTOCK PRODUCTION AND EXPORTS

Periods (Averages)	Production	Exports	Ratio of Exports to Production (Percent)
	(Millions of Pesos at 1950 Prices)		
1900–04	4,152	2,177	52
1920–24	8,724	4,148	47
1925–29	9,945	5,179	52
1930–34	10,546	5,043	48
1935–39	11,531	4,984	43
1940–44	13,401	3,441	26
1945–49	12,756	3,652	29
1950–54	12,482	2,658	21

SOURCE: U. N., Economic Commission for Latin America, *El desarrollo económico de la Argentina*, México, 1959.

TABLE 6

RATIO OF FOREIGN CAPITAL TO AGGREGATE FIXED CAPITAL, 1900–1955

Years	Domestic Capital	Foreign Capital	Aggregate Fixed Capital	Ratio of Foreign to Aggregate Fixed Capital (Percent)
	(Millions of Dollars at 1950 Prices)			
1900	4,327	2,020	6,347	31.8
1909	7,716	5,250	12,966	40.5
1913	9,007	8,230	17,237	47.7
1917	9,537	7,980	17,517	45.6
1920	10,164	7,300	17,464	41.8
1923	11,961	7,100	19,061	37.2
1927	14,450	7,580	22,030	34.4
1929	16,639	7,835	24,474	32.0
1931	17,942	7,640	25,582	30.0
1934	18,559	6,920	25,479	27.2
1940	21,795	5,570	27,365	20.4
1945	23,394	4,260	27,654	15.4
1949	30,378	1,740	32,118	5.4
1953	33,279	1,870	35,149	5.3
1955	34,924	1,860	36,784	5.1

SOURCE: U. N., Economic Commission for Latin America, *El desarrollo económico de la Argentina*, México, 1959.

TABLE 7

CAPITAL, EMPLOYMENT AND PRODUCTIVITY, 1900–1955

Periods (Average)	Capital (Millions of Pesos at 1950 Prices)	Employment (Thousands)	Gross Product (Millions of Pesos at 1950 Prices)	Capita per Person Employed	Product per Person Employed	Product per Unit of Capital
				Pesos at 1950 Prices		
1900–04	44,606	1,996	10,756	22,348	5,389	0.241
1925–29	140,280	4,288	33,184	32,715	7,739	0.237
1940–44	173,130	5,517	45,908	31,381	8,321	0.265
1945–49	187,963	6,261	57,009	30,021	9,105	0.303
1955	231,737	7,348	68,769	31,537	9,359	0.297

SOURCE: U. N., Economic Commission for Latin America, *El desarrollo económico de la Argentina*, México, 1959.

INDEX

Index

DUE